T0295683

Transforming the B2B Buyer Journey

Transforming the B2B Buyer Journey

Maximize brand value, improve conversion rates and build loyalty

Antonia Wade

KoganPage

First published in Great Britain and the United States in 2023 by Kogan Page Limited

2nd Floor, 45 Gee Street
London
EC1V 3RS
United Kingdom

8 W 38th Street, Suite 902
New York, NY 10018
USA

4737/23 Ansari Road
Daryaganj
New Delhi 110002
India

www.koganpage.com

Kogan Page books are printed on paper from sustainable forests.

© Antonia Wade 2023

The right of Antonia Wade to be identified as the author of this work has been asserted by her in accordance with the Copyright, Designs and Patents Act 1988.

ISBNs

Hardback   978 1 3986 0682 1
Paperback   978 1 3986 0680 7
Ebook   978 1 3986 0681 4

British Library Cataloguing-in-Publication Data

A CIP record for this book is available from the British Library.

Library of Congress Control Number

2023930939

Typeset by Integra Software Services, Pondicherry
Print production managed by Jellyfish
Printed and bound by CPI Group (UK) Ltd, Croydon, CR0 4YY

To Nick, Holly and Freddie
with love

CONTENTS

Antonia is currently the global Chief Marketing Officer for PwC. PwC builds trust in society and solves important problems. It has offices in 155 countries, employs over 280,000 people and is one of the leading professional services networks in the world. In this role, she leads on brand strategy for one of the world's most trusted companies, creates PwC's flagship global campaigns and runs an integrated client-facing technology stack.

Before that, she was CMO at Capita, at that time a £4 billion consulting, digital transformation and business services company. In two years she led the refresh of the brand and transformed the sales and marketing function to generate £5.8bn pipeline in 2020.

Prior to that, she led the global marketing team at Thomson Reuters, transforming it from a loss-making function into a productive team, delivering 17 per cent of gross sales and 34 per cent of pipeline – making $14 for every $1 invested in marketing.

She spent 10 years at Accenture, where she led global marketing strategy for their £2.5 billion+ operations business to accelerate sales, drive customer loyalty and raise brand within the market. She also led internal communications for 50,000 people.

She is a regular speaker on the marketing circuit – on change, data, technology and client insights. She is also on the boards for ITSMA and Propolis – both of which champion all that is great about B2B marketing – and she is a mentor for the Marketing Academy scholarship programme.

Antonia is passionate about B2B marketing and building high performance teams. She loves solving business challenges and driving strong, creative ideas that can build real differentiation and brand profile.

ABOUT THIS BOOK

I find the challenges of B2B marketing compelling and endlessly fascinating, which is why I've chosen to specialize in it for more than 15 years. It's a highly varied discipline – complex and emotionally engaging, requiring mental agility and the ability to predict or read the subtle signals that explain a buyer's thinking. It brings together creativity, commercialism and analytics in a way that is unique within a business environment. As a B2B marketing practitioner, you have an exciting role positioned between buyers, the people who influence them and your business stakeholders. Buyers need information to direct decision-making; your sales and product teams want to get their message to market in a high impact way – and marketing owns the levers that connect these two. When done well, marketing helps buyers get value at every point of engagement with a company and it can be the critical component for the growth of a business. I fundamentally believe that marketing should make money, not cost money, and that it can be one of the most efficient and buyer-friendly ways of building future pipeline. Crucially, it can offer invaluable insights into how buyers are making decisions. Knowing how to maximize potential in marketing will be the marker of companies that will succeed now and in the future.

This is the book I wish I had had when I was a manager and senior marketing manager, looking for ways to add more value to my client and drive commercial return for my company. I wanted to be able to better explain how my teams were driving revenue and how interesting and complex B2B marketing done well can be.

In this book, I offer a way of designing the multifold aspects of your marketing strategy and plan, a way of working out how to resource against it and a way of talking to business stakeholders so that you can help build confidence in what you and your teams are driving. It is based around a buyer journey framework that differs from the traditional marketing funnel, which I hope brings a fresh way of thinking about B2B marketing.

My experience has been predominantly in professional services and technology, but when I look across the B2B landscape, I think that there is something in here for any marketer trying to drive revenue, support business strategy and deliver outcomes for their buyer as well as their business.

The book is in three parts:

- Part One explains why it is time for a new approach to the traditional funnel and how to diagnose what is holding B2B marketers back. It provides an overview of a new buyer journey framework, detailing what buyers are trying to do in each phase and then reflects on how B2B marketers should respond. I then deep-dive into each phase in a structured way with sections on content, channels and metrics appropriate for that phase. I also make suggestions about how to move the buyer from one stage of the journey to the next.

- Part Two brings it all together. It talks about the fluctuating nature of client buying groups at each stage and what this means for how you target them and assess whether your marketing is well invested and yielding return. I offer thoughts on how you can design the overall journey in a way that provides insights into your buyer's process. It also suggests how you can use the buyer framework to decide where to invest, the importance of creativity, how to get buyer insights and how to avoid things going wrong.

- Part Three takes a buyer journey view of brand, outlining how to direct and justify brand investments according to what brand is doing for you at each stage of the buyer's process. It provides insights into how to use the framework to make good decisions about using and choosing technology. It also outlines the challenge of return on investment (ROI) in B2B marketing and offers thoughts on working with agencies. Finally, it shows how to use the buyer journey to build a new, productive relationship with sales, that is more relevant for what today's buyers need from your business.

There is also an appendix which contains some helpful templates: marketing strategy, events strategy, agency briefing and a marketing competency framework to help you manage your team. I also offer some thoughts on managing your own core skills as a B2B marketer and developing your personal brand.

Throughout the book, I've included *Insider Insights* from people who live and breathe B2B marketing at PwC, EY, Accenture, ServiceNow, Salesforce, Optimizely, Stein IAS and NCR Group. They have been where you are and have succeeded in transforming the fortunes of their companies by repositioning how marketing adds value to the buyer and their organizations.

I hope this book helps you build more confidence in marketing with your stakeholders, drive incredible growth for your business and create amazing experiences for your buyers.

A NOTE ON TERMINOLOGY

Different industries use different terms. I have decided to use these terms throughout the book:

- *Client* to mean client or customer.
- *Buyer* to refer to individuals who are in the process of buying solutions or services at any stage: *Active Buyer* denotes the phase when they have secured budget to spend and have a shortlist of prospective companies from whom they will buy.

For when you need advice fast

This is a long book! And while I hope you read it all, I know that sometimes time is pressing, and you need quick ideas to help you work through what to do. Table 0.1 (overleaf) provides a guide to how to use this book when you're in a tight corner.

TABLE 0.1 Top tips and where to go in the book

I need to...	Top tips and where to go in the book
Work out how to allocate budgets into brand vs lead generation	This is an ongoing conversation in B2B marketing, with many competing voices. I don't think that it is a binary choice between future demand and today's sales. In the moment, it feels like a good idea to pivot to the immediate term, but brand investment can have as much impact closing pipeline as driving future business performance. • Chapter 11 gives you a view about how you talk about the value of brand investments against each part of the buyer journey as well as data to back up your conversation. Of course, there are choices to be made about where to put your money, which I go through in this chapter, but if you subscribe to the view that not all your buyers are in market to buy at any one time, this should give you some useful insights. • Redirecting money can harm today's pipeline as well. Figure 7.1 gives you a good set of data and rationale for how to justify why switching off brand investment entirely not only harms your future demand generation but also your likelihood of winning over current buyers. • Look, too, at the Insider Insight from a sales leader in Chapter 13 about how sales conversations can be a leading indicator of the success of investments into brand.
Talk to sales about the role that marketing plays in helping them	The role of marketing and sales, including hand-offs, has changed dramatically so be bold in how you advocate for the modern buyer when looking at process, hand-offs and the roles that marketing and sales are playing. • I reference some useful data points in the introduction that will help you make your case. • Use Figure 13.1 to discuss the mutually reinforcing roles that marketing and sales play across a buyer's experience of your company. • Talk about who does what, how you'll hand off between you and what good *looks like* (Part Three) so that you're aligned from the outset. • Read the advice from a senior marketer at Salesforce in Chapter 10 and from the NCR sales leader in Chapter 13.

(continued)

TABLE 0.1 (Continued)

I need to...	Top tips and where to go in the book
Manage budget reduction conversations	First, it happens to all of us, so don't take it personally! Marketing funds are not fixed in the same way as other functional budgets, so it can be a place that finance teams challenge. It is a pragmatic business question; you need to be structured about how you have the conversation. • To start with, try to have a fact-based discussion about the sense of retaining marketing budgets (Chapter 13). • If that doesn't work, figure out where against the business strategy marketing can really help. Often this is believed to be at the sales conversion end of the journey to help with short-term conversion: but it might be that sales can deal with that while marketing supports the longer-term business aspirations. • If you know it is going to be a tough year, look at how you might spread investments into agencies on a fixed-term basis, so you don't need to make people redundant. Advice on how to work with agencies is in Part Three. • Events are often the most expensive outlay for a B2B marketer – Guide 2 in the appendix gives some thoughts about how to ascertain their value and challenge your organization's thinking on them.
Understand whether to embark on an account-based marketing (ABM) programme	The clue as to whether you should embark on this is in the profile of your business. • If a large percentage of revenue is in a small number of clients – so losing them could be punitive for your business – or if your growth is dependant on increasing wallet share from current clients, this could be a good strategy. • Look at how many of your existing clients are buying multiple services from you – this will also help you indicate whether there is an unmet business need for marketing to be involved. Chapter 8 goes through the benefits of building loyalty, and how to use my buyer journey framework to create new business in existing accounts.
Create a marketing strategy	The buyer journey outlines the content, channel and metrics appropriate for where the buyer is in their journey – rather than what your business wants them to do. • Look at the content, channel and metrics sections in Chapters 4 to 8 – they will help you work out your strategy for each stage. • Each company will weight the different parts of the buyer journey differently, but this should give you a starting point on content, channels and metrics, which will help you build out your plan. • I've also put a template in the appendix on how to write a marketing strategy (Guide 1) – this has been one of the most requested things I get asked by mentees and previous teams.

(continued)

TABLE 0.1 (Continued)

I need to...	Top tips and where to go in the book
Make decisions about technology and data acquisition investments	You can't do effective, targeted marketing without good data and strategic use of technology. The challenges of it are multifold though. • In Chapters 4 to 7, I talk about the fluctuating target market group for each stage of the buying process, and how to use it to ascertain whether you have the right data to target your marketing effectively to everyone who matters in the buyer's process • In Chapter 12, I discuss how you enrich data in order to make sure your marketing is well targeted and how you can extract insights from your content to help you shape strategy, target market insights and capture data. • Finally, I devote Chapter 12 to how you use the B2B buyer journey to make decisions about what technology to choose and how you need to flex processes as well as train the team in order to take advantage of the investments you've made.
Choose an agency	Choosing an agency – for capacity or capability – is an important decision given B2B marketing budgets and the fact that agency teams might be representing marketing to senior stakeholders. • Essential things to consider are in Chapter 13, as well as a view from an agency on what makes a great client. • In my experience, lack of ROI from agency spend has come from poor briefing, so I offer a tried and tested template in Guide 3 of the appendix.

ACKNOWLEDGEMENTS

This book draws on all my experiences – good and bad – of being a B2B marketer. You learn as much from your mistakes as you do from your successes. So to all the teams I've worked with, the people I've worked for and the mentors I've had along the way, thank you.

I'd like to specifically recognize everyone who helped me with this book: my invaluable editorial support Louise Hannah, who not only read this innumerable times, giving great advice, but also kept me cheerful when I thought it wasn't close to being finished; and the incredibly creative Helen Grainger, who took reams of tabulated content and turned them into beautiful illustrations. Thanks too to the team at Kogan Page for all their support in publishing the book.

To all the people who contributed to the Insider Insights: Michael Stewart, Jo Burgess-Gibbs, Peter Thomas, Gemma Davies, Kirsten Allegri-Williams, Jo Pettifer, Tom Stein, and Ismail Amla: thank you for adding your wisdom to this book – it's significantly better for it. I feel lucky to know so many brilliant B2B experts and have learned a huge amount from each of you.

To my readers, Ilona Steffen Cope, Anna Reeves, Kate Owen, Melissa Booth, Nicola Catlin, and Nicola Marsden. I so appreciate all your comments, thoughts and suggestions: any you gave me made the book better, anything I didn't incorporate properly is shame on me! To Mindy Gibbins-Klein, who got me started, to Tim Dickson, who helped with early structuring, and to Fiona Czerniawska from Source Global Research for her thought leadership – thank you, all.

To my mother, who supported all my decisions while I was beavering away, and to my sister and brother without whose encouragement I would have given up long ago.

To my children, Holly and Freddie, who tolerated distracted weekends, but were still constant cheerleaders for what I was trying to do – thank you for believing in me. And lastly to Nick. Not only could I not have written this book without your support, but I also wouldn't have had the work experiences needed to conceive it if not for such an amazing husband. Thank you for supporting me in all my ambitions, being my partner in parenting, making me laugh and giving me confidence.

PART ONE

01
Why do we need a new buyer journey framework?

Changes in B2B buying and some of the challenges embedded in responding to these in traditional ways are heralding a new age of marketing. Since I started doing marketing, there has been talk of the funnel. There are strengths in this as a mental model. The concept of converting as much of the interest as you can through stages to an ultimate sale helps bring focus. Thinking through what makes buyers engage at the outset then working through where you might take them next is helpful to marketing and sales teams. The downside of a funnel is that many assume a singular set of buyers going through a rational series of choices. I suggest in this book that instead of a funnel, think about it as a framework, where people at each stage and the information they need change in each part. The strategy, tactics and measures flex according to the buyer objectives at each phase, and it is possible for individuals within the buying group to be in a number of phases simultaneously depending on their role – or, in fact, for the individuals in each phase to be entirely different from the preceding ones.

There has been much written about how fraught the buying process is. Reputations hang on the line as people make expensive decisions on behalf of their company, which take months, even years. This means you need a new, better way of explaining to internal stakeholders how the benefits of marketing align with in-year objectives so you can build a genuine lever for growth in the short and long term.

In the past, the role of B2B marketing was to support sales. Typically, businesses would offer their products and services into the market, under the assumption that buyers knew what they wanted. The goal was a simple one: get your brand in front of them; move quickly to explaining features and benefits; then hand on to a salesperson. Companies focused primarily on how they sold to customers rather than responding to how they wanted to buy – it was a transactional relationship. In more relationship-based businesses, the role of defining what a buyer might want was vested in account teams, who would try to bring the appropriate solution to the specific needs of their contacts in the buying organization. Marketing's role here was to provide opportunities to deepen relationships via hospitality, events or support a sales motion with collateral. This is still the case in some organizations. While this is changing, some of my counterparts continue to struggle with marketing being classed as a cost centre rather than a real driver for revenue.

There are many reasons for organizations to rethink marketing – but the critical ones are that the way buyers make decisions has changed. You're competing for attention with the business to consumer (B2C) companies, which means the expectation of a smooth, intuitive and human buying experience across all channels.

The number of people involved in buying decisions is growing and changing

Buyers come in different guises with different needs. Typically, they initiate a buying process in one of two ways:

1 *Senior people, taking a telescopic view*: they spend time thinking strategically about macroeconomic issues such as how to manage the physical risks of climate change, customer digitization or workforce trends that may affect their business in the longer term, then work out whether they need to do anything about it. Their problems are ambiguous and what they need to do isn't straightforward or well understood. They need to work out what the problem statement is for their organization, decide whether they need to take any action now and whether they need an external third party to help them.

2 *Functional buyers with a clearer problem statement*: they may have bought similar services many times before or have a more straightforward challenge to solve. Where they have a well-defined problem, such as needing to find a software solution for payments or needing specific technical legal advice, they will spend less time defining their requirements at a high level and instead go straight into the market with specific information needs – often with a supplier shortlist in mind. This also happens where there is an incumbent provider who isn't working out and the buyer is looking to switch.

Whatever they are doing, it is rare for buyers to go it alone. Where individuals in companies are sole budget owners and decision makers, they will engage with peers or people in their teams to validate or inform their opinions. Making decisions on behalf of a larger company is an even more precarious endeavour – it can make or break careers – so people usually try to mitigate this risk. They are mindful of their internal reputation and want to make the best choice for their company or advance their position because of making the decision. Businesses form buying groups with defined roles and accountabilities, which need different levels of information. This is particularly true where complex or expensive services are being bought – or if the implementation of that solution might touch several departments in the buyer's organization. Consider buying a marketing automation solution – a buying group could comprise a few sub-teams within marketing itself, then may include sales, IT, procurement, maybe even finance depending on the price.

Not only are buyers forming groups, but they are also getting bigger and more complicated. Recent data shows that the number of people who are part of each buying decision has changed. According to research firm Gartner (2022), in a typical firm with 100 to 500 employees, an average of seven people is involved in most buying decisions Other varied sources suggest that anywhere between 11 and 15 people are involved in any decision, up from four to five a few years ago.

This paradigm makes it almost impossible for even the best salesperson to know and respond to the functional and individual needs of all the buyers targeted by your company. Marketing is a much more efficient and scalable way to do this. My framework accommodates the fluctuations in buying groups, considering what individuals within them need at each point to move their thinking on.

The way that buyers make decisions has changed

It is well documented that buyers are going much further down the decision-making path without contacting sales reps and are looking to digital channels to garner information, insights and points of view. Gartner data shows 94 per cent of B2B buyers research products online before talking to sales, and the CEB (part of Gartner) states that buyers are typically 57 per cent of the way through their decision-making process before engaging with sales (Gartner, 2022). This has been a trend for some time but has been exasperated during the Covid-19 pandemic and the demographic shift in buying groups. Over 45 per cent of B2B technology buyers are 25- to 34-year-olds (TrustRadius, 2021). Digital channels, typically owned by marketing, are critical to educating, informing and translating buyer interest into action. This means often B2B marketers know things about the buyer that others in the business don't, for example how much time they spent on the website, what the key words they searched for were, and what is occupying them as evidenced by the pieces of thought leadership they read. These insights are invaluable, and yet they aren't being used to create a differentiated experience for the buyer, or for your business to learn more about their decision-making process, or to help sales better improve their approach. To do this well, it is vital to take a buyer journey view first rather than working back from a sales target as you create strategy and plans.

The attention economy has altered

The rise in digital channels and mobile means B2B brands are competing for share of eyes and minds not only with each other, but with B2C brands too. Digital marketing experts estimate that most Americans are exposed to around 4,000 to 10,000 ads each day (Simpson, 2017). Added to this, your target audience receives incredible personalized experiences from B2C brands, and can buy from them seamlessly through whatever app they are on. These companies put huge effort into generating and analysing customer data, then use it to make sure they're putting exactly the right products in front of the customer at exactly the right time and through the channels they prefer.

B2B buyers are starting to expect this level of customization and relevance, but know their experience falls short compared to the easy, relevant standard of B2C digital platforms. Research by Salesforce (2018) found that 72 per cent of business buyers expect vendors to personalize engagement to their needs, 69 per cent expect Amazon-like buying experiences and 67 per cent have switched vendors for a more consumer-like experience. B2B buyers' experience as B2C consumers has shaped their perceptions of just how easy it should be to get up-to-date information as well as choose and buy goods and services online. And as more learning and buying activity shifts to digital channels, comparisons to digitally advanced companies is unavoidable. This is exacerbated by the fact that 73 per cent of those involved in decisions to purchase services for their companies are millennials (*Almquist*, 2018), and this age bracket cite internet search and vendor websites as their top means of researching products and services. B2B firms need to catch up.

Buyers will increasingly expect marketing to be highly correlated to their needs, which change depending on context, such as where they are in their decision-making process, the role that they're playing and individual preferences. Cutting through the noise involves innovation. B2B marketers need to align insights with creativity and a strong sense of brand identity so their company's offer can stand out in the sea of noise. Additionally, some B2B companies have started to invest in digital customer experience as a differentiator, spending 72 per cent of their budgets on digital marketing (Gartner, 2022). This means your competitors are likely to be on the move, and if experience matters to your buyers, you will lose revenue if you don't act.

The impact of channel consistency

Most buyers want a level of consistency of experience in the delivery of your solution to them. The rise of expectations in pre-sales experience means that marketing has become a benchmark for your company's ability to deliver what they promise to the buyer. While in the past it was frustrating for a buyer to have a great meeting with a company's senior executives then go on a poorly updated website, or receive a generic email, these days it can lead to mistrust in your company. At best you look disorganized, at worst like you don't care about the customer experience. It is also important for your brand as there may be different individuals from a buyer's company involved in each phase – you can't assume that any brand equity or experience that you have built during one phase automatically carries to the next.

Although we are yet to see it in B2B marketing, I predict that this expectation will start to be exacerbated if buyers already spend a significant amount with your business. If I expect a personalized experience from companies I spend a few pounds with, how long before clumsy marketing from someone I spend hundreds of thousands or millions with is considered unacceptable?

Each of these factors means a new way of thinking about the funnel. The buyer journey framework accommodates the complexity of the buying group and how they engage with content and channels. It assumes that you must be expansive in your messaging, adapting for influencers within the buyer, as well as giving guidance about whether you should embark on client specific, account-based marketing.

What is holding B2B marketing back?

Despite its place at the sharp end of buyer interactions with the business, much of B2B marketing remains tactical. Plans are often written around specific initiatives – an industry event that everyone must be at, for example, or a piece of thought leadership that comes out regularly every year. They are reactive to what the organization thinks it needs in the short term, like marketing noise to introduce a new product and drive client leads. Or they are heavily correlated to the financial year with those milestones dictating the rhythm of activity – like a heavy blast of prospecting emails during the final sales quarter of your financial year – with little heed to when the buyer is in the market looking for services with budget to spend.

These may be valid anchors in the plan – moments that will galvanize internal energy or external market attention – but as isolated actions will not drive revenue growth. Additionally, they will waste money and cement internal perceptions that investment in marketing doesn't yield results. There is no substitute for basing your plan of action on defining the full buyer journey and understanding how buyer needs for information change as they move closer to becoming a client.

There are several other areas to think about as you're reshaping the reputation and impact of B2B marketing within your company. These include your budget cycle, your role as a profit rather than a cost centre, and the relationship with sales.

Marketing budget cycles are out of sync with market buying cycles

B2B marketers are fishing in a finite pool of opportunity. The time between purchases for many goods and services can be significant. Research by LinkedIn's B2B Institute suggests that corporations change service providers such as their principal bank or law firm around once every five years on average. That means only 20 per cent of business buyers are *in the market* over the course of an entire year, which translates to something like 5 per cent in a quarter – or 95 per cent who aren't in the market (B2B Institute, 2021b). Those not in the market to buy at this moment also need marketing to but will not deliver in-year leads or revenue, which is likely the primary metric that marketing is measured by. All too often, any investment in marketing is highly scrutinized or challenged as companies look for immediate return tied to direct sales leads and in-year targets. Outcomes and metrics used to quantify any return on investment in brand are muddied with campaign or pipeline metrics, which sets brand activity up to fail.

In addition, as the buyer moves through the journey – from speculating about whether they need to do something, to prioritizing and acting, to considering high-level options, to seriously comparing vendors, the information they need from you will alter. What mattered to them at the outset will change once they are at shortlist stage as their thinking will have evolved throughout the journey.

Balancing brand-building activity with lead generation is challenging in a B2B environment, as it can be difficult showing the revenue impact of long-term brand investments. Typically, budgets are set annually but the return can be many years out. As such, B2B marketers need a way of talking to their companies about this and building trust in long-term outcomes as well as the short-term returns. It is key to link brand activity with demand generation using the buyer journey. If you don't look at the whole journey, you run the risk of being irrelevant just at the point that relevance matters most, i.e. when the buyer has budget and is ready to spend it – something that will be discussed throughout this book.

The challenge of volume versus value

With complex services, it is likely that the amount of people with the scale of problem and budget to solve it is reasonably small. There has been a predisposition for marketers to use volume metrics to explain the success of their campaigns – often driven by a more consumer marketing led view of what good looks like. However, it can be that small is beautiful in B2B marketing. A precise, very well-targeted campaign to a small number of real decision makers may well be more lucrative than a far-reaching imprecise wave of marketing, but B2B marketers need to reframe how they have talked about success historically.

In addition, many established businesses have the bulk of their revenue coming from a low number of important clients. These clients are also going to be the driver for much of a business' future growth: either through cross-sell to get more share of wallet, or by co-creating products and services. Account-based marketing (ABM) – which I cover extensively in Chapter 8 – has risen in popularity given this paradigm, but it is hard to show attributable ROI on deals already in the pipeline. Doing ABM is expensive too, so B2B marketers need to explain the value of redirecting funds from prospecting new business.

Marketing as a profit centre not a cost centre

Marketing is still seen as a back-office support function in many B2B companies. It isn't always clear how marketing makes the company money – and marketers struggle to talk about the impact of what the function is doing in these terms. Changing the way that teams talk about how to create value, as well as instilling a level of confidence across the function and tying marketing activities better to the buyer needs are all critical to the success of a modern B2B marketing team. If you're not a profit centre today, that should be your aim in the next three to five years.

A new relationship with sales

I come on to talk about this in Part Three of the book but given the critical mutual dependency of the two functions as well as the historically poor relationship, this is fundamental to your change journey. Traditionally, B2B marketing focused on parts of the journey with sales owning other parts. This led to friction between marketing and sales, particularly in the passing over of leads – with marketing derided as money wasting and sales accused of being underappreciative. To transform your buyer journey, you must fundamentally rethink this. In the buyer framework, no part of it is owned 100 per cent by marketing or sales. Buyers are increasingly looking to marketing owned channels to understand how businesses can add value to them. A pre-pandemic Gartner survey of buyers of complex solutions only spent 17 per cent of their time interacting directly with sales teams (Gartner, 2020) – so if they have three vendors to speak to, the share of time they spend with your sales teams is more like 5 to 6 per cent.

The companies that do best are those that work in true partnership with each other and figure out how to collaborate in the right way across each of the stages, with a view to fulfilling buyer needs rather than focusing on hitting sales targets alone.

A new way of thinking about your buyer

Your challenge as a B2B marketer is to ascertain where a buyer is in their process, rather than pushing them indiscriminately to sales. You need to provide information they need for the phase they are in and try to nudge them to the next stage. Your role is to make sure that they can access the content they need at the point they need it, through the channel that works best for them.

Divided into five phases – Horizon Scanner, Explorer, Hunter, Active Buyer and Client – the buyer journey framework recognizes the specific buyer needs and behaviours at each stage while linking them all together to create an end-to-end content and channel strategy which can be measured and adapted at each stage according to tailored metrics.

This is the foundation for long-term B2B marketing success. It means you improve the client experience and don't lose them by going dark at critical decision-making moments. You can better support your company's strategy, driving and protecting revenue. You can spend money in an efficient way, as you'll be using the right channels rather than broadly distributing your message in a haphazard, expensive way. You can make marketing plans more agile because you're designing them to learn about what the buyer is doing. This means you can test and course correct as strategies succeed or fail, as you were deliberate in what you were trying to achieve at each part of the journey rather than just focusing on part of it.

Last but certainly not least, it means that you can talk to your business about the importance and impact of marketing in a way that is concrete and tied to metrics they care about, elevating your team's reputation as revenue drivers.

IN SUMMARY

- The way buyers make decisions has changed. You're competing for attention with the business to consumer (B2C) model, which means the expectation of a relevant and human buying experience across all channels.

- Instead of a funnel, think about a framework where buyer needs change in each part. The strategy, tactics and measures flex according to the buyer objectives at each phase, and it is possible for individuals within the buying group to be in a number of phases simultaneously depending on their role, or for the individuals in each phase to be entirely different from the preceding ones.

- The framework is divided into five phases – Horizon Scanner, Explorer, Hunter, Active Buyer and Client – the buyer journey framework recognizes the specific buyer needs and behaviours at each stage while linking them all together to create an end-to-end content and channel strategy which can be measured according to tailored metrics.

- Buyers come in different guises with different needs. Typically, they initiate a buying process in one of two ways: as a senior person taking a telescopic view or a functional buyer with a clearer problem statement.

- It is rare for buyers to go it alone. Where individuals in companies are sole budget owners and decision makers, they will engage with peers or people in their teams to validate or inform their opinions. Businesses tend to form buying groups with defined roles and accountabilities, who need different levels of information.

- It is vital to take a buyer journey view first rather than working back from a sales target as you create strategy and plans.

- In the buyer framework, no part of it is owned 100 per cent by marketing or sales. The companies that do best are those that work in true partnership with each other and figure out how to collaborate in the right way across each of the stages.

- Typically, budgets are set annually but the return can be many years out. B2B marketers need a new way of reframing how to deliver long-term outcomes as well as the short-term returns.

02

The buyer journey framework: what buyers need

In this chapter, I summarize the five stages of the B2B buyer journey and how the buyers' objectives for engaging with your company differ in each one. Thinking solely about one part means you miss opportunities to provide future value or may put more of your scarce marketing resource towards something that has less chance of providing a strong return. Skipping parts of it means you give an awkward, inconsistent experience to your buyer, who may infer that you are difficult to do business with as a result. And if your competitors are better at thinking about buyer needs at each point than you are, you will be at a disadvantage as the choice is made.

The complexity of the B2B buying landscape juxtaposed with the challenges that marketing has in demonstrating its impact on delivering business strategy and growth means there is a serious case for adopting a buyer-journey approach to marketing. Of course, B2B marketing funnels aren't new, but I believe this particular framework is effective as it considers each phase as something that happens with a specific audience over a period of time, and considers how they link together rather than seeing every engagement with your company as an immediate buying signal. It factors in the post-purchase part of the journey as this can be fertile ground for growth for many B2B organizations. It also offers guidance for types of content that are effective, channels to consider and metrics appropriate for each phase. This last point is particularly important – if your activity lends itself to building rapport with a group of senior client executives over a period of time, but your plan is measured primarily on lead generation, then you will fail to deliver and will lose trust internally. Being able to define the objectives against a framework shared with sales will help both parties prioritize which stages of the journey to invest in, and will help assure mutual success.

The five phases of the buyer journey

There are five distinct phases which capture the buyer's needs and thought process at that particular time. Buyers typically enter the framework either in the first stage

(Horizon Scanner) or third stage (Hunter). The former tend to be senior people looking for insights into a new problem before moving through the rest of the phases. Buyers in the latter stage tend to have a well-defined problem and know what they want.

Horizon Scanner

Most businesses have senior people in strategic roles assessing how market trends or innovation will help them grow or shape their business. I call them *Horizon Scanners* and they are likely the first group of potential buyers to cross your company's radar. Their objective is to seek opinions and insights to stimulate thinking inside their company about growth or competitive advantage. They need data, points of view and expert opinions. The sort of questions they might be asking themselves are 'How might emerging customer trends affect my strategy?', 'How shall I use technology to secure future growth?', or 'How could I make my workforce more productive?' They aren't looking for answers and they're certainly not looking for a sales message; they are looking for ideas. Even once an idea is lodged, they may not decide to prioritize it immediately or at all. They need you to provide thought leadership not solutions, which means your goal is to position your company as an expert and authority while taking the opportunity through strong branding, clever messaging, and channel selection to make your company memorable. Horizon Scanners may not at this stage know what your business does, or they may know it for something other than the immediate issues that are preoccupying them. It's likely that your company's representatives are not directly in the room or in the discussion, so it's important that your brand is known to third parties who they might talk to at this stage – analysts or peers. Thought leadership needs to be available in channels that you don't own (like third-party publications or events). Public relations is important – some of your thought leadership needs to be designed to appeal to journalists, which means it needs an angle. You can't just put out flat content; it needs a new insight or data point. Horizon Scanners will likely come across your brand tangentially rather than seeking you out. They may also not be the ultimate economic buyers; they could be senior people who will delegate the decision-making to their teams.

Explorer

The second phase of the buyer's journey is likely to involve a set of people in the company who will be formulating the problems they need to solve at a high level. I call them *Explorers*. Having decided they need to do something different to address new problems or opportunities, they will be looking to define a point of view relevant to their organization and prioritize it against the other commitments they have made to shareholders, employees or customers. To do this, they are seeking opinions and ideas about what other companies are doing – which could be in their sector or not. They might need information to pull together a high-level business case or secure resources to start scoping problems in more detail. They will also be deciding whether the problem is sufficiently complex that they need to get third-party support. In many sectors – particularly professional services or technology companies – the biggest competition you face is your customers deciding they can go it alone, that they can postpone the decision to a later date or not act at all.

Hunter

There are two ways buyers get to this stage. They can have been through the first two stages, decided they need to do something different, adapted their business strategy and made the internal business case. Alternatively, they will enter their buying journey at this phase directly. This happens when they know what business product or service they need. They may have bought it before and be looking to switch suppliers – or may have a specific requirement to do something, for example because of regulation. If they enter at this phase, their problem statements are known and they have a clear idea of what their requirements are.

Whichever route they are on, once they get to this phase, I call them *Hunters*. They are getting familiar with – or already know – the range of possible solutions. They are actively researching options and surveying the competitive landscape. They want to know whether you have the solutions they need, what your track record is in delivering it and what sets you apart from your rivals. They are looking for technical expertise, opinions and evidence that your solution is specifically designed to help them, as well as detailed information and proof points.

Active Buyer

Typically, buyers will shortlist a smaller set of companies they think can do the job. At this point, they are seriously considering your services, actively comparing you to your competitors and are doing due diligence. I call them *Active Buyers*. They will want specific information relevant to the product or service they are looking for. They may initiate a procurement-led process. They need to understand specifically how you are better than your competition and will want practical details of what you offer and timely responses to requests for information. They may ask for pitches and will expect access to the right people within your organization. They will also want to ensure there is a good cultural fit – and that they can trust you to deliver what you say you will.

Client

The last phase of the journey is post purchase once the buyer has become a client. So much marketing effort has gone into getting them to this point and often they are then left as the service gets delivered or product gets rolled out. However, the very start of a relationship can be precarious as it moves from sales to contracting or delivery. A negative experience can damage your reputation because it is a fraught period for the buyer – they need to demonstrate to the rest of their peers or team that they made a good decision on the company's behalf. Once the solution is being implemented, buyers need help building loyalty within their own business for your company's solution or with driving adoption for the solutions that they've bought. They want to be able to give feedback which may help you improve your product or services immeasurably. Finally, they may have colleagues who would benefit from working with your company too – but don't know how to connect you. For example, your company may have very strong relationships with the finance part of the organization but also offer solutions for HR. As the finance director hears problems articulated by their colleagues in the HR function, they want to help and would advocate for you because they trust you to deliver, if only they knew that you offered those types of solution.

Fluctuations in your audience at each stage

Often in marketing strategy documents, there is a singular buyer with clear pain points identified. This buyer journey framework suggests that having a narrow view may not be appropriate. Across each stage of the framework, your TAM and audience type may change quite considerably. This affects the type of information that you may want to give: strategic thought leadership versus detailed functional information for example. Additionally, the number of people at each point will inform your targeting strategy and how you contextualize response metrics. For example, if part of your campaign is positioning a new strategic idea to prompt thinking with a set of senior buyers, he number of people you may be marketing to might be very small so measuring high volumes of traffic to a web article is misleading. I come on to talk about this more in Part Three.

FIGURE 2.1   What buyers are looking to do at each stage of their process and the types of information they need

	WHAT BUYERS ARE LOOKING TO DO	WHAT TYPE OF INFORMATION THEY WOULD LIKE
HORIZON SCANNER	• I'm in a strategic role and am assessing how market trends or innovation will help me grow my business	Opinions, discussions and insight to shape future strategic decisions.
EXPLORER	• I know the problem I'm trying to solve at a high level • I'm defining a point of view and the outcomes I want to achieve • I'm prioritizing whether to do anything, what to do and if my company needs outside help	Options, opinions, high level business case details, industry points of view, case studies.
HUNTER	• I know the business service I need • My business challenge is well understood as I have been through the first two phases. Or I know what I want as I've bought it before and my problem is well defined or there is an existing vendor • Familiar with the solution landscape and researching and comparing to competitors to see what sets companies apart	Detailed information, proof points, case studies.
ACTIVE BUYER	• I'm seriously considering your company and doing due diligence • I want to have a conversation or enter a procurement discussion • I'm looking for specific information to support this	Specific answers, RFI/RFP response, access to right team.
CLIENT	• I want to get more value from your company • I want to know whether there are other relevant solutions my company can buy • I want to be treated as a valued client and know that my feedback will be listened to	Tailored content, relevant new solutions, robust feedback mechanisms.

As you start to build your marketing strategy, make sure you diagnose the buying stages and start to size them. Understanding what they need, by stage, to move their thinking on is the foundation of your plan.

IN SUMMARY

- There are five phases to the buyer journey framework: Horizon Scanner, Explorer, Hunter, Active Buyer, Client.
- Horizon Scanners tend to be a small, senior audience, often C-suite, looking for ideas, opinions and insights to shape future strategy.
- Explorers are formulating problems that need to be solved at a high level. They have senior roles and are looking for case studies and industry points of view.
- Hunters either get to this point because they've been through the first few stages, or enter the journey at this stage directly, skipping the previous two. This is because they already know or are getting familiar with what they are looking for. They tend to be functional leads who want detailed information and proof points.
- Active Buyers are seriously considering your services and comparing you to your competitors. They are often functional leads supported by a buying group who will help execute a decision, such as finance and procurement. They need answers to a specific set of questions.
- Clients value tailored content and robust feedback mechanisms. It is important not to drop the ball as soon as the deal is done – they still need content and information that will help to build the marketing company's profile internally and ensure they are seen to have made the right choice. They are also a fertile source of new revenue as will be covered in Chapter 8 when I focus on account-based marketing.
- Your TAM is likely to change throughout the stages and it is important to adapt the content and activity accordingly.
- View the buyer framework holistically and not each section in isolation. A journey is exactly that and you risk giving an inconsistent, awkward experience to your buyer by skipping parts of it.

03
The buyer journey framework: the B2B marketer's role

As covered in the previous section, buyers are trying to achieve different things at different phases of the journey. In this chapter we will look at how B2B marketers need to respond, ensuring channel and content choices align with what the buyer needs at each stage. Looking at it in this end-to-end way will also help you decide how much resource you need to put against each phase, agree with stakeholders where to focus and determine what return you should expect using appropriate metrics for each phase that have also been agreed by the sales team and wider business. You need to both cater for the stage they are in and should be trying to nudge them to the next stage of the journey, amassing as much insight about them as possible while they move through the process. As you do this, plan a number of hypotheses in advance that you will test against – I come back to this in Part Three of the book when we bring it all together.

Horizon Scanner

 During the Horizon Scanner phase, your objective is to help create or address undefined buyer needs. Placing your experts and thought leaders strategically into the buyer's ecosystem means you can build trust and a stronger reputation with both them and the people who influence them, such as market observers, peers, regulators, or journalists. You can help shape their thinking on issues by giving fresh insights. You may be able to create a market for your services by helping buyers uncover a potential new challenge or re-evaluate the urgency of a problem. It is a chance to educate buyers at a high level about the breadth of your capabilities – helpful if your brand is well known for one thing but you want to grow market share for other services. For example, PwC has a strong and long established audit, tax and consulting business but in some markets is best known for audit and tax. Engaging senior buyers with solutions too early – as sales teams may want to do – is counterproductive. Your role as a marketer during this phase is to keep the conversation at a strategic level about themes and issues that matter to the buyer and to get your messages into the channels they are engaging with.

Explorer

When buyers are in the Explorer phase, your objective is to create a market for your solutions and an imperative for the buyer to engage with your company. In this phase, procrastination, inertia, or the belief that they have the internal resources to do the job themselves are key challenges, particularly if you are in professional services, or an agency, or outsourcing environment. In the technology space, buyers may think that they can continue with their existing systems for a bit longer. You are trying to encourage them to prioritize the challenge you have a solution for against their existing commitments and convince them that they need to engage a third party – i.e. your business – to help them. Positioning your experts continues to be very important. Buyers might or might not know how your company can help them – and will want to know whether you have relevant insights from previous work in the area, or strategic points of view on what is happening in the market. The thought leadership and points of view you provide should target specific challenges for an industry, sector, country, or business function. In practice this looks like moving from a high-level point of view on 'Will capital solve climate change?' to 'Retooling banks for sustainable lending', for example. The channel will vary according to buyer preference but the interest you create should start to drive early leads and build future pipeline. Activity at this stage should maintain the conversation with key buyers as they evolve their thinking. When developing content for this and the next phase as you nurture leads, it is critical to have enough new things to say on a particular topic so you can keep engaging with buyers, regardless of how long they want to spend in this phase.

Hunter

Once a buyer has decided they need to act and is actively researching who to work with in the Hunter phase, you need to differentiate yourself from the competition and demonstrate that your solutions will deliver the outcomes they want. Do this by showing them that you understand their problems, that you have helped clients solve them before and that your teams can deliver what they need in the best way. You have the chance to position your company as easy to do business with, as well as convince the buyer that your solution better suits their requirements than others in the market. As they shortlist companies that they will select from, help them find the information they need quickly and connect them to your experts or sales teams, especially where they have questions that need answering or specific research requirements. If you are successful, you will differentiate yourself from your competitors in the buyers' minds as they approach the start of the procurement process and make a buy/don't buy decision, which may mean you are ahead as they shortlist. Your company may even be able to help them shape their scope, which gives you a huge competitive advantage. You have the opportunity to reduce the time spent in the pipeline by nurturing leads so they feel inclined to buy and are *warm* for a sales conversation.

Active Buyer

Once you are on the shortlist and they are in the final stages of the buying process, you want to win. Marketing can help buyers decide faster by supporting sales activities, providing the relevant information across digital channels – even allowing them to go as far down the process as they would like digitally. This includes detail about your expertise and credentials if you are in a professional services or complex services environment, or if you sell products, the information should focus on features, benefits or technical specifications. The goal is to make it easy for people to buy from your company and remove any barrier to driving revenue, even enabling them to buy from you directly through digital channels if appropriate. This is likely to be either a highly human-driven part of the process with sales or account teams taking the lead with pitches or direct sales meetings, or a highly digital one if your product lends itself to that. While current B2B marketing tends to assume that buyers will choose to buy products digitally and services from people, research indicates this is changing. According to Gartner, B2B buyers spend only 17 per cent of the total purchase journey with sales reps. And 44 per cent of millennials prefer no sales rep interaction at all in a B2B setting (Gartner, 2020). Coupled with the fact that many companies are seeking to expand their portfolio by offering digital solutions – companies may need to look again at the profitability of a time intensive, costly salesperson-led approach to this phase.

Client

Your objective once you have moved your buyer to being a client can be multifold, depending on what type of business you are in.

- You may need to drive loyalty and adoption for your services so that you increase revenue and keep competitors out. There may be a period of dissatisfaction at the early stages of a tricky implementation or through a period of discovery that your team needs to make. Marketing could help provide value to the client as they onboard your company as a new supplier.

- It may be a very efficient way to drive growth by finding new buyers within that client group for other parts of your portfolio. You know their business strategy well and are already proven to be able to deliver projects within their unique internal environment. You want to help them get best value from your organization by ensuring they know the full breadth of what you offer.

- Your company may be able to harness expert feedback from your client on your business strategy, product roadmap or team performance. Using marketing to deepen relationships can help generate positive client references or improve net promotor scores (NPS).

- It may make sense to build deep relationships with individuals at client accounts given the churn in the employment market; they could become invaluable advocates for your company as they get promoted, or introduce you to new business as they move to a new company.

Traditionally, account management has been the preserve of sales, but the last few years has seen the rise of account-based marketing (ABM), which is an approach that brings highly relevant insights, content and solutions to clients based on what you already know about them to add value or drive new pipeline. Whether you go for a full ABM programme, or do a lighter touch set of marketing activities, I would encourage you to consider this group of buyers within your marketing strategy. I will cover in Chapter 8 how you can decide how much time and resource you should put into it.

Each journey is different. Not all B2B buying decisions go through each stage at the same depth or rate; they might not go seamlessly from one to another either, as buyers don't always think in a linear or logical way as their business strategy shifts, the market changes, or new individuals join or leave companies. Decisions may also be delegated meaning the people you have been marketing to may switch to someone else mid-cycle. While buyer journeys vary, by keeping the framework top of mind – and understanding clearly which stage they are in or are about to be in means you will be better able to give buyers what they need when they need it.

Three types of metrics

Building an appropriate set of metrics for each phase is essential: it helps you to measure your return on investment, keep your plan on track and make decisions based on accurate information. However, it is important to use the right metrics.

FIGURE 3.1   Summary of the framework: what a buyer is trying to do and how the B2B marketer should respond

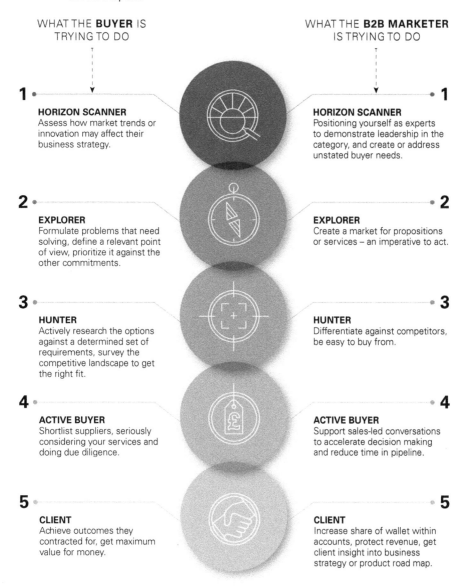

WHAT THE **BUYER** IS
TRYING TO DO

WHAT THE **B2B MARKETER**
IS TRYING TO DO

1

HORIZON SCANNER
Assess how market trends or
innovation may affect their
business strategy.

HORIZON SCANNER
Positioning yourself as experts
to demonstrate leadership in the
category, and create or address
unstated buyer needs.

1

2

EXPLORER
Formulate problems that need
solving, define a relevant point
of view, prioritize it against the
other commitments.

EXPLORER
Create a market for propositions
or services – an imperative to act.

2

3

HUNTER
Actively research the options
against a determined set of
requirements, survey the
competitive landscape to get
the right fit.

HUNTER
Differentiate against competitors,
be easy to buy from.

3

4

ACTIVE BUYER
Shortlist suppliers, seriously
considering your services and
doing due diligence.

ACTIVE BUYER
Support sales-led conversations
to accelerate decision making
and reduce time in pipeline.

4

5

CLIENT
Achieve outcomes they
contracted for, get maximum
value for money.

CLIENT
Increase share of wallet within
accounts, protect revenue, get
client insight into business
strategy or product road map.

5

When taking on new teams in the past I have found that there is a proliferation of numbers being presented to senior leaders, in a confusing way without enough context to know whether marketing is having an impact or not. Saying that a piece of thought leadership has 70,000 hits on a website sounds like it should be good. But if your target audience was seven million, it starts to look like an underperforming campaign; or if your solution is niche and could only be bought by a few thousand people then 70,000 looks like poor targeting. Outlining the target addressable market at each phase of the buyer framework with relevant objectives and results is much clearer and gives better insights into whether the strategy is working.

I often find too that metrics are jumbled. To help with this, I find it useful to think about metrics across three groups:

- *Input metrics*: this is what you and your team are executing, for example the number of blogs, events, pitch documents and demo videos. It is a measure of how productive the marketing team is.

- *Outcome metrics*: these are things that line up to your business strategy; either revenue related, such as pipeline value and won revenue, or client measures like NPS or brand equity. These align your marketing strategy to your business strategy and show return on investment.

- *Indicator metrics*: these help you track whether you are likely to hit your agreed targets. There is always a lag between activity and outcome, sometimes a long one. The decision-making process can be complex and slow at the Horizon Scanner and Explorer phase, meaning the pipeline won't convert for months or even years. In this instance, it is helpful to have indicator metrics so you can adjust if you need to dial up (or pull out of) activities that you've committed to. It also means that you can show progress to the business and manage their expectations in the knowledge that you are having an impact that will lead to the desired outcome.

At each part of the buyer journey framework, you'll measure different things depending on the objective. In the next few chapters, I'll cover how to think about input, outcome, and indicator metrics at each stage. These should roll up to an overall set of targets aligned to business outcomes, but if you try to measure the impact of the full buyer journey marketing with one number – for example, leads – you will put most of the marketing activity to one part of the buyer journey rather than taking a holistic view, which will damage your ability to drive sustainable, profitable revenue growth in the longer term. In the next chapters, as I go into more detail about each of the five stages of the buyer journey framework, it will become clearer which metrics are appropriate to use, along with selecting the right content and channel strategy.

How to work out whether a buyer is the progressing through their process

You can use insights from the market, existing clients, and internal stakeholders to work out how you will recognize when someone is moving from one phase to another and where any handoffs to sales teams should be. For example, if someone moves from strategic thought leadership to case studies on how you've helped a client solve a problem, it might indicate that they've prioritized dealing with a particular issue and are starting to understand how people have solved it in the past – i.e. moving from Horizon Scanner to Explorer. Or if they have started to spend time looking at detailed product information, they are indicating that they're ready to buy. As the buying process moves increasingly to digital channels, in marketing you hold a rich and powerful source of information about when buyers are on the move.

Critical to reframing your organization's objectives to align to the buyer experience is to embrace the mindset that no part of it is 100 per cent marketing and 0 per cent sales or 0 per cent marketing and 100 per cent sales across any phase in the journey. Marketers need to play a role in driving purchase and loyalty, sales need to help with profile raising with Horizon Scanners.

Some sales teams like to take leads very early in the cycle – particularly if they want to make a more consultative sale. Some effectively want a buyer on the end of a phone ready to sign a contract before they'll accept it. I would argue that taking the lead too early or expecting it to be so overly nurtured are both suboptimal, but having the discussion and a clear, documented agreement is an essential starting point. This will also enable you to identify, recommend and track marketing targets which are appropriate for each stage, given insights, support strategy and above all will help you get things done and be seen as an equal partner. Getting alignment up front means that you can focus energy and deliver insights about the buyers that matter most.

Putting together a shared plan across the buyer framework means that you will be aligned in how you show up in the market and will mean that you are able to drive revenue faster. It will also mean that you can share insights so you improve how each function operates, it aligns marketing expenditure to sales effort and allows you to set realistic timeframes for when the impact of marketing will be felt in the sales pipeline.

IN SUMMARY

- During the Horizon Scanner phase, your role as a marketer is to keep the conversation at a strategic level about themes and issues that matter to the buyer and to get your messages into the channels they are engaging with.

- During the Explorer phase, positioning your experts is key to convince buyers they don't have the expertise to solve an emerging problem themselves. It is vital to maintain a conversation with them via more tailored thought leadership and case studies.

- During the Hunter phase, you need to differentiate yourself from the competition and demonstrate that your solutions will deliver the outcomes they want. Client testimonials are essential here as can be connecting the buyer with one of your experts or a member of the sales team to answer questions on specific requirements.

- During the Active Buyer phase, B2B marketers should focus on supporting sales activities and ensuring the relevant information is available digitally.

- During the Client phase, drive loyalty, advance account-based marketing to grow share of wallet and use these clients as advocates to influence others and to give you feedback on your marketing strategy.

- Building an appropriate set of metrics for each phase is essential: it helps you to measure your return on investment, keep your plan on track and make decisions based on accurate information.

- Create a shared buyer journey strategy between marketing and sales to agree activity, metrics and when to hand over leads. Having a joint hypotheses on when a buyer is moving to the next phase of the journey is critical to this.

04
Horizon Scanner

Of the five phases of the buyer framework described, this can be the most challenging for B2B marketers. In this chapter I look at the content and channels to use to reach them, the metrics that will guide you and how to manage the wider business' expectations. Given the complexity of this phase, and how intertwined the C-suite is with regulators, policy makers and other influencers, I include an Insider Insight from Michael Stewart, Global Corporate Affairs and Communications Leader at PwC, who expounds the critical relationship between corporate communications and marketing.

This is a tricky part of the framework as in many cases the client doesn't know what they want – or even if they want anything at all. Executives are thinking strategically about the long-term health of their business, rather than about specific needs. They are scanning what's happening within their sector, and more broadly across the market to work out which macroeconomic trends such as technology, demographics, supply-chain bottlenecks or climate change will require them to shift their business model, and what other things they need to do to achieve their near-term financial targets. Their objective at this early stage of the journey is to get information to inform their strategy; your objective is to get your company's brand and messages in front of them by positioning yourself as an expert in their field or category leader in the market, offering helpful insights or new ways to think about problem sets. The benefits of doing this well can be multifold. As well as building your reputation and standing in the market, you can position your company as able to help buyers think about what they want to do, which could mean you are brought into discussions ahead of a formal procurement process. By educating buyers, you can differentiate yourself from competitors at an early stage, which could improve the chances of being considered later once they've decided what they want to do. Engaging with senior executives and buyers means you are perceived as more strategic, which may help you as they delegate decisions to their teams.

In the Horizon Scanner phase, you need to engage potential buyers through high quality thought leadership and that means content that is relevant, rich in ideas and an inspiration to action – and definitely not a sales pitch. Source Global Research (2021) found that during the pandemic, as business leaders faced new challenges in ambiguous circumstances and had to make decisions with little information, 51 per cent of executives spent more time-consuming thought leadership.

Once you know your target audience, develop a strategy to reach them in this phase. Prospects in senior roles will likely be looking for information from independent third-party sources rather than directly searching for opinions from a specific provider. They operate in an interconnected ecosystem, which includes their competitors, peers, direct teams and other teams in their business, as well as external market actors like journalists, analysts, regulators and policy makers, so make sure you have a stakeholder map with an outreach plan that covers these groups too.

Spend time identifying just who your target market is. Use your business strategy and engage your internal stakeholders to work out carefully who you are trying to reach, what sector they are in, where they are geographically and how many of them there are. If your company sells highly complex, expensive services, it could be that only a few people in the world are likely to be interested in acquiring them. In such a case it would be a waste of money to devise a wide-reaching advertising campaign, and much better to concentrate your resources on precisely targeting a narrow audience instead. As you have internal discussions, be wary of settling for sweeping statements like 'everyone in a C-suite role' – that may be true, but it is not particularly helpful from a targeting perspective as you go into the market with new ideas. Bear in mind that the individuals involved may be in high-level influencing roles, not the ultimate buyers that your company will work with day to day.

Articulate clearly what problems your company solves, then use this information to help extrapolate or refine what topics you can legitimately talk about. Michael has a very helpful three-part framework that he explains in his Insider Insight in this chapter. For example, your experts may want to talk about a number of topics that a business executive has on their minds, but you should use your business strategy to select a few that could generate future pipeline for your services. If you are still building your brand, and your experts are not well known in the market, work with partners or industry associations to lend credence to what you are saying.

Content

The importance of developing good thought leadership in the Horizon Scanner stage is paramount. In a professional services study by Source Global Research (2021), 16 per cent of buyers that found thought leadership particularly useful went on to buy services from that company, and 33 per cent said that thought leadership had the greatest impact in forming their perception of a firm.

Thought leadership gets your brand, point of view and subject matter experts (SMEs) into the buying process as potential clients start to shape their response to strategic challenges before they've even defined what they are going to do. Getting in front of them early gives you a competitive edge later in the process. Your buyer is speculating about whether something is important, so your thought leadership should inspire action – or create a new sense of urgency around a topic. Without this, your content is likely to fall flat. As you think about your editorial focus, consider what exactly you want to be a thought leader in and who your experts are, and hold yourself to a high bar in terms of quality and activity.

What you should talk about

People in your organization will have lots of ideas on a wide range of topics and are likely to have specific passions or areas of expertise. However, be careful what you choose to put out there. Think about where your brand has permission to play. Your internal experts may have amazing points of view but if they're not related to anything you sell, at least indirectly – or if buyers who know their market well don't think your opinion is relevant – you will have to spend a lot of money promoting the content to raise its legitimacy, which won't give you the right commercial return. As Michael states in a few pages, 'Be selective, avoid blindly supporting "pet" projects and seek strategic justification'. There is little point in producing thought leadership that doesn't encourage buyers to think about their challenges in a new way. It isn't helpful and won't be remembered. Your thought leadership needs to be memorable as it might take a buyer some weeks or months to decide that they want to do something about the issue.

As you design the content, use social listening, existing clients, and client teams to guide your thinking. Look online to find out what key target clients are talking about. Read the articles in the technical, functional or sector-specific publications they are likely to be reading. Look at the topics covered at the third-party events they are likely to be attending. These will give you good insights into what your buyers care about.

Then review what your competitors are doing, and what angles they are taking so you can find topics that feel new, unexplored, or differentiated, which will cut through the noise. Build a content pipeline that stretches over a sustained period – one-off articles or surveys may get a spike of interest, but any advantage will be eroded if you can't quickly follow up with more insights. Lastly you need to work out who in your organization will help you create the thought leadership. Horizon Scanners, whose problems are ambiguous and at this stage not fully defined, are starting to make complex decisions with imperfect information. Any decision they take carries a level of risk. When the level of that risk goes up, their tendency is to buy from experts, so this is an important opportunity to set the tone of your ongoing relationship.

Promoting experts – and their thought leadership – powerfully in the market will help your buyers. But you need to choose them carefully. I often see people positioned as experts who haven't contributed regularly to industry discussions and events, or even written about the topic more than once on their own channels. This erodes your reputational value and makes buyers sceptical about your company's understanding of the level of expertise needed to help with deeply technical and risky problems. Instead, identify the eminent thinkers among your subject matter experts and position them to become the voice of your business on the topics that matter to your buyer. Ask them which issues genuinely interest them, then match this to the list of topics you've created from your external research. Form a contract with this group and get them to commit to a certain amount of content on a regular basis which you can rely on, monitor via an editorial calendar, and put marketing effort behind promoting. Make sure that they have the foundations in place to build their profile in the business community, for example an up-to-date LinkedIn profile, active Twitter account and connections to the right industry associations or group – and support them with a plan for getting their content into the right channels.

Being content with your content

As you review the quality of your thought leadership, hold it up to a high bar. Here are some questions to ask yourself:

- Is it interesting? Is it new, or have others already flooded the market with this point of view? Does it have a point of view, or is it bland? Are you telling the audience something they already know or will your content help educate them in some way? Is it something exclusive, for example proprietary research, commissioned surveys, or a new voice or a fresh perspective?

- Is it different? Is the article telling them something that they are not hearing from one of your competitors?

- Is it legitimate? Does it feel like it has been written by one of your buyer's peers with the same level of expertise, including vocabulary and terms, that they'd expect?

- Does it need to be timely? Sometimes it is better to have something less well formed but of the moment, rather than a perfectly crafted piece that's late to the game. Try to segment your internal thought leaders into those who can respond fast to market changes and those that produce deeper insights that need time to develop or an extensive data collection exercise. There might be opportunities to prepare two pre-approved articles ahead of a market event with two possible outcomes, enabling you to go to market quickly when the result is known. For example, when my team was marketing during Brexit, we knew that it would either have a yes or no outcome so prepared content for both eventualities, allowing us to be quick off the mark once the decision was announced.

- Is it accessible? Use what you've researched and what you know from talking to clients or internal teams to think about what tone or style the audience likes. Understand the media they read and the channels they pay attention to. Consider too the format – busy senior stakeholders may not want something onerously long, so is it digestible if your audience travels frequently? Does it look good or stand out from the rest of the market?

- Is it memorable? They may be in the Horizon Scanner part of the process for months or years, so dipping in and out with peaks of content and nothing in between won't make you memorable enough as they move into the next phase. Having a distinctive point of view and steady flow of ideas will help you build credibility with this group over time.

- Is there enough of it? Whichever way you want to promote your expertise, make sure you have enough content to do it – and a reliable stream of new content coming over time otherwise you won't be able to establish yourself firmly in future buyers' minds. If you're worried you won't have enough content, you can generate new ideas for your SMEs – for example, is there an upcoming regulation which you might have expertise in? Or a sector-specific trend that you could develop a point of view on? Get creative about what is happening more broadly in the world, and how you can use interest in it to create an associated point of view. For example, my team used the anniversary of the first moon landing as a platform for talking about innovation and women in STEM (science, technology, engineering, maths). You may also be able to cut the content differently to get more mileage out of it, for example by splitting survey data into a series, or getting a response to your point of view from an outside source or a client.

Often businesses talk about moving their relationship up the strategic curve within their client. Achieving your objectives in this stage will help you, but it takes time, effort and commitment from your organization.

Channels

Once you have content, having a promotion strategy is vital. Many organizations go to huge trouble to develop great content but neglect to spend enough time or money making sure it gets in front of the right people. Look at your internal production to distribution ratio: how much time and effort gets spent creating thought leadership as opposed to getting it into the hands of the right prospects at the right time? Too often, thought leadership is published with a fanfare of promotion that then falls away fast as your marketing organization moves onto the next thing. The chances of you producing a piece of thought leadership at the exact moment that a prospect is considering the topic are quite small. Many businesses spend all their money on big bursts of promotion for marquee content rather than being *always on*, which allows buyers to easily discover it when they need it.

All buyers operate in an ecosystem that includes people beyond their own business and who shape their thinking as they look for trends or new ideas. They want to hear from experts and understand what their peers, market observers and suppliers are thinking about when it comes to macroeconomic topics and themes. You need a way to identify what these forums are and then try to get your content and credentials into them. Bear in mind too that buyers may not want to engage directly with your company's account teams in this part of the cycle as they don't want to set the expectation that they will go on to buy from your company. But they do want to hear from your experts. Given Horizon Scanners are looking for insights, not solutions, it is likely that your channel strategy will be skewed towards third-party (earned or paid) channels as this will be their first port of call as they develop their thinking. Third parties may be better placed to bring your point of view into the conversation, even if your executives aren't there. Senior people don't always look to the supplier community to help them articulate the problem, as they don't want to incur a debt of obligation later in the process. They will instead look to external points of view. Cultivating the right relationships with analysts, journalists and regulators will help you: but you need to be consistent, or this will backfire. Making stakeholder outreach part of your business as well as your marketing strategy may be fundamental to you being considered in this phase at all.

EARNED

- Media: executives thinking about their strategy in the Horizon Scanner phase will likely read publications like *The Wall Street Journal*, the *Economist*, *Bloomberg*, or the *Financial Times*, or they may look at publications more closely relevant to their function or sector. Find out what they are reading and build relationships with those journalists – either directly or in collaboration with your corporate communications team. Offer data or insights to relevant journalists or suggest your thought leaders provide comment or co-author pieces for the publication.

- Industry analysts: depending on your sector, these groups will work with your audience, speaking to hundreds of different people across a range of roles, and can have a huge influence over buyers and end-user professionals. It may make practical sense to assign your experts to these analysts to keep them regularly updated so the analysts can represent you accurately as they are advising their, and your, buyers.

PAID

- You can also place paid media advertising in the outlets cited above, which is an effective way of getting your message to senior executives. Remember at this stage it's about promoting your thought leadership, not your services.

- Media sponsorships and partnerships is the next stage on from pure advertising and helps you more deeply align your thought leadership/messaging with the external outlets that Horizon Scanners rely on to inform their opinions.

- Third-party events: there are likely only a small number of events that senior people in your audience will congregate at. See if you can take a keynote slot, sponsor a content stream, have a client round table or host some hospitality. Negotiate with the event organizer to have your thought leadership promoted through their channels pre and post event.

- Peer networks: offer to sponsor, or ask to attend, these networks which buyers often join to meet their peers and discuss common trends or challenges. By accessing their community, you can play a visible role in supporting the sector's thought leadership agenda. If you can't sponsor or attend an event, some of which deliberately exclude vendors, perhaps initiate a thought leadership campaign around the topics to be discussed and promote it to those involved.

- Alliances or partners: use any established relationships with them, particularly if you think they have a better respected brand in the buying group you are trying to target. Can you showcase your thought leadership alongside theirs through a joint event or promotion via their digital channels, for example, or directly through their sales teams?

OWNED

- Your company's broader networks: how can you harness the power of your leaders, account and sales teams who may be connected to your buyers' peers to promote, share and 'like' your company's thought leadership? Outline clearly to your internal audience what you're aiming to achieve by positioning yourself as an expert, then make sure they get all the latest posts, blogs, articles and opinion pieces.

- Your own social channels: though this is cost-efficient, it is worth making sure that you think carefully about what the purpose of the channel is, who it is for and how you balance the internal demands of this channel.

- Direct mail can also be effective if you have a book or whitepaper that feels helpful to the buyer; but these perform better if sent in a personalized way from someone senior in your business rather than being a generic email that isn't thoughtfully followed up.

Working with corporate communications

Positioning your brand in this juncture of the buying journey is likely to be a shared endeavour with corporate communications. You are marketing to a group of senior people who congregate and share ideas with peers in conversations your executives might not be party to. Driving up brand perception helps achieve reputational and commercial goals, so you are likely targeting the same external audiences and asking for time from the same internal stakeholders. As Michael Stewart shares later in this chapter, your audiences expect you to be in lockstep with your colleagues – even if you don't have the same reporting line. Both teams' successes are inextricably linked with each other. As he remarks, 'communications and marketing leaders have to ensure there is consistency – understood internally and communicated externally – about the company's different roles as employers, corporate citizens, suppliers and partners.'

You want to be giving clear, consistent messages about what the company cares about and what it does. Content that appeals to Horizon Scanners will also be interesting for broader stakeholders who influence their decisions and vice versa. Sometimes the person on the receiving end is both a buyer and an influencer into other buying groups.

Start by jointly defining the total audience for both teams and what you think that these buyers, influencers, and market observers will need at different points of their engagement with you. Think through what issues you will support because they are core to your purpose and strategy, but be selective, using the services you already provide. This will help you focus the organization and not scatter the market with your company's beliefs and opinions that perhaps aren't being backed up by your company's actions. Otherwise you risk reputational risk, such as being accused of greenwashing or being held up as hypocrites and ultimately this brand erosion is bad for your commercial success.

Across your campaigns, define which topics and channel activations will be owned by marketing, which by communications and which are shared. As Michael remarks, it doesn't matter who owns what, but roles must be clear, and teams need to be collaborative. Agree up-front some governing principles, for example which types of messages take priority across social media, or how many times you think it makes sense to communicate to a specific group in any given time period. Doing this together means you can uncover any gaps and minimize the risk of sending out mixed messaging that could confuse Horizon Scanners.

Agree too the operating rhythm between teams and – critically – what your internal stakeholder map is and who will communicate with them. As I mentioned, it is in both your interests to look like a seamless machine so tripping over each other when talking about progress, results or new ideas won't help.

A company's brand and reputation hinge on many things, not least the way marketing and corporate communications collaborate. Get it wrong and you'll duplicate effort, create internal tensions, even disrupt commercial operations; make the effort to understand each other and develop a smooth, cooperative relationship, and you'll drive strategic and stakeholder alignment to great advantage.

INSIDER INSIGHT

Michael Stewart, Global Corporate Affairs and Communications Leader, PwC

In this Insider Insight, Michael Stewart, Global Leader of Corporate Affairs and Communications at PwC since 2019, draws both on recent experience with one of the world's largest multinational professional services firms and on earlier spells as a partner at McKinsey and Global Vice Chairman of Edelman, where he advised numerous global organizations.

CLARITY OF ROLES

As an outside adviser I found many of the communications and marketing teams I came across were unclear about their mandates and how to divide up the labour. To overcome that sort of dysfunction, marketing and communications must reach a joint understanding of the company's strategy, how they intend to promote it, and how they plan to engage with stakeholders. What's the purpose of the business? What does it want to be known for? When do things need to be done together (by communications and marketing) and when executed separately? How to reconcile complementary perspectives? How to deal with friction among stakeholders? In cases where both functions are involved, who's on point to deliver what?

Communications and marketing leaders must ensure that there is consistency, understood internally and communicated externally, about the company's different and sometimes contradictory roles as an employer, corporate citizen, supplier and partner. There has to be a continuum – teams can't afford to think of audiences as having distinct needs, but as being connected via a common message.

COMMERCIAL REALITIES

It's all too easy for marketing and communications to operate in silos, engaging with stakeholders in isolation from other teams. It's also possible to lose sight of the ultimate goal. At PwC, functional leaders spend a lot of time discussing regulation, public policy, and broader societal issues in the context of the firm's commercial aspirations and strategic objectives. Any position we take on carbon taxes tomorrow, for example, needs to be compatible with the way we might want to sell an ESG (environmental, social and governance) service or provide advice to our clients. The best companies don't just have a short-term horizon, they are thinking about the products they might launch, the people they might attract, and the regulatory environment which would most help them succeed way into the future.

SOCIETAL ISSUES

As I see it there are three points on the grid. At the top there are the issues that you have to support because they are core to your purpose and strategy and to the sort of service or product offerings you're likely to make in the medium to long term. Leaders must engage with these wholeheartedly, though what exactly they are will be different at a mining company to what they are at, say, a financial services organization. Then there is the set of issues driven by the personal passions either of top management, or employees, or clients, or any or all of these. Such issues require tough decision-making – how do you make them sustainable and justifiable if they do not map directly to your strategy or to your budget? Be selective, avoid blindly supporting 'pet' projects and seek strategic justification even if it is not immediately obvious. Climate change was a good example at one financial business I know – there was no apparent strategic reason to get involved in the debate but when leaders thought harder, they realized that the sort of talent they expected to hire over the next few years would likely be committed to this topic. The third rung of the grid is for topics that, however important to individuals or even leadership, are clearly at odds with the prevailing behaviour of the business. Companies that don't pay adequate wages, for instance, will simply lack credibility if they actively enter the debate on income inequality tempting it may be, these sorts of options should be avoided.

Try to keep this sort of categorization of societal issues top of mind. Without it, it will be hard to make sensible decisions when the next big thing hits the headlines.

DANGERS OF MIXED MESSAGING

At one company I used to work with, whose communications and marketing were normally remarkably coherent, there were two near misses. In one case it became a marketing imperative to drive sales at one of the group's more lacklustre businesses. This led to the development of a marketing campaign – at a cost of tens of millions of dollars – which had a punchline that, while not overtly sexual, was at best controversial and at worst provocative and offensive, just when the MeToo movement was drawing attention to workplace bullying and sexual violence. Marketing was so focused on its commercial priorities that it failed to spot the reputational risk.

The second instance highlighted how corporate affairs can also be blinkered. Marketing leaders were trying to close an important acquisition at a time when one of the company's social affairs teams was seeking to raise the company's profile in a debate that had recently become politically charged. From a broad reputation point of view there was a rationale for the company to get involved, but had the intervention gone ahead it would have had severe business consequences.

Left in their silos, the marketing and corporate communications teams in this company would have incurred huge reputational risk. Remember that trade-offs between purpose, policy and sales are even more important in periods of economic stress when corporate affairs is likely to be more intensely focused than usual on reputation and marketing is trying particularly hard to grab commercial opportunities.

REACHING THE INTERNAL AUDIENCE

Sometimes the content a company puts out in their name, whether it be on social media or in Tier One publications like *The Wall Street Journal* or *Financial Times*, is more important for those inside the company than outside. It's a validation of the messages employees have been hearing in other formats about what's important, and it's a way of cutting through the incredible noise to reinforce values. Letting a thousand flowers bloom with content is not helpful from a positioning perspective. Allowing too much proliferation creates an impression that everything matters, and nothing matters.

SEGMENTING CONTENT

Corporate communications, through the dissemination of content that is compelling (natural, organic, authentic and shareable), acts as the company's external brand ambassador. Segmentation is critical here – what's going to be compelling for Gen Z and sharable on Tik Tok and other platforms will be quite different from what very senior leaders want to read and share (both the content and the channels). By tailoring content towards different audiences, you'll achieve both high volumes in terms of hits and stickiness in terms of audience engagement.

DISTRIBUTION AND CHANNEL OWNERSHIP

I'm agnostic on whether marketing or corporate communications own channels, as long as there is a continuum across, and a partnership between, the different functions. I've seen effective companies where all social media content and asset creation is owned by marketing, and other effective companies where it's all done by communications. Whoever owns it must deliver across the whole spectrum and spend the resources in a way that reflects this. If social media is owned by marketing and marketing teams do not understand how to engage with policymakers, regulators or broader stakeholders, the model is broken. What works for a 27-year-old consumer, after all, is unlikely to work for somebody on Capitol Hill in Washington DC. Worse still is replicating or duplicating roles in the two functions, which will only drive up cost, undermine the impact of everybody's messaging, and lead to brutal cost cutting when the downturn comes.

All this calls for close collaboration between leaders. Earned media is probably a channel and an audience best owned by corporate communications – but both functions will want to be active in it. There's a world of difference between pitching an opinion piece to an international publication on thought leadership (something likely to be handled by a communications professional with good relationships with key journalists), and negotiations over a paid promotion for a new product in a trade monthly (where marketing will probably have the inside track).

It's not about competition for budget or access to leadership. Both sides will have a greater impact if they understand why they need the other one.

As Michael astutely observes, done well, the partnership between corporate communications and marketing can mean that you can mutually reinforce each other's goals and help guard against 'pet projects' that don't support the Horizon Scanner or your company's broader strategy. Below I talk about the metrics that can be used to determine successful investment in this part of the framework – a win for both teams might be to align marketing and communication measures so that the budgets secured can go further in achieving both your reputational and commercial goals.

Metrics

In this phase of the buyer journey, you are unlikely to acquire concrete new leads – in fact, if you peg the success of your thought leadership to this part of the buying process then it will make your efforts seem ineffective. Remember, your objective is to elevate conversations with senior executives, creating conversations to improve your reputation. You want to position your company as experts to create or address unstated buyer needs.

If you want to extend your reach as a brand, this is a critical stage of the relationship build between your company and the market, but it can be hard to know what to measure and communicate in a way that feels valuable to your stakeholders. It is essential, however. It might feel easy to make short cuts here and in the next phase, but that could dramatically impact your future pipeline. Here are some suggested metrics in the three groupings I outlined earlier in the book:

FIGURE 4.1 Horizon Scanner stage metrics

INPUT METRICS Measure of how productive the marketing team is	INDICATOR METRICS How likely marketing are to hit the agreed targets	OUTCOME METRICS How marketing performed related to the marketing and business strategy
Number of journalist conversations	Requests for data or comments	Raised profile of your brand: • Number of third party articles featuring your thought leadership or experts • Mentions in target publications • Media share of voice
Number of articles, blogs, points of view developed, number of proprietary research pieces, number of social posts, money spent on promoting thought leadership e.g. through media	• Number of social mentions/ shares/likes • Number of social followers from clients/prospects you want to engage with • Number of people willing to take part in surveys or follow up interviews • Number of interactions with named influencers • Reads, downloads, views, shares, likes of thought leadership	Associated your company with topics buyers care about: • Number of people in your target audience engaging with content • Amount of time spent engaging with your content
Number of third party or industry events / webinars you speak at, number of keynote speeches	Number of sign-ups for your sessions	Directly engaged buyers with your proprietary content: • Attendee numbers • Face to face engagement metrics e.g. number of touch points with key buyers • Anecdotal and qualitative feedback • Client requested follow up conversations with your experts

Moving the buyer to the next phase

You don't know how long a buyer will be in this phase. Deciding what to focus their business's valuable resources on takes time, and tough choices often require a lot of research. They may want to spend time looking at a plethora of information; or doing something about future issues might not be top of their priority list. But if – and when – they are ready to move on, you need to be ready for it. When driving people from a third-party source into your own channels, think about what you want the buyer to do next. You may want to offer them more thought leadership on similar topics, so create a series and proactively offer a couple of articles or points of view to go to next. Or you may want to give them the option to look at content related to the next phase of the journey to see if you can move them on, for example by joining an upcoming round table on the topic you're hosting or speaking to one of your experts. Ideally, particularly if they are on your digital channels, you'd do both so they can choose their own next steps and you maximize your chances of catching them if they are ready to move.

IN SUMMARY

- The Horizon Scanner is the most elusive of your targets, but if you're selling complex or strategic services, they will be one of your most important.

- They are top-down influencers in their organization, responsible for strategy and prioritization so will be critical in establishing whether there will be a project at all. You want to make sure if they do decide to act, you will be credible in future stages.

- At this stage your buyer is speculating about whether something is important, so your thought leadership should inspire action – or create a new sense of urgency around a topic. It is definitely not a sales pitch and should not look or sound like one.

- You need to have great content from experts who are passionate about their subject, have interesting points of view that feel fresh and different and have a lot to say so you can keep your company's expertise in the market over sustained periods of time.

- Third parties are essential channels as buyers often don't want to engage with sales or account reps directly in this phase.

- Work in lockstep with corporate communications: you share external audiences, channels and internal stakeholders, and your successes are mutually dependent.

- Be patient! This phase is important to your business but can take time – sometimes years. Don't lose heart and redivert money into short-term lead generation as you will regret it in the future.

05
Explorer

Once senior executives have started connecting strategic issues to opportunities that will drive their business forward or to a problem that may impede their growth, they will start refining their thinking about the issue. In this chapter we will look at the importance of creating an urgency to act, positioning yourself as having the skills and knowledge that they don't have internally to solve the problem. Positioning your experts continues to be critical at this stage: in this chapter Joanna Brown, Director of Communications and Engagement at EY, gives some sound advice about how to choose what to talk about in the market and cultivate a rich set of subject matter experts that you can rely on to showcase your category leadership and company insights.

Explorers are making a particular challenge or opportunity relevant to their business and are seeking to understand what others are doing in their industry, sector or function. They may also look at what's happening in other geographic areas or at businesses with similar interests. Having decided that they need to do something different, they will prioritize it against the other things they have committed to do in the short and long term. They know the problem they need to solve at a high level and are defining a point of view about implications, as well as the outcomes they want to achieve. To do this, they are seeking opinions and ideas about what other companies are doing, whether in their sector or not. They might need information to pull together a high-level business case, or to secure resources that will start scoping problems in more detail. Buyers are looking for suppliers and other third parties to provide insights that will help them build, enhance, or refine their business case. They might or might not know that your company can help them, so you need to think about which channels you use to promote your content depending on how well known you are for providing solutions to their problems. You can position your expertise, grounded in an understanding of the problem they are facing, which will make you seem relevant and empathetic. They are determining whether or not to do something, then whether to go externally to buy something. Often, they decide not to: research estimates that the consulting market in the UK could be 20 times bigger than what it is currently – the gap is where buyers decide either not to act, to postpone a decision or to do the work themselves (Source Global Research, 2021). Your role is to help create an imperative to act. Explorers are early leads – so by demonstrating you have relevant experience to help them achieve their business outcomes, you can start to build an impression of what you'd be like to work with. And again, this means you may get the chance to engage with them ahead of a formal procurement process, which will give you a competitive edge.

The buyer group may expand at this stage as senior executives start to engage their teams or others within their business to help decide what they are going to do. In the Horizon Scanner phase, you developed thought leadership in line with your business strategy targeting specific, relevant members of the C-suite or other senior executives. To determine content and channel strategy for the Explorer stage, start with the senior executives you were targeting then work out which functional head job roles report to them to build out your new target market groups. For example, if you're selling HR technology and have targeted your thought leadership in the first phase to Chief Human Relations Officers (CHROs), you will need to think about those surrounding that CHRO, who might be pulled into the process at this stage. This includes people in their immediate teams – heads of payroll or heads of talent – and their business partners, for example people in IT who might be asked to help identify how to solve the problem that the CHRO has. Build out your new addressable markets and size them so you know how many people you are looking to target in this part of your campaign. Given this, when you think about what type of information they like and channels buyers prefer, you may need to have two branches to your content and channel strategy. In the example above, consider how HR thinks about IT and vice versa. It might be that you need to flex your content and format approach to each audience too. For example, you may predict – or use previous campaigns to inform your view – that HR professionals prefer written content heavily aligned to their sector, whereas IT professionals are more likely to look at sector-agnostic content in video format.

Explorers want to be educated about what market problems mean for them and their business areas specifically. They also want to be reassured others have either faced these challenges and successfully overcome them or are currently going through them and could help shape their thinking. This education process can be lengthy: it depends on how much capacity they have to learn about something new versus tackling today's delivery challenges, or whether they are leading or following the market in addressing these issues and how well resourced they are. They may need to convince lots of other people internally to do something different and – in the case of professional or managed services – that they should use a third party as opposed to doing it themselves with existing resources. Winning work depends on you being able to start linking what clients need to what you have: but be warned – this takes time. You will need to manage expectations internally about the volume of leads you will create in this phase and how quickly you'll create them.

Content

Explorers want to know how other people have addressed the problems they are prioritizing. You are creating an imperative for them to think and act differently. Whereas Horizon Scanners are looking to see what might happen and what trends may affect their business, buyers at this stage have decided something is important and they might need to do something; they just don't know yet whether they need to act now and be convinced that they need someone to help them. They are looking for opinions, high-level case studies, research or insights that help shape their thinking and will support their decision. Thought leadership continues to be vital, and you want to inject urgency and show them that you have the expertise they don't have themselves that will be critical for their success.

It is important to research what your target buyers think at this stage and use it in your messaging. For example, if your buyer is looking to improve their speed to market, then content around agility, digital capabilities or innovation will be interesting. If they are looking to create efficiencies, then talking about process, operations or supply chain management will get their attention. You will need to actively link your content from the Horizon Scanner stage and make it relevant to the new phase of their process.

Try to include data or insight that makes it relevant to the industry they are in, the functional role they play, organizational size or geographic reach. This phase is about beginning to build a bridge between high strategic themes and getting ready to buy between the Explorer and Hunter phases of the framework.

There are several formats that can be effective here:

- *Opinion pieces*. These allow you to showcase your expertise but in a way that doesn't feel sales oriented. These should build on what you've done in your Horizon Scanner phase and make it sector, function or geographically relevant depending on what matters to your target audience. Gently promote your company's services at the end of the piece in case the buyer wants to move fast or if they are ready to move on to the next phase but the piece itself should be *solution agnostic*. Buyers will want to hear that you have expert opinions and are part of a conversation. They will be observing trends and gathering insights but may not be ready to buy, so giving them lots of information about your services at this stage doesn't help them. Giving them insights and a reason to accelerate their internal thinking, or an understanding that they may need a supplier to help them solve it, will be more constructive.

- *Industry insights and market trends*. This sort of content allows you to position yourself in the buyers' minds as a credible player in the market. It also gives your subject matter experts important, relevant information to comment on in their thought leadership. You want to show understanding of the specific industry, functional, organizational, or geographic challenges your buyer is facing as they start to think about what their own role might be in helping their company address the issues in front of them.

- *Digital diagnostics*. I like to use these in conjunction with surveys that are useful data points for your buyers but often don't have anything particularly new or insightful to say. You can use a diagnostic tool where buyers enter information about themselves, such as functional area, region, role level and organization size, which then gives them access to survey data relevant to them. This is more valuable for buyers as it gives them a benchmark of their own performance or capabilities – and can help you by injecting urgency into their buying process.

- *High-level case studies*. At this point in the journey, remember, buyers are still not looking for detail about what you do. However, offering them a high-level, strategic example of how you have worked through these challenges with another company can be helpful. Focus on the earliest phase of the project you choose to write about and show how you thought through the problem with the client, how you agreed the first pragmatic steps, and how you advised them on their broader approach or overall strategy. If you don't have case studies about this early phase of thinking, outline how your company would approach a problem. Demonstrate how you would engage with buyers, give examples of the questions you'd ask, and show how you would go about putting together a group of experts.

Consider at this stage offering specific Explorers exclusive access to content – or introduce a unique layer of insight tailored to their needs. For example, if you've done a survey on the impact of changes in workforce trends, you could add something extra for those with globally diverse, remote employees as opposed to those with office-based staff.

This is an important opportunity to demonstrate you deeply understand the buyer's problem and the peculiarities of their sector, function, or country they operate in. This makes you relevant, memorable and shows that you can guide them in framing up what they need to do. If you get this right, you can get onto shortlists you wouldn't otherwise be considered for and accelerate other parts of the buyer process having established yourself as knowledgeable and trustworthy.

Across the Horizon Scanner and Explorer phases you need thought leadership – and plenty of it. Cultivating a bank of experts within your organization who you can draw on to create and curate content is essential. Joanna Brown, who has more than 20 years' experience successfully working with executives in a number of professional services companies, offers some advice about how you choose what to talk about, encourage relevant experts, maintain narrative control and deliver content that resonates.

INSIDER INSIGHT

Joanna Brown, Director of Communications and Engagement, EY

At the time of interviewing, Joanna was Director of Executive Engagement and Partnerships at Tata Consultancy Services and has spent more than 20 years driving content development in marketing roles at big international companies (EY, Accenture and Capita). In this Insider Insight Joanna discusses why leading B2B companies should nurture and manage their subject matter experts as conference speakers, round table conveners, authors of high-quality articles on thought leadership, or a mix of all three. She explains where to get started, how to deal with big egos, and what incentives to offer reluctant executives.

THE IMPORTANCE OF EXPERTS

If you're trying to make top people in the company famous you first have to establish that they really are experts and that they have a clear point of view, ideally based on a good track record and a certain level of seniority in the business. It's possible to glue on a fake persona but authenticity will always be more convincing. I like to get to know the budding stars by following their profiles and interests online, meeting them in the office, listening to how they talk and seeing what topics make their eyes light up. Those that just don't have it come across without conviction. There's a world of difference between these speakers and the ones that are really animated.

LINKING TO STRATEGY

There's no point having someone who's passionate about something if what they're passionate about is not relevant to the business. The people who represent the company have to talk or write about topics that reflect the organization's drivers and its business strategy. And they must choose the right audience. Are they going to be a global colossus and speak at Davos, will they be better at intimate round tables, or should they avoid the camera and stick to publishing articles? It's important to know which executive will come across best at an opening event, which will wow audiences looking for academics, and who should be fielded to talk intelligently and cogently on a current affairs programme.

NARRATIVE CONTROL

Don't just have people scattered across the media and conference circuit talking about anything they like, particularly if there are a lot of mavericks in the company. Talk to the CMO and CEO so they understand why this is important – and reinforce your message. Everyone in marketing these days realizes there must be a common look and feel in marketing materials. Finding a strategic, common narrative with appropriate tone and register is key to this.

Executives interested in promoting their own profile are hard to control but if you can win their support by helping them find good opportunities you have a better chance of harnessing that energy. Show them what good (and bad) looks like, perhaps by filming the audience occasionally rather than their presentation and highlighting moments of engagement or turning points when they're looking at their phones. Find advocates in the organization – preferably one or two senior, and co-operative, people who you have helped to be more effective and powerful speakers. Where possible use data to show the impact on their pipeline.

SHRINKING VIOLETS

At the other end of the spectrum there are experts who have plenty to say but are reluctant to put their hand up. At one of the companies I worked for we had just such a senior manager: intelligent, hardworking but nervous. We knew she had great potential but rather than throwing her straight into a major event she started with some internal activities, moved to chairing conversations at our own round tables, and finally stepped up to external conferences. At first, we chose a safe one where we knew the audience was friendly: that gave her a chance to grow her confidence. My advice would be to provide the support and training but not rush it.

NO MONOPOLY ON WISDOM

There's a widespread assumption, particularly among companies that don't have a lot of content to hand, that all thought leadership has to be their own. But one of the most successful campaigns I was ever involved in explicitly drew attention to other companies (not direct competitors, admittedly) and the intelligent things they had to say. There's no harm sending someone a TED talk if it's addressing a topic of mutual interest or inviting a prospect to an external event and perhaps using the ideas discussed there and a dinner afterwards to bring them up to date with your own thinking. Far from being a sales pitch you've helped them tap into a wider ecosystem of conversations.

MAKE CONTENT COMPELLING

No one has to read something just because it has a big company's name on it. Content has got to be engaging – there's nothing worse than opening up a piece of thought leadership to be confronted by dense and dark prose, free of anecdotes and everyday language. Use journalistic skills and call on agencies and professional writers to help get the right tone if you don't have good internal experts, though my advice to marketers would be to hire more people with strong writing skills.

Too much B2B thought leadership and marketing is identical – articles open with the same ponderous sentiments or go to the other extreme and become flippant. In an ideal world nothing should be published without sign-off by an editorial board, formal or informal. Bring in a set of external eyes from time to time, an accommodating client who will tell you truthfully if the tone is right or if there are too many clichés. Examples and anecdotes enliven an article, as does flagging or emphasizing the key messages as you would when engaging a child in a story or entrusting a friend with an important piece of information. Look through an article before publication and ask if all the information provided is really essential, and if not lift it out, or put it into a footnote or a boxed-off Q&A at the end.

TAILORED MESSAGES

It's useful with small audiences to know where readers are on the buyer journey. Are they about to make a purchase? Have they only just set their budget for the year or are they at the end of the financial year and needing to spend money in a hurry? What issues are preoccupying them? What is the background noise in their heads that they can't dislodge but which the content and ideas you are supplying will help them address? If you're sending them an article, will they read it at work (when it can be more serious) or on the train?

INCENTIVES

People who you want to encourage to develop their ideas into conference speeches or thought leadership pieces are sometimes reluctant because they'd rather spend the time with clients, or they just think the effort isn't worth it. You need to convince them that being involved will help them find their next job, or show them that 12 organizations read their stuff or gave feedback on their presentation and three are now in discussion with sales. They'll know they're making an impact when they're invited to events without having to pay for sponsorship.

Channels

With complex solutions, buyers are looking for new suppliers infrequently – and given churn rates in senior roles, may only buy your solution once during their tenure. So, they will consult third parties who are close to the supplier market – analysts, industry observers, third-party advisers and peers – for help. When thinking about your channel strategy, you will need to blend earned and paid channels with your own proprietary ones. Like Horizon Scanners, Explorers are looking for insight rather than solutions, so you will probably need to invest more in third-party than owned channels. The balance will depend on how well known you are in the market for providing solutions – which will allow you to focus more on your own channels – and whether there are reputable sources that your buyers look to for advice on specific topics.

EARNED

- Media: At this point, executives are likely to rely on publications relevant to their function or sector. Use your target job-role list and find out what they read. Build relationships with journalists. This way, you are more likely to be able to get your subject matter experts quoted in the piece or writing the article themselves for more niche publications.

- Analysts and third-party advisers: these may be providing commentary on issues and trends in the market that affect your buyers at this stage. They are often seen as a trusted, neutral source of information, so identify who they are, what role they are playing and make sure you keep them briefed on any new things that you're doing or thought leadership you have. This will help them give an accurate view of your company's services as well as point to helpful points of view from your experts to any explorers.

- Peer networks: there will be a plethora of organized peer networks to choose from – on and offline. Make sure you know what these groups are and that your SMEs are well-connected within them. They need to be active participants – so agree at the outset what this looks like and what they need from you to support them. This can be a place where offering *exclusive* early access to content that you're producing can help the SME attract interest from the buying group. Some do not let suppliers in, so try to build relationships with the organizers and send them some of this early access content. This will enable them to add value to their membership while getting your brand and points of view to your buyers.

- Opinion formers and first movers: think about whether you can give trendsetters and market shapers exclusive access to your thought leadership or experts. If you're in a product environment, give them an early look at innovations, or let them be part of a beta testing group so you can get their feedback as you develop the product. This way they will feel invested in your success.

- Alliances and partners: if they are better known than you are with your target buying group, use their established relationship with buyers to showcase your thought leadership in their channels or via their sales teams.

PAID

- Paid media: this is a way of promoting your content directly into the channels your buying group is looking at, or to them directly through LinkedIn. If you are advertising your content, make sure that the promise of the advert is fulfilled by the receiving page on the website – looking at bounce rates or time on page will help you work out if this is the case.

- Third-party events and webinars: keep a keen eye on what is in the market – and who is attending them, as senior executives do not give up their precious time easily. Start by ensuring that your target market is attending, that the quality of attendees is high and that they are people you wouldn't be able to access otherwise. Make sure you send your subject matter experts, not salespeople – and ensure you have follow-up content that builds on the event topics. Given you're targeting senior buyers at this stage, you will need to agree a follow-up strategy. If your executives have met a senior buyer, think through who contacts them afterwards and what new insights you will offer to keep the conversation going.

OWNED

- Create a community: launching a group of like-minded and interested people, perhaps unified by job function, sector or country can be an invaluable way for buyers to learn from one another and for your company to position itself as at the centre of like-minded thinkers and problem solvers. What's attractive here for those buyers that are invited is that it's hard for them to do it themselves. Such an initiative should also help you get insights into how buyers are thinking about their problems that you can then share with sales, product experts or account management teams. Make sure that you have experts attending these events or calls – though make sure that they are about relationship building and not selling. If they become too much about product placement, demonstrating a service, or overtly showing case studies of previous successes, you will lose credibility and the group will fail. Get it right, though, and you will gain a huge advantage over your competitors as buyers move to the next stage. The value to participants will increase if you summarize the insights from each session and feed it back to them after the event. In this way, you're continuing the conversation. For example, I take part in a monthly CMO peer group which discusses a wide range of issues from creativity to inflation. The follow-up summary has incredibly useful insights to share with my team about what others are doing – as well as what CMOs at our clients are thinking about.

- Run your own proprietary events and webinars: bring together people with similar job titles in the same sectors to discuss a specific topic you've done research on. So if you've just done a survey on European regulation, you may want to bring together a group of Chief Risk Officers to discuss the themes. This will help you promote your content and raise your brand profile. If you are able to, capture the discussion and package it: you get data about your report, insights into how it is relevant across different organization types and greater return on investment for your content as you can extend its shelf life.

- Your company's broader networks: as with the Horizon Scanner phase, look at how your leaders, account teams and sales are connected to your buyers (it might be that there are more connections as the buyer group expands). They should promote, share and 'like' your company's thought leadership – but it would be better still if they offered opinions or if they encouraged engagement from the audience. If they know people in the expanded buyer group, then they may be able to email something relevant to start the conversation.

- Email: unsolicited spam is never effective, but if an email comes from someone that the buyer knows – or if it has something extremely different or useful to say, then it can work. In my experience, email alone won't get great traction, but it can work as one of a blended series of tactics.

Metrics

Your objective is to generate a market of interested parties for your products or services, create an imperative to act and get yourself considered as they start getting serious about buying. This will help your business find new revenue streams and establish multi-year pipeline. Having good contact data is the cornerstone of effective targeting so as your target addressable market expands, being able to collect more data in the form of contacts is also an indicator of success at this phase. You are gathering more early leads to be nurtured, so don't underestimate the power of having good information as you cultivate interest through this stage and into the next.

FIGURE 5.1 Explorer stage metrics

INPUT METRICS Measure of how productive the marketing team is	INDICATOR METRICS How likely marketing are to hit the agreed targets	OUTCOME METRICS How marketing performed related to the marketing and business strategy
Number of opinion pieces, blogs and articles in third party publications	• Number of positive media and social media mentions (ideally from targeted client group) • Content performance: number of read/share/view of materials or time spent on assets, website visits (from target clients), organic search, visits to opinion pages on your website • Email open rates	Raised profile of your brand: • Number of articles featuring your thought leadership or experts • Articles featuring your thought leadership or SMEs in target publications Associated your company with topics buyers care about: • Number of people in your target audience engaging with content • Amount of time spent engaging with your content
Number of keynote speaker or panel slots	• Number of acceptances for sessions, number of attendees • Audience feedback	Expanded reach: • New buyer contacts made for nurture campaigns • Number of follow up discussions initiated
Proprietary research pieces and number of events or webinars that you run to promote them 1	• Number of positive media and social media mentions (ideally from targeted client group) • Content performance: number of read/share/view of materials or time spent on assets, website visits (from target clients), organic search, visits to opinion pages on your website • Email open rates	Established your company as a trusted advisor: • Attendee numbers at your proprietary events Associated your company with topics buyers care about: • Number of people in your target audience engaging with content • Amount of time spent engaging with your content • Face to face engagement metrics e.g. number of touch points with key buyers
Number of industry bodies or social groups part of	Industry body advocates, how active you are in these (e.g. how often you're asked to present)	Industry analyst mentions

Moving the buyer to the next phase

During this phase of the buyer journey the B2B marketer's job is to incentivize action. As you execute across the channels discussed in this chapter – using content types appropriate to Explorers from the buying organization – think about what you want them to do next. Don't leave them hanging. If you have conducted a market survey and provided interesting insights, make explicit what the message is and implications for buyers. Quite often, I see that B2B marketers are not thinking through this part of the journey; they develop interesting thought leadership but neglect to direct readers to the next step either with an associated piece of content or an offer to follow up with the author. Always think about how to nudge them to the next piece of content or activity that they could engage with.

IN SUMMARY

- Explorers know the problem they need to solve at a high level and are starting to look at what others are doing in this space as well as define the outcomes they'd like to achieve.

- They are not yet sure if they can manage the problem themselves or would benefit from further support. Your job is to inject a sense of urgency and demonstrate your expertise in this area via your own content and channels as well as reputable third parties.

- Your target audience may start to broaden to include parties who could have a vested interest in finding a solution, such as finance, HR and procurement.

- Explorers are early leads, but you are still at the beginning stages of the B2B buyer journey, so you may need to manage expectations internally about the volume and how quickly they can be converted.

- Like Horizon Scanners, Explorers take their time. Don't give up on them and redivert spending to those that feel closer to buying something; these Explorers are the basis of your future growth.

06
Hunter

Once buyers reach this phase, they know what they want and are starting to look at possible solutions or providers. In this chapter we will look at how you can stand out compared to your competitors, the wider buying group you will be marketing to, as well as how to create more interactive content and identify a strong buying signal. Your role as a B2B marketer is to improve your company's chances of being chosen by making sure your buyers have as much relevant information to match their specific needs to your propositions as possible. Help yourself too by being very clear about how your services are better than the others in the market. You may have been engaging with individuals in the buying group through the Horizon Scanner and Explorer phases, but if they are replacing an existing solution, or if they have a very well-defined problem, they may be starting their process at this point and encountering your company for the first time.

As we've already ascertained, the B2B buying process is complicated. Buyers are going through a journey and a series of internal processes and decisions about which you may have little knowledge. Insights that you've gleaned in the previous stages of the journey – and any information you can get from the sales team – will be essential.

In the Hunter phase, particularly in cases where problems and solutions are more complex, the risks high, and the costs significant, buyers typically form a cross-functional group to manage their thinking process and assess who should be shortlisted or considered. This means your audience will expand again, sometimes significantly. There is likely to be a primary buyer who is leading the process because it is their team that will benefit from the purchase, or because their role requires them to be the expert that is buying it on behalf of the company. They will bring in members of their teams, associated groups like finance or IT, and in large organizations it is typical to have procurement running the actual process. Buyer roles at this stage could include:

- Someone – or a small group – who scanned the market and prioritized this as a problem they want to solve via the Horizon Scanner and Explorer phases. They own the business process which generates the need that your solution will solve. They are accountable for making a decision. They will primarily be interested in technical ability and whether they like you or not because they are the ones who will need to work with you day in and day out. They will want to make the right choice for their company and be held in high regard internally for making a good choice.

- People from enabling functions – such as finance or IT – who will share the responsibility of getting the value from the services you deliver and could be critical to the success of the project so have their own needs from a supplier, which may not be well articulated in the brief.

- Internal influencers. These could be senior or junior – but at some point, unless you are selling directly to the CEO or owner of the business, they will either be supporting the main buyer directly or their views will be an important – if undefined – factor in the choice made. Brand and reputation are critical to ensuring that this group is well-disposed towards your company – I'll cover more on this in the brand chapter later.

- Purchase process owners – usually procurement – who are there to make sure the decision-making is fairly and effectively run – and that any due diligence is met.

You need to understand the client context to make sure that you are generating marketing plans that meet the needs of all involved in the buyer's process. For example, if you're selling into large corporates people can't buy anything without going through procurement, whereas single executives in a small private business can make major investments on behalf of their business. The way they are going to buy the same product or services from you changes depending on their internal constraints or freedoms. You need to understand this well so your targeting will be effective, and it will vary by industry sector, company type or organizational size. Do research by speaking to sales teams and existing customers, which will give insights into who is involved as you shape your marketing strategy.

Even where the buyer isn't forming a formal group, or if their requirements are more straightforward, it is rare that they will make a unilateral decision without speaking to their teams and peers. Making sure that your offer is well understood by those that influence the decision is still important.

Buyers are comparing you to your competition and looking to shortlist a group to choose from so they may be starting to engage with your sales teams. However, they will be using indirect channels too as buyers prefer to do lots of discovery themselves before talking to company representatives. I cited some examples of this in the introduction – research suggests anywhere between 57 per cent (CEB, 2012) and 70 per cent (Miller Heiman, 2018) of the decision is made before contacting a vendor.

Making major decisions on behalf of a company is a high-stakes game. It is fraught with risk. Careers can be made or broken because making a mistake is hugely costly – and buyers may be tied into that bad choice for many years. This means that third party endorsements, from peers and other market observers, become very important, as does evidence that you deeply understand their business and have done something similar – successfully – before.

Work through which of the buying group job profiles you will create content for, how you will understand the things that are important to them, then play up the relevant messages in your content. It is also important to ensure it's easy for them to distinguish what is good about you versus your competition. If you have a marketing automation system that looks at the seniority of prospects as well as the number of touch points, look at how you are weighting these variables. The task of finding out the details of a product or service may be delegated to more junior, technical experts in the buying organization, so if you see a drop in the seniority of those you are dealing with this may be a more serious buying signal. Model what you think may be happening in the buyer's organization as they get into the specifics of choosing and shortlisting, and make sure you adjust your scoring in line with that.

Research firms can help you understand this, and sales will also have great insight into what your competitors are doing. Make it easy to find information about your company through search optimization, advertising, executive LinkedIn profiles or your own websites. Finally, remember that all engagement with your content in this phase is a buying signal – and a clue about where they are in their process. Tracking and follow-ups are critical. Map out what you expect someone in this phase to do then use technology to give you insights into what your buyers actually do against what you had predicted. You need highly responsive and proactive strategies if buyers ask for information. Sales should be lined up to talk to buyers if needed and if someone downloads content then a well-thought-out email should follow. Likewise, if they attend an event, make sure it's clear who will follow up and how. Sales need to be well briefed on the campaign and its objectives so they can continue the conversation in a way that feels seamless for the buyer.

Content

Given the level of risk associated with their decision, at this stage of the journey buyers want to be armed with facts, data and testimonials that reassure them your company has previously addressed and solved the type of challenges they face. Think about what proof points you have that will be relevant and aligned to what drives choice. Deploy your subject matter experts who, as Joanna Brown explained in her Insider Insight, know the challenge inside out and can demonstrate their wisdom and expertise. The buyers responsible for delivering the work will want to see that you have done it before for organizations that have similar problems, while others in the buying influencer group will be interested in credentials and high-level benefits.

The first and most fundamental thing is to make sure your client value proposition is clear and easy to understand. As a marketer you should have a deep and detailed understanding of what the business challenge is that your product or service is solving, and how your proposition stands out. What is your client value proposition? Is it very clear what the benefits are in a language that your audience understands? Why should someone want it? Why is it better suited to their needs than nothing, or what they already have or what your competitors offer? What makes your product/service valuable and how would you prove it? Too often, value propositions become mired in hyperbole and jargon – or have been reviewed by so many people they've become bland. Take the time to get this articulated really well – otherwise you will lose your buyer at a critical stage.

Research is critical to informing your choices. Survey your customers and prospects to understand what their drivers of purchase are and what matters to them in this phase of the framework. Once done, make sure you play up those attributes within your marketing and sales literature. If, for example, technical expertise and cost are the primary reasons that someone would buy from a supplier, you need to bring these to the fore. If corporate responsibility is a cost of entry, then you need to make sure your company's progress against sustainability goals is clearly explained. If industry expertise is important, use words and terminology that show your technical understanding of the sector's issues. If functional experience (HR, finance, supply chain or marketing) matters to your buyers then articulate your experience here in a way that is easy to understand and relate to. Look at the questions or requests for information (RFIs) you have received in the past and see if there is a pattern of information requests which would indicate the answers aren't being provided on your website or in sales-focused collateral. Filling in these gaps will help raise the perception that you are easy to do business with.

When creating content, think about how you will play up certain messages depending on what matters to the buyer. They will have specific things they are looking for as they narrow down who they want to work with. By understanding these, B2B marketers can tailor materials to align with them so the buyer doesn't need to do the hard work of matching what they need to what you have. These typically fall into four main areas:

1 *Fundamentals*: the things that really matter to the success of the project or service being bought, such as expertise of the account team or specific transformation experience. What these are and what you highlight should be informed by insights from surveys of clients or internal teams, are likely to be common to the buyers of groups of services and products and should be played up in your case studies and testimonials.

2 *Rational drivers of choice*: these give buyers confidence that you can do what you say you can. They could include your company's ability to deliver on large projects, or its knowledge of the buyer's sector. They should feature across your marketing and communications because the whole buying group – not just the programme sponsor at the buyer – will likely be looking for evidence of them.

3 *Hygiene factors*: again, these may not be explicit but could include things like diversity and inclusion, expertise or geographic spread. These are table stakes – you will be quickly ruled out if you don't have this. Offer information about these aspects of your business to the buyer at this stage to ensure you remain considered as an option. They may not ask your company for this directly, but not having the information there and accessible might mean they assume you don't have these things, which will get you ruled out.

4 *Emotional drivers*: essential, given the high risk position your buyer is in, but unlikely to be outlined in any formal documents. It could be your company's values, cultural fit, or how collaborative you are.

Another thing many B2B companies fail to do is talk about what they are like to work with. Rarely do services companies use net promoter scores or qualitative comments from customers to infuse marketing materials, which is surprising for people-to-people services. Product companies – and B2C – do this as a matter of course, but it is rarer to find when people are buying consulting or professional services solutions. Buyers want to know what you are like on a human level and how you will approach their problems. In this high-stakes environment, they want to be sure they can trust you, much of which is based on intuition, chemistry and likeability. Make sure you detail what you are like and how you work – as well as the *harder* facts like number of clients, number of countries you operate in or number of employees – particularly in your digital channels, which tend to be underused for this type of information. Talk about how you think about problems, how you build and maintain relationships with a client and how you attract or retain great teams. Doing this will differentiate your company from competitors and make it more attractive to buyers who've not worked with you before.

At this stage buyers are comparing you directly against your competitors. Services companies don't generally like to explicitly claim that they are better than their rivals, but you can still convey that message in a subtle way. Know who all your competitors are. Look at what they offer, then ask your internal teams what sets you apart on each of the drivers of choice. Use what comes back as input to describe your company's approach and its solutions or products. If your technical expertise is deeper than your competitors, or your solution set broader and this is perceived to be important by buyers, bring this to the front and centre of your marketing.

Remember that this is a highly stressful time for the buyer burdened with making the right decision. Try to understand their concerns and what information you might offer to mitigate them. If you don't know, make some educated assumptions: most people feel reassured knowing that third parties think you are credible, that you have evidence of doing the work before and that you have the right level of experience to do the job. You can achieve this through:

- Third party endorsements like analyst reviews and rankings. Make sure you brief analysts on what you have that is new and interesting for the market so that their review will be current and representative. Share case studies and important or strategic wins. This is particularly important given most companies don't change their suppliers for technical infrastructure or professional services advice very frequently. With current tenure rates within companies, it might also be the first or only time that this particular buying group is making this type of decision for this company. They might have outdated information about your services and will look to analysts to give a neutral but informed view of what suppliers are providing in the market, and how good they are at it.

- Awards. Most sectors have them, so enter your products and solutions. Buyers will see award wins as a mark of prestige, and it helps them feel reassured that you have a solid offering that is well regarded within the broader market. It makes it feel safer to choose you. There is the additional benefit here of making your internal teams feel good when your company wins something or is highly placed.

- Showcase key wins and any partnerships you have so that buyers can see that you are someone that others want to work with: do this on your own channels and if it's a major win it could be worth taking out an advert in key third party publications and working with corporate affairs to promote to relevant press.

- Testimonials from existing clients that articulate their problem, how you approached it and what the outcomes were. These are vital for account teams and buyers, but they can be difficult to get. A good time to try is when you've successfully hit a key milestone in a contract and there is goodwill on both sides: ask your sales leads to flag these opportunities and galvanize teams to ask clients for credentials. It can help to have it in account team objectives, or to make it a regular agenda item for quarterly business reviews. Another way to do this is to invite clients to take part in events so that potential buyers can hear about their experiences directly.

- Case studies: these are critical at this juncture and should be easily accessible to the outside world via your website, and internally to your sales colleagues. Good ones will outline the situation that your clients were in, how you approached the problem, what you did and the results. Think about how you highlight the value of your product or service for the main buyer and for the people they are buying on behalf of. For example, the value of a customer relationship management (CRM) system is different for a salesperson who is using it to get insight than it is for a P&L holder looking to manage pipeline.

- Very specific and more technical thought leadership articles, blogs or case studies: in these your subject matter experts should go into much greater detail than what you published in the Explorer phase, allowing you to show off a much deeper understanding of regulation, process, industry or change management, for example. At this stage buyers are likely to read more deeply as they seek to understand how your expertise can drive value for them.

- Proof points: buyers tend to like data, so make sure you've highlighted successes, scale or benefits in a numeric and easy to understand way. Use data points, perhaps based on the ratings derived from a customer survey. Actively differentiate your company by emphasizing key strengths in your materials. Use numbers and make it easy for a buyer to see why what you have is better. For example, if you know your software product has more insight and analytics features than its competitors, run a survey of the market to quantify how important this is to successful businesses, then incorporate the findings in your literature with statistics about the depth of your product capabilities.

- Decision-making aids. These include benchmarking tools, calculators or interactive diagnostics that help buyers understand the scale of what they need to do and enable you to give them something helpful to aid their thinking. Design your content in a way that solicits buyers to tell you a lot about themselves so you can learn about buyers in this group and share specific insights with your sales teams.

- Look for trigger event opportunities to instigate a marketing and sales campaign. At a market level this could be volatility, macroeconomic trends or regulation changes. At a company level, this could be new appointments in the C-suite, financial activity like M&A, hiring surges or office location changes.

- Map your company's services to client problems and create conversation starters for sales teams to have more strategic discussions with buyers.

- Use white space analysis to identify look-alike buyers to your existing best clients. This will help you target your messages and prospects more precisely.

Across all of these, use insights to make your marketing distinctive and stand out. This is a competitive field, so there needs to be something that aids memorability or helps you position yourself as innovative at a critical stage in the buyer's experience of your company.

As an example, while I was working at a previous company, the European Union brought in the Solvency II directive which introduced a new framework for insurance firms. This was a great opportunity for us to position our data services. We wanted to position our capabilities, make the most of this market opportunity and find ways to get high-quality leads into pipeline quickly. We started by hosting events about the regulation, inviting senior compliance buyers and regulators. The regulators were frequently asked by buyers how they would know if they were ready enough to meet the new standards. This gave us the idea to develop a unique piece of content aimed at Hunters. They knew the problem that they needed to solve but were looking for help in how to size and implement the problem. Our team conducted a survey of those companies we felt would be most advanced in their thinking, based on a number of factors including how large their compliance teams were and whether they'd been fined for regulatory breeches in the past. Rather than just publishing the research findings and making them available for download, we built a digital diagnostic tool with a series of questions that the Hunter had to answer. We then gave them a personalized PDF report comparing their answers to our benchmark companies across eight dimensions, which they could use with their boards to help secure additional resources and to help their teams prioritize activities. This was shared with our sales teams. Buyers got a rich source of tailored information to help them make an internal business case, while our sales specialists got insightful leads enabling them to have more productive conversations and reduce time in pipeline. Our testing didn't stop there. We also used social listening to inform the campaign's visuals: risk practitioners were talking about *drowning in regulation* and a *tsunami of new requirements* so we introduced a water theme and A/B tested against traditional office photography. These water visuals dramatically outperformed the more standard ones in terms of open rates, so we adapted all our materials to align with the themes.

The principle underlying the strategy of the campaign above, and the way that I like to think about materials designed for this part of the journey, is to be helpful. Making decisions on behalf of your company is difficult. Are you giving useful insights or tools to help them think differently about the problem?

Don't forget the broader buying group in this part of the framework. Procurement, finance and IT may be involved in making the decision and their specialists will need different types of information. As you consider the dynamics of the buying group, make it easy for the enabling functions to understand the value you provide given they may not have specific expertise in your area. While the decision makers want to know how your company will work with them to implement the project, others in the group need to know at a higher level how your products or services will benefit the organization. Think about designing assets for them directly. Understand from sales teams and existing clients what is important to the diverse members of a buying group, for example where finance may want to understand value for money, IT may look for specific platform expertise. B2B marketers rarely cater for this broader audience at this stage of the journey, though individuals other than the lead decision makers can be much more influential than you realize. Being mindful and respectful of their questions and needs will set the right tone as you go into the buying part of the process. Any way you can help the lead buyer to educate them will ultimately help you. I saw a good example of this once when being marketed to by a marketing automation company (Rothman, 2015). Their insight was that a key part of the buying process would be the conversation between the CMO and C-suite, particularly the CFO about funding. They wanted to be useful and to help deliver value to their buyers at this stage. They created a business case document covering the key points a CMO should make; how to align the potential purchase with business strategy and how to calculate and forecast ROI. It was designed to help the CMO be more convincing and secure funds, giving value to the buyer and ultimately helping the marketing automation provider to win business.

Finally offer plenty of format options for your content. Your buying group has broadened, so too have the ways in which people will want to access your information. For any article that you publish online, do an executive summary and a longer report, offer a diagnostic, create a podcast, infographic, or slide share. Don't just count on one format working. Use your technology to monitor how people are engaging with materials: what are they looking at, how far through demonstrations do they get, and is video proving to be more appealing than using a brochure? Track who is showing interest, e.g. by gating parts of your content (assuming that doesn't affect drop-off rates), and pay attention to how buyers are getting to these pages, for example whether they are searching for specific product names or more generic searches. Look at where they go to after looking at your materials – and if they come in and out of your website quickly, then you aren't addressing their needs correctly.

Alongside this, continue to seek feedback from existing clients – particularly those who are newer to your organization – to help shape the materials you produce. As sales do win/loss reviews add in some questions or do the outreach directly from marketing. What helped them decide to choose you? Ask them whether there was an asset that was particularly useful, a data point that stood out for them, or a piece of content that really affected how they came to a decision. Listen too to what surprised them about your company and think about how to remedy it. Perhaps they didn't expect such a high quality of expertise or found that you had a broader range of services or features than they expected. If so, bring this out more strongly in your materials.

Channels

Buyers are actively researching so information about your solutions needs to be easy to find and show up where they expect it to be. Use direct channels like email, events and social media to promote content and make sure it is easy to access through your owned channels. Driving people to your website is essential, as you can showcase relevant expertise and experience through detailed proof points, case studies or more technical thought leadership then start to track how they move from one piece of content to the next, their preferred formats and engagement rates – all of which will help you learn about the buyer as well as improve your content strategy.

Whatever route buyers take to get to your website, harmonize what they see when they get there with how they got there. So, if you've promoted something about your transformation capabilities, make sure that what they see when they click through is an appropriate piece of content, not just your home page or something more generic about all your capabilities. If they have come through a high-level search, offer them a mix of brand and campaign content. If they've responded to a campaign message, take them to a campaign landing page but add some prospecting content or built-in data capture to try to get them to give you information that your marketing and sales teams can act on.

Buyers are trying to get to know your services so will be more responsive to proprietary events – particularly if it is a good opportunity to see your team or product in action. Roadshows or webinars, particularly where the content is related to compelling market events, can be great ways of engaging groups of buyers in an efficient way. Equally, if the sales team has started engaging with buyers but the conversations have stalled, an event can be a good way to kick-start the conversation. You can use events to showcase happy clients, give a sense of the calibre of your subject matter experts and outline how you approach challenges at a high level. They should give buyers a better idea of what you'd be like to work with, appealing to their key emotional as well as rational drivers for choice.

They will also be researching and comparing you through third parties too, so make sure you continue to incorporate indirect channels into your strategy:

EARNED

- Engage with the analysts that rank products and services across your competitor set: ensure they have the most up-to-date information about you and have had a chance to speak to your senior executives or clients. Invite them to come into your offices to see how you deliver work in practice. This will help them get an up-to-date view on what you have and where you're investing for success.

- Forums that bring together technical experts: many IT buyers, for example, have regular meetings and industry bodies that get deep into discussion about solutions to specific challenges and which external suppliers might best provide the answers. Even if these sessions are closed to suppliers, send the organizers any relevant thought leadership as it might be shared in the forum – or they may invite you to be a guest speaker. If you know when they happen and what the topics are, create thought leadership and post onto your site, promoting it immediately after the event.

- Awards: in this part of the framework, specific technical and expertise-driven awards work well.

- Alliance/partner ecosystems: make sure your services are promoted on their website and that their sales teams have a good understanding of what you offer so they can endorse you when buyers ask their advice on who to work with.

- Peers: even if they are competing, your buyers will be well networked and able to give opinions about suppliers in the market. It can also be helpful to build an alumni network for people who have left your business as some may have gone to the buying side. Make sure they have the latest information about your business and keep them up to date with your strategy, investments, key wins and client successes.

PAID

- If your buyer is responding to a known business problem, it is likely that there are reasonably niche publications that cater to them as a group (for example specific websites about regulation catering to legal services). Use this insight to produce and place direct advertising on the website about the solutions or products that you have against specific case studies. This is different to the advertising that promotes your content for the Horizon Scanner and Explorer. It needs to precisely match the buyer demand to your supply in a direct, simple way.

- Invest in search terms that your buyers actually use rather than what you call things internally. When joining a new company, most people remark on how much jargon is needed – it can be surprising how quickly you become sensitized to the way that your organization talks about things!

OWNED

- As mentioned, your website is key here. Make sure that the pages are kept up to date, regularly review traffic, bounce rates and keep optimizing. Often the more descriptive pages in the site are left to infrequent reviews compared to campaign specific or home pages. Even though the volume of visitors to this part of your site will be lower than the home page, they are likely to be the most interested in buying something – you may have a volume/value dynamic. If someone has gone to the effort of getting to this page and is reading it, they are likely an interested lead so you should prioritize giving them an excellent experience.

- Social channels: continue to promote your experts but you might select a different group who focus more on the *how* than the what/why. Showcase real examples of projects and how your experts rose to the challenges in their own words.

- Proprietary events: if you're running webinars, try to do them in your web environment. Have registration hosted on your site and promote your services alongside – if people are signing up to very specific, technical webinars this is not the time to be shy about what you could offer to add value to them. Promote your services in any information you send out post-event.

- Email: be direct about product or service benefits and how you're different from your competitors. This could be what you do and how you do it: typically, you will compete on price, speed or expertise.

Whichever channels you choose, consider what you will do as your buyer responds to it. When creating your buyer journeys, make sure you have thought through all the eventualities and have an action plan for what you'll do next. For example, if you are organizing and promoting a webinar, think through how to react depending on what the buyer does:

1 Registers for the webinar and attends. Clearly these are your most interested group, so what are you going to do as a follow-up? This can range from having a sales call through to sending a summary and an invite to a further webinar, but you should be looking to add more value than just saying thank you. Then how will you engage with them next month? Over the next six months? Should it be different to what you would have done if they hadn't responded to your webinar invite? Do you put them back into the prospect list or do you do something to move them along the pipeline?

2 Registers but doesn't attend. They were clearly interested but got waylaid by something important. Do you send a recording of the webinar? A summary? An opportunity to follow up with the webinar experts from your business or an alternative date for similar/same content?

3 Doesn't register but opens email. They had some interest so your message worked at a high level, but the webinar failed to attract action. Do you want to try a different channel or topic for this cohort or try running the webinar at a different time or day?

4 Doesn't open email or register. Try to engage a prospect a few more times – but each time, try something new – so perhaps a different call to action or different tone of voice, so that you learn more about what your customer base responds to – though of course you need to stop after three to four attempts in order not to alienate someone who might be important at a later date.

Putting yourself in the buyer's shoes and having a good set of next steps depending on how they engage with your channels is critical to ensuring that you make a return on the money you've invested, and that you've given enough options to cater to what the buyer wants to do. This could be the *make or break* part of the journey, so you need to make sure that you take particular care of the buyer in this phase.

The more straightforward your products or services are, the more likely it is that buyers want to do more discovery themselves online – they may even want to purchase through ecommerce – so making details of products and services accessible digitally is important. Make sure you:

- Show the product. Include screenshots, recorded webinars, slide shows, recorded product demos or digital inside views where buyers can navigate themselves through the product features.

- Clearly articulate the benefits to the customer, both at a general level (emphasizing speed and cost, for example) and a more specific one. How has it been designed with the buyer in mind? Start with the key features up front then give more information as the buyer scrolls down the page, culminating in technical specifications if necessary.

- Have a clear call to action. This is usually a request for product details, a *contact us* form or a telephone number/email that will be monitored constantly by a team that has clear key performance indicators (KPIs) for both responding to the prospect and for giving feedback to marketing about the quality of any leads coming in through the channel.

- Give sales teams attending or running an event where they are showing demos compelling give-away materials that outline key features/benefits and ensure that they follow up quickly with anyone who is interested in seeing more.

Metrics

You are trying to increase profile of services, encourage proactive client contact and generate pipeline, or be invited into a formal procurement process. It is essential to differentiate yourself from competitors and go into the next stage as the preferred option. Buyers need to believe that your company will be easy to work with, and as a marketer you can help create this impression by making sure that information is interesting, accurate and clear, easy to find and helps build confidence that your company could do the job.

FIGURE 6.1 Hunter stage metrics

INPUT METRICS Measure of how productive the marketing team is	INDICATOR METRICS How likely marketing are to hit the agreed targets	OUTCOME METRICS How marketing performed related to the marketing and business strategy
Number of proof points: case studies, benchmarking tools, decision making aids: (e.g. calculators, competitor table), product collateral with features and benefits	• Number of enquiries • Engagement with diagnostic tools • Engagement with product information/case studies • Organic search • Email open rates • Visits to product/service – or campaign landing pages	Established new lead flow: • Number of new contacts • Number of Leads Revenue growth: • Unweighted pipeline • Conversion rates Improved commercial effectiveness of your business: • Length of time in pipeline • Value of deals/sales
Number of events – road-shows, webinars, third party	Event attendance	

Moving the buyer to the next phase

If every engagement is a buying signal, your sales and account teams need to actively respond at the right time. Formalizing what a strong Hunter signal looks like and deciding where you want to take them next should be done in conjunction with sales so you are aligned on what a good lead looks like and how your company should continue the conversation. Agree what the timescales are for getting back to someone who has asked for information, entered details on a website or attended an event, all of which is critical to making sure your leads are nurtured effectively. Knowing when to engage someone into a sales conversation can be tricky, so keep the feedback loop strong in this phase, which will also help you decide the best way to follow up.

Your marketing should be designed to capture contact details. As well as having strong calls to action on every piece of content, think about how you will follow up from a marketing perspective with people who attend a webinar, have seen a demo at a booth at an event, or downloaded content. Capture their information as they sign up or request more details, and make sure that you and sales have agreed KPIs on who will follow up. If sales are stretched or struggling to meet the KPIs, perhaps marketing can provide aircover. It may be that a well-crafted email with an attached case study about specific benefits to one of your existing customers will continue to keep your company front of the buyer's mind until someone more actively pursues the lead. Even when buying signals are strong, sales do not always pick up on leads, particularly if the sales and marketing functions don't have a strong relationship, or if there is a history of marketing passing on leads too early before they are ready. Make sure you have regular feedback sessions with sales about what you are both seeing at this point in the journey – if leads are not actively interested and engaged, you may be getting the wrong type of prospect, or they may be at an earlier stage on the buyer journey. In this case you may need to review your strategy and plan to redefine what a marketing-qualified lead looks like.

IN SUMMARY

- Hunters are clear about what they want and are starting to look at possible solutions and providers.

- They may have been through the first two stages, but if they have a well-defined problem, they may be entering the buyer journey at this stage and be encountering your company for the first time.

- Your buying audience has broadened once again – typically into a cross-functional group – and you may now be engaging with *heads of* as well as their team, and potentially procurement.

- It is likely they are considering several options and so you are being compared closely to your competitors. It is essential therefore to differentiate your offering as much as possible while making sure you have plenty of content that demonstrates how your propositions map to the buyer's specific needs.

- Third party endorsements are particularly important at this stage as is evidence you understand their business and have successfully solved similar problems previously.

- Driving Hunters to your website is essential so you can track how they are engaging with your content.

- All engagement with content at this stage is a buying signal – work with sales to identify what looks like a strong Hunter signal, agree how to nurture the relationship and always follow up in a timely, appropriate way.

07
Active Buyer

People in this phase are committed and in the process of making a difficult choice. In this chapter I talk about the various roles played within the buying group, how to cater to them and how to work hand in glove with sales to get the deal over the line. I also include an Insider Insight from Peter Thomas, former Global Marketing Director, Accenture Innovation on how to think about structuring marketing teams to support bids and what it takes to do this successfully.

This phase is fraught with risk for the buyer as it can be career-defining for those involved. If it is an expensive decision, there will be a high level of internal scrutiny. Chemistry between your two businesses is important, as you may be working together on complicated problems for several years. Buyers will be engaging with your sales representatives or account teams, as well as any pitch materials and your marketing content, all of which need to work in concert with each other but sometimes don't. You want the buyer to select your company and marketing can help seal the deal by giving them specific information, making sure detailed features, benefits and specifications are readily available, thereby removing any barrier to choosing you.

Across the whole buyer journey, but particularly as they enter the final stages of their decision-making, B2B marketers should be thinking about the context that the buyer is operating in, specifically against the three simultaneous roles they are playing.

1   As a representative of the company that they work for. They are looking for alignment between their organization and the suppliers they work with – a good cultural fit or a similar view on key societal issues like climate change or diversity, for example. You should be looking for ways to create a sense of shared values to build trust.

2   As a member of a buying group, with a defined role within it. If they are the main person responsible for buying the solution, or their teams are direct users of it, they will need to know that the product or service will meet their specific requirements. As cited in previous chapters, this group also includes influencers who are interested in the outcome of the purchase – for example finance, procurement, or IT. To succeed, you need to show them you can understand their specific needs and demonstrate how you'll fulfil them.

3   As individuals in their own right who use specific channels that appeal to them, want information to be personalized to a greater or lesser degree, like content to be delivered in a certain format, and react in a personal way to tone, style or imagery. Doing this well involves creating a connection at a human level and can lead to stronger relationships too.

I mentioned in the previous chapter the concept of your marketing touching on the functional, rational, hygiene factors and emotional needs that buyers have. As they move into this phase, the emphasis of each will change – and the hygiene ones are likely to have gone away as they were a gating factor to get you into this stage of the process.

Analysis by Source Global Research (2021) looked at what mattered to buyers of professional services versus what the professional services companies believed was important in this phase. They identified 16 attributes as being important in clients' overall decision-making (detailed in Figure 7.1). All the attributes mattered, but they're ranked in terms of their relative importance, from most important to buyers (top right) to the least important (bottom left). It is notable that things that were important in the Hunter phase are less important now because they've been considered at an earlier stage. To put it another way, your company wouldn't have made it this far without these, so you don't need to reiterate them as strongly in this phase.

The attribute strength dots show the overall performance of professional firms. Again, the further to the right it is, the more buyers say that companies in the market are strong in that specific attribute. The main message here is that companies generally overemphasize on attributes that matter less to buyers in this phase and are seen to be relatively weak on those that clients value more – and which are more likely to be differentiators (Source Global Research, 2021).

While this research is about professional services, the messages are relevant to other fields: once you are on the shortlist and being seriously considered, don't waste the precious time you have with the buyer – directly through sales or indirectly

FIGURE 7.1   The relative importance of company attributes when clients are shortlisting (professional services)

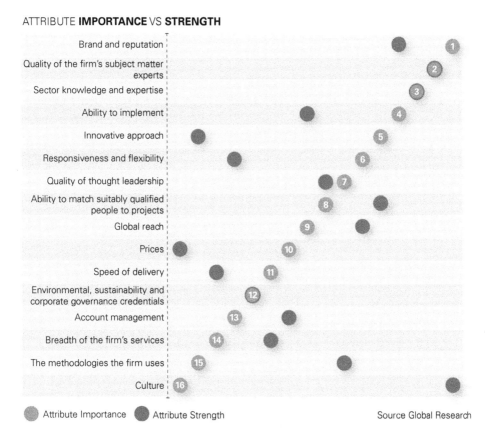

ATTRIBUTE **IMPORTANCE** VS **STRENGTH**

⬤ Attribute Importance   ⬤ Attribute Strength

Source Global Research

through marketing – reinforcing what got you here at the expense of what will differentiate you in this part of the framework. Not seizing the opportunity to align what you have with what buyers need at this critical phase could render all your efforts to this point fruitless.

Once you are at this stage and are being downselected for an expensive purchase, there is no shortcut to research and insights. If you are a complex solution, there will be a defined, known buying group, so work with the sales team to understand what they are interested in, their track record and their views about your company versus your competitors. Use data from analysts – like the set above – to inform your pitch materials and marketing collateral. If you are in a more transitional business, test and learn about the right balance of functional, rational and emotional content as your buyer is edging ever nearer to a purchase.

Content

As you think about the content, work through what makes sense against the roles the buyer is simultaneously playing.

Representative of their company

They are playing an important role in representing their company's culture when buying services from your business. Having a clear brand promise and strong reputation gives a safety net to this high-stakes decision. Remember they will have to *sell in* their decision to the rest of the organization, so anything marketing can do to clearly explain the end value to their various stakeholders will help them.

As I mentioned in the previous chapter, how you work with different types of clients or how you will approach a set of problems is interesting to buyers. Note though from the data in Figure 7.1 that your internal culture may be less important here – it could have been evidence that you are able to attract and retain talent, which is important pre-shortlist but now they are more interested in how you are able to align to or work within their culture. This becomes critical again when you're selling more services into an existing customer. You are already able to factually demonstrate this, and it is a huge differentiator as it minimizes buyer risk – I will talk about this more in the next chapter on marketing to clients.

Member of a buying group

If it is a significant purchase, you will typically know precisely who is involved in the group. Peter Thomas in his Insider Insight talks about the difference between bid support and ABM, citing 'the deal team you are working with will have a specific set of things they want to communicate to a highly targeted set of people'.

For smaller or more straightforward purchases, you will need to work with sales and review previous successes to understand which job roles are typically involved formally or informally at this stage. Understand the functional factors that will drive their decisions to help you to stand out over your competitors, remembering that they are likely different to what got you to the shortlist. Be prepared to challenge your existing views and bear in mind the following:

- At this stage they are looking for whether you have the specific skills, experience and expertise to help them get it done, so give detailed case studies with specific results.

- Understand how your services are perceived by your buyers (existing customers can help you here) and talk about it explicitly. For example, if you are regarded as having a high level of expertise, refer to your credentials often in all your materials.

If you're thought of as a leader in customer service, put in facts and stats about responsiveness and quote the positive feedback from other clients.

- Third party endorsements are hugely important, so actively work with supportive clients to get quotes that you can publish online and in any sales materials. Other data points that can help build confidence include number of clients, number of repeat clients, geographic coverage, number of employees and awards won.

- In case studies, articulate specific times when you helped clients solve problems differently or where you went above and beyond what was in the contract to help them solve their problems or get a better outcome.

- Some of the buying group will be supporters of your competitors and you are being compared toe to toe with a small number of suppliers. As you articulate how you are different to your rivals, address specific points head-on, so if your competitor is known to have excellent account management, make sure you get customer testimonials which demonstrate how good your teams are – and how that made the difference to the outcomes they achieved. Try to downplay the competitor's advantage too: if their software is known to be easy to use and yours isn't, but you have better data instead, show how this depth of data made a real difference to clients and trumped usability when it came to longer-term benefits.

- Remove any barriers to you being chosen. The buyer will have specific questions through the process, so ask the sales team what these are likely to be and make sure the content you have on your website and marketing literature targeted at this phase covers those questions and can be found easily.

- Proposition or product pages on your site are probably rarely updated, but they might prove critical to whether you are chosen, so it will pay dividends to pay more attention to them, tracking bounce rates and how far into the pages people go. I talked about this in the previous chapter. Try to diversify the experience too, with videos or charts, to make them stand out against your competitors.

- Take the opportunity to bring parts of your offer to life. At one company, we created 360 virtual tours of our delivery centres, with profiles of people who worked there and an opportunity to connect with them in real time.

- Consider how you show up during the Active Buyer process and whether it is well aligned to your value proposition. If you know that innovation and technology skills are important to the buyer, using flat brochureware in direct sales materials or on your website undermines your statements that you are highly digital, or insight driven.

I mentioned in the previous chapter that procurement, finance and IT may be involved in making the decision and that their specialists will require different types of information. Their needs are likely to be very functional at this stage and they will want detailed fact sheets or tech specifications. Understand from account teams what is important to these members of the buying group – for example, value for money or technology expertise – and play these features up in materials you are designing for them.

Often B2B marketers let sales do the hard work at this stage, but if you are smart, you can also help your buyers get the information they need and position yourself positively in the process. Having confusing information which is hard to find gives the impression you're difficult to do business with – and those playing an influencing role in the purchase will be looking to marketing materials to confirm their views on your brand and your capabilities, particularly if they aren't the ones directly engaging with your company's representatives.

Individuals in their own right

Of course, your buyers are individuals with preferences in their own right. You will have been getting insight from earlier stages about what format preferences groups of buyers have. Use these to shape your content, optimizing for what you know worked in previous stages. If you don't have good insights, think about what type of personality that profession or sector typically attracts, then work out what channels and messaging will appeal to them. If they are a group that tends to be analytical, provide links to external sources to reinforce your content. The design should be data rich with many proof points and numbers. Be brief, concise and to the point with no marketing jargon. If they tend to be more friendly and casual, then make your tone conversational, using anecdotes or stories. Despite tailoring for audience, review to make sure your company is showing up consistently to the group, in line with your brand attributes and with no disconnect between the marketing and sales experience. If your marketing is creative but your sales highly technical and serious, you will come across as two different companies, which is unnerving for a stressed-out buyer.

Channels

Buyers are actively investigating you, so as well as speaking directly to sales, they will continue to do their own research and be trying to get as much information from your channels as they can. Ensure content is well laid out across your owned channels, clearly labelled and easy to navigate. There are lots of tools available for you to track what people are doing when they come to your site, and as a test you can also run exercises with potential buyers or new recruits within your business where you set them scenarios to see how easy it is for them to get what they need from you. Make sure that your credentials are easy to find on your website as that is where buyers will typically be looking for this type of information as they are researching you. Design online experiences that really draw out the specific benefits to your buyers in the role that they're playing. Given you don't always know the relative importance of different internal influencers on the buying group, give as much information as you can across multiple formats. Point procurement to areas you have had reviewed by your procurement teams. Direct primary buyers to areas with video content so they get a sense of what you're like to work with, as well as testimonials from their peers or accolades from awards that they respect.

The main emotional connection will be through any face-to-face engagements they have with your sales or account team. Make sure they have as much insight as possible about the topics buyers have been engaging with upstream and can easily access the latest marketing collateral or pieces of thought leadership. If you've encountered some of the individuals in any of your earlier marketing activities – for example they've been to one of your webinars or events – let sales know which and what topics they'd engaged with.

Of course, for many B2B companies, the pitch or the bid process is where sales can look to marketing for support. Depending on the level of support you are being asked to give, as well as the size of your team, it is worth having a frank conversation with sales about how much effort you put into this part of the process as opposed to the earlier parts, where you are building new pipeline. As Peter explains below, it is important to set expectations as unless you have a large and well-funded team, doing the intensive sales support that is needed in this phase can be all-consuming. He suggests how to set it up for success if this is the best place to put your resources and how to ascertain what to focus the team's efforts on. If your metrics are about pipeline versus revenue, be pragmatic about what you can do in this part of the process and manage expectations accordingly.

INSIDER INSIGHT

Peter Thomas, former Global Marketing Director, Accenture Innovation

In this interview, Peter shares his insights into setting up an effective bid support function, how to decide what to support and the type of skills needed to do it well. He draws on more than 30 years' experience building and delivering client-focused programmes for major global organizations, including as Global Innovation Marketing & Communications Director and European CMO of Accenture, as well as his time at the Rugby Football Union, Bloomberg LLP and Hill & Knowlton.

THE CASE FOR A BID SUPPORT MACHINE

The critical thing is not to try and apply a standard traditional campaign model when supporting bids. The skills and attitude needed are very different. At Accenture, we started to get real traction and momentum behind bid support when we recognized three things: firstly, bid support account managers need to only do bid support. This is because bids come quickly, often without notice, so they are very hard to plan for. If you try to do it alongside other campaigns, it won't work. Secondly, they are high intensity so when you're doing them, it's very hard to do anything else if you really are going to provide what the business needs. Thirdly, you need to provide them with a dedicated support team including creative and data analytics people, for example.

We used to run bid support via the industry marketing function. So, if there was a big bid in a sector, that industry marketing team got assigned to work on it. Because of this model, we found that many people were doing two jobs half well. Instead, we created a bid support machine – a specialist team moving from one bid to the next, rather than moving industry marketers in and out of bid support alongside their BAU campaigns. Once we had this SWAT team model, we deployed them on one bid after another. A lot of the processes and tools needed to support a bid are repeatable as the key components of a bid are pretty standard: messaging, client-specific targeting, audience insights for example. Today, professional services and law firms tend to have pursuit marketing teams, which are separate from core marketing teams because bids require this type of resourcing model – a team who can brilliantly execute a set of repeatable activities that come in high intensity bursts. This is really quite different from traditional campaigns, so it is important to acknowledge that and think about how you will organize to deliver it effectively.

GETTING STARTED

In the early stages, when you're building a bid support function, there may be times when you have to convince the business to bring marketing in because they're used to doing the selling on their own. Sales challenge why marketing is needed to close deals: a common view we came up against in the early days was that marketing didn't understand sales and should focus on top of funnel lead generation. But, as ever, with marketing, there will be some heroes and early adopters who get it – likely the same people in your organization who are always open to the value that marketing brings. Secure their support and get started and as you build success cherish them and make them famous. By doing this at Accenture we were able to prove reasonably early on that if you had a marketing team doing proper, organized bid support, you stood a 30 to 40 per cent better chance of winning; which was a metric that helped start to convince sales they should engage with us! Over time that success becomes self-referencing, and you start to see other sales teams thinking 'Oh, maybe I should try a little bit of that.' There will come a tipping point though (which you need to look out for) which is when you're seeing more demand from sales than you can support. When that happens you need to change the conversation with sales leadership to define priorities, recognizing you'll never have infinite marketing resources.

As you look to convince sales of your approach, it can be helpful to create a toolkit that showcases the suite of capabilities that you bring: for example, understanding the bid audience using deep insights, personality profiling, interests, your views on their personal brand. Then include message development and creative. Keep examples of how you would develop the win message with a creative that really pops, so they start to understand that you're not talking about a brochure or an event, which is the classic sales view of marketing. Have in your kit bag existing proven case studies of what marketing interventions look like at each stage of the life cycle of the bid. This isn't just about keeping buyers warm and fuzzy while the bid process is happening, it's right into the bid itself and in the immediate aftermath. With a toolkit, you will find it becomes much easier to showcase what you can do.

HOW TO DECIDE WHAT THE TEAM SUPPORTS

Once you've created the team, be disciplined about where you put them – they are a valuable resource. Don't fall into the trap of all bids being equally important. Put in some very strict criteria for where marketing is going to get involved. Inevitably, it tends to be size that matters. So, for us, very often these will be outsourcing or technology services deals – you're not going to bid for 100-million-dollar consulting contracts very often. That being said, sometimes we decide to prioritize strategic opportunities. Landing a reasonably sized new deal in a new account could be strategically more important than a $200 million deal in a client where there isn't much more growth. You can't work on everything. It's worth considering whether you can produce processes and templates that you give to bid teams to help them do their own version – that means that you can add value even to those you're not directly supporting.

FUNDING

With tight budgets in marketing, remember, bids often have their own funding. In professional services the business development funds are often very large, dwarfing marketing funds, so find ways to access them. We have a mechanism where if the business wants to pay for it, we will deliver it – through our core marketing resources or agencies – as a paid for service outside our core budget. In addition, there are now creative agencies that will help you with messaging workshops and creative delivery. We would provide the costs of bid support and the business development teams would decide whether they'd pay for it out of their budget, or not have it.

THE ROI OF BID SUPPORT

At a macro level, it's the easiest area in the world to measure ROI. You either win the bid or you don't. But of course, it is resource intensive so you need to balance out how you allocate budgets and people across the breadth of where marketing could add value. None of us have infinite resources, so it comes back to priorities – you have to work with the business to make choices. Be clear that if you over-index on bid support which, of course, the sales team would love you to do, you have a completely unbalanced marketing portfolio with not enough effort going into sustained brand building or pipeline building. At the start of each year, establish what your priorities are overall and where bid support fits across the whole. Then set the criteria about where you will and won't support bids. You can't afford to have 50 per cent of your people suddenly focused on just this area because other things won't happen – you need to be clear what the opportunity cost of not supporting brand, recruitment, marketing or pipeline growth will be.

THE DIFFERENCE BETWEEN BID SUPPORT AND ABM

Bid support is separate from the ABM teams in Accenture today. When you're supporting a sale, it's all about what's going to win us this pitch, right here right now. The deal team you're working with will have a specific set of things they want to communicate to a highly targeted set of people. Account-based marketing sits somewhere between that and traditional campaign marketing. It is much more consistent and long term and targets a wider set of people, looking to open doors to new business or drive loyalty within existing contacts. In a bid you're often only really trying to influence a handful of people versus 10 to 20 companies in many ABM programmes.

WHAT GOOD LOOKS LIKE

In one bid, the team created a complete messaging platform to frame how to bring the capabilities to life within the client account. This informed everything – from the assets used in the bid, to the pitch, to the events done before and after. They created a fully immersive, bespoke 360 virtual tour of our delivery centre network and co-branded the floors of the actual centres (which the client was visiting in person) as if we'd already won the deal. In another, for an airline company, the bid packaging was an online check-in, the room was decked out like an air cabin with the round windows and each person that came in from the client got a passport with profiles of the people on the team. In another, we did out-of-home advertising using messages about Accenture that aligned with their core values around the client headquarters – throughout the train station and all along the route to their office.

WHERE BID SUPPORT HELPS AS PART OF YOUR CAREER DEVELOPMENT

Bid support is best thought of as something you do as part of your career trajectory – it is not a career path in its own right. Typically, people do it for two or three years; partly because it's tiring and intensive when it's happening and partly because it isn't a path to getting into the global marketing leadership team. We see high performers going into these SWAT teams to learn more about sales, the bid process and how to be part of a fast-paced, agile team, but then get to a point where they need to go and do something else with the skills they have learnt.

To do it well, you need to understand the sales process and have a sort of fellow feeling with the sales team – a passion for commercials and a *win at all costs instinct*. The skills needed to be a great account manager are confidence, and competence with data. Confidence because you are trying to reconcile and manage the desires of a sales team which are often out of kilter with the budget they have or what's achievable in a short time frame. You'll be dealing with a very intense sales team who may not know much about how marketing works. Sales leaders on these big opportunities tend to be reasonably senior and those big beasts of the sales jungle are difficult to deal with. Junior marketers will struggle to bring the right level of influence into a fast-paced, high-stakes dynamic. For a lot of these sales guys, this is their personal and professional reputation on the line. If they are leading a 100-million-dollar bid and don't win it, that's their career knocked back two years. It's high stakes for your business and the individuals involved – like it is for the buyer themselves. Competence with data is key too: the more you can make decisions that are data driven or use insights to give you the edge against your competitors, the better the end result will be. You tend to find that marketers drawn to this type of work are extrovert, decisive and comfortable with sales environments.

BUILDING A RELATIONSHIP WITH SALES

As you're thinking about building a different relationship with sales more broadly, consider whether you start building that relationship with bid support – which gives a tangible direct benefit and builds alignment fast against their critical priorities – or get the campaign and demand mechanic functioning well first. The latter option might be better as great bid support cements marketing as being sales enablement. Additionally, if you start with bid support, you build extremely close relationships with individual salespeople, but not with the sales team as a whole. If you're not careful, your relationship grows at an account level, not at a macro level. If you want to get close to sales, the best way is for the marketing director and the sales director to sit down and work out how their functions are going to work together across the buyer journey, how much ownership they each are going to take of each other's responsibilities, then bid support becomes one articulation of the overall partnership.

Metrics

Everything else you've been doing has led to this point. Whether you win or lose, getting feedback from sales is critical. Get involved in the win/loss reviews or debriefs and discuss whether there was anything marketing could have done to give more information, or better detail, or positioned the brand differently. If you won, ask if there were any particular marketing content or channels that stood out or helped give your business the edge.

FIGURE 7.2 Active Buyer stage metrics

INPUT METRICS Measure of how productive the marketing team is	INDICATOR METRICS How likely marketing are to hit the agreed targets	OUTCOME METRICS How marketing performed related to the marketing and business strategy
• Number of bids supported • Number of pieces of collateral produced • Number of product videos and demos • Virtual office tours or pitches	• Engagement with collateral – amount of sales focused content viewed and time spent on collateral • Feedback from sales or clients through purchase process • Number of demos watched, software downloads	Improved market share, competitive advantage and revenue impact: • Closed/won business • Win rate improvement • Reduced length of time in pipeline (revenue hits earlier)

IN SUMMARY

• Both buyer and supplier have the most to win or lose from this phase: for the buyer this can be career-defining depending on the outcomes produced by the relationship. It's a financial investment with high levels of internal scrutiny for them. This is the time when marketers need to bring everything together, so the buyer feels comfortable committing and reassured you are the right choice compared to competitors.

• There will be three main roles the buying group will be playing that you need to focus your content and strategy around: representative of the company, member of the buying group with a defined role and individual in their own right.

• They want to be sure you have the skills, experience and expertise to help them with their challenge or opportunity, so give detailed case studies with specific results. Peer testimonials and relevant awards can be particularly useful in this phase as reassurance.

• You need to demonstrate you have the right chemistry with the buyer and are showing up as a strong, preferred brand.

• Pay attention to proposition/product pages on your website as they may prove critical to being chosen. Ensure they are up to date, that you're tracking bounce rates and how far into the pages people go.

• When setting up a bid support function, work through the types of people you need and the repeatable processes they will deploy – think SWAT team, not a side-of-desk activity for campaign or brand marketers.

• Whatever the outcome, always have a debrief to learn what worked and didn't so you can take these lessons forward.

08
Client

I've split this chapter into two sections. Firstly, to finish the buyer framework, some thoughts on the value of building loyalty. Secondly, and perhaps more lucratively, how to use the buyer framework to generate new revenue streams within existing clients.

SECTION 1: BUILDING LOYALTY BY MARKETING TO EXISTING CLIENTS

You have good reason to want to keep competitors out – your client was hard won, and you want to drive value for them by making sure they have the best experience of your company. Helping them explain the benefits of working with you to the rest of their business when under scrutiny in the first few months of delivery, through to riding the inevitable storms of professional relationships will help you retain business longer, create advocacy with the wider market and support any renewal or up/cross sell that you may want to do within that customer group.

SECTION 2: GENERATING NEW PIPELINE: USING BUYER FRAMEWORK WITHIN EXISTING CLIENTS

When it comes to delivering more value through selling additional services, your business should have an advantage: you know a lot about their strategy, so have a head start in making other solutions relevant to their needs. You may well know their

Horizon Scanners, have come across many of the influencers before, maybe even communicated with Explorers and Hunters directly. We have talked about the importance of peers in these three stages – and who better than their work colleagues? You are already demonstrating that you are able to work within their unique culture – so you should be able to prove to new parts of the client business that you can fulfil some of the needs outlined in the Active Buyer chapter.

Both aspects are key because in many well-established B2B companies, a large proportion of the revenue comes from a relatively small number of important clients, so it makes sense to focus a disproportionate effort on them. There is clearly a business case both in cementing their loyalty to prevent them switching to a competitor and in trying to expand your share of wallet. They come under the umbrella of account-based marketing (ABM), an approach that has risen in popularity over the last few years in B2B marketing. I include in this chapter an Insider Insight from Gemma Davies, Head of ABM and CXO Engagement at ServiceNow, a software company that helps companies manage digital workflows. She gives advice on how to get started, some tips for success and how to think about attribution of marketing effort.

What is ABM? A summary

ABM is a strategic, integrated approach to driving long-term growth with customized marketing programmes for specific, named accounts. There has been plenty written about ABM, so this is a highly abridged version of what it is. ABM focuses marketing resources on your biggest clients to drive loyalty and to increase share of wallet. It makes sense as many established companies get most of their current revenue – and future growth – from their largest existing clients.

The principles are to simplify and streamline cross-product up- or cross-sell in a way that feels like it is a direct benefit to the customer based on your precise understanding of their needs; and provide the *personal touch* – to make your customers feel great about being your customers so they advocate for you with their peers.

Although it is called marketing, done well ABM is a highly collaborative, joint endeavour with the account or sales teams – sometimes with the client themselves. To be successful, you'll need to form a close partnership with sales to gain deep insights about your buyer at an individual as well as functional and organizational level. Without personalization across the whole buyer framework, you won't achieve your objectives.

ABM makes a lot of sense if your company has a large percentage of revenue – and growth ambition – in a small percentage of existing clients. Bev Burgess cites in her illuminating book *Account Based Growth* that in many B2B companies around 80 per cent of profitable revenue comes from just 20 per cent of customers. Driving loyalty makes sense too. Her research found that losing one tier-one customer can mean finding up to 256 tier-four customers (Burgess, 2022). The cost of losing hard-won major customers can be punitive for established businesses.

ABM is resource intensive, so take care when choosing the accounts that you will focus on. There are two dimensions for you to consider when making a choice:

1 An attractive account, with strong revenue potential and a sizable internal market for the solutions you offer.

2 An engaged internal account or sales team – one that has strong existing internal relationships, a good understanding of the dynamics within the buyer's account, capacity to help you design content and a willingness to try something new.

A bespoke client marketing strategy brings together messaging, storytelling and customer journey management so that you are bringing insights, value-add content and credentials to buyers within the account in a way that makes sense for their specific business needs. Accounts on the ABM programme should get curated, filtered, and personalized content and assets so they get only the most relevant information through channels that you know work best. Often this channel is the sales or account team, so having a clear pipeline of content aligned to their activities is paramount.

As mentioned, this chapter is split into two sections: the first finishes the buyer journey framework as it is a continuum of the relationship you've been building with this set of buyers over a long period. The second section focuses on generating new pipeline, and I suggest how to use a truncated version of the overall framework in a more tailored way for existing clients. Both approaches should be done in lockstep with the client relationship and sales teams. All research into successful ABM programmes – and my own experiences – shows that for it to work, a new type of teaming with your internal stakeholders is needed. If marketing is thought of as a nice to have, a means of accessing more money for corporate hospitality or an extension to the bid support team, then ABM simply won't work. If you get it right though, the upsides of ABM should be felt by clients, account teams and your marketing team:

- *Clients*: buying is a risky business. Choosing a supplier who has already proven they can operate effectively within their environment and will do what they say they will – as well as having internal advocacy already – minimizes this risk hugely. They will feel better understood and enjoy a bespoke experience thanks to tailored research – an approach that puts them in the centre of the solution. Your conversations with them will be focused more on key issues and challenges than on what's being sold.

- *Account team and/or sales*: ABM can help shift client perception from vendor to trusted partner and adviser. Clients get a broader understanding of your offerings, strategy, and solutions through personalized marketing so that sales conversations are more strategic. Marketing may be more effective than sales at expanding reach into a client – building relationships with senior executives that it is hard for sales to access. Driving loyalty can mean advocates are more comfortable positioning you across the organization as a partner in tune with their needs.

- *Marketing*: ABM aligns marketing and sales functions in a new, unified way that is entirely based around the client, building stronger relationships with shared objectives across the two teams. It can also create greater insight into how marketing assets are being used and what's resonating in the market, as well as provide opportunities for client advocacy which helps elsewhere in the framework.

In this context, ABM investments can yield significantly greater returns than other forms of marketing expenditure for companies. The IT Services Marketing Association's (ITSMA) ABM Benchmarking Study in 2022 states that 73 per cent of marketers agree that ABM has led to measurable improvements in account relationships, 65 per cent in revenue and 40 per cent in reputation; 52 per cent reported significant improvement in account engagement and 39 per cent in pipeline growth (ITSMA, 2022).

Section 1: Building loyalty by marketing to existing clients

As mentioned in the introduction to this chapter, winning the work might not be the time to rest on your laurels: clients still need marketing attention as they seek to justify the decision of engaging you with their wider business stakeholders to prove that it was a choice well made. They are personally invested in the success of the work you're delivering. You want them to get disproportionate value from your company. Some of this will be factual, some will be felt; either way, marketing can add value to the relationship to the client in each of their *guises* – company representative, functional buyer and individual with specific needs – in a number of ways.

Additionally, as your client relationship matures, your competitors can use price, business development budgets, persuasion, or market changes to tempt your client away. And they will always be looking for opportunities. Relationships can sour where deals are subscription or service-based and must endure over a lengthy period. System outages happen, services don't get delivered on time, teams don't get the results they want in the timescales to which they committed. Clashes of opinion are possible; individuals within client and account teams change. These and other problems can drive the client to look elsewhere for support or help. If they feel like they've had personal and professional value above and beyond contract delivery, that can help shield you from these competitive advances. Perceived value can also help you raise prices – or protect pricing in an economic downturn.

There are benefits to marketing in supporting loyalty building: client advocacy, peer-to-peer recommendations, feedback into your marketing strategy or creative and case studies, all of which are critical content or channel components of the buyer journey framework as evidenced in previous chapters. Think too how fluid the job market is. Senior executives move roles often and building the right type of relationship with them as individuals as well as the company they are in today may mean a double win for your business if they move to a new organization.

It is time consuming, however, so unless you are well funded with an explicit remit to do this, it can be harder to prove ROI here than in generating new business. If you are to support this type of activity, ensure you have contracted well with your business, agreeing up-front what metrics matter over longer time horizons (usually well over a year, which is the typical marketing budget cycle) and how you will protect the funding that you have allocated to the work. You also need to be clear about the offset of allocating resources to this work, and the impact it will have on lead generation.

Content

You want to drive loyalty, so clients become ambassadors for your business within their company and externally in the wider market. Marketing's objective at the outset of the relationship is to support them in showing that they made a good decision choosing your company. According to the peak-end rule, our memory of past experiences (pleasant or unpleasant) does not correspond to an average level of positive or negative feelings but to the most extreme point and the end of the experience (Kahneman, 2000). As the client relationship transitions from sales to delivery teams – which may comprise different people from your organization – it can feel jarring. In one of my roles, we looked at customer satisfaction in the months immediately post-signature and found that relationship scores had plummeted. At this critical point for the client – when they were having to justify their decision to their peers internally and onboard a new supplier, they felt the positive experience they'd had of our company through the sales process had diminished. We set up a marketing programme to provide air cover while this transition happened, ensuring clients were catered for at two levels: an individual professional level, including inviting them to exclusive executive events with peers who had been through similar change, and at an empathetic level, to help them bring their organization with them as they rolled out a new technology. This included useful materials for their end users, bespoke microsites, and experience days in their offices.

A more scalable version of this could comprise a logged-in area of your website for all clients as they onboard, with tailored information for both procurement and end users. If you do this, you have a model you can efficiently extend to other clients, getting maximum investment for minimal additional expenditure after the initial outlay. If you have more complex services, a tailored site with client teams and roles, interesting case studies and upcoming events or thought literature may be appreciated.

Given the importance of the first months of a contract, consider whether you need to add a marketing lens into your company's onboarding process. Act as an adviser, use your marketing skills and client insights to make materials more engaging and in line with their buyer experience to date. Diversify the experience using video or info-graphics then use marketing automation tools to track what formats work. Marketing can also help clients with adoption programmes, strategy workshops, and introductions to other clients who have begun their transformation.

Over time, marketing can play a role in keeping clients loyal by giving packaged-up good news stories to share within their organization, helping them to mark milestones and finding ways to shine a spotlight on a project's success externally. This will help your client to feel validated in their choice and proud of the progress they've made. Everyone wants to look good, and you can position your customer as an early adopter, innovator, or highly outcome-focused leader. Take time to understand their formal incentives. One measure of success for your client might be the take-up of or satisfaction with your product or services. If so, work with them to create bespoke events at their offices to drive up usage or adoption – or offer to do one-to-one coaching with executive teams.

Once you have created advocates, build heroes out of them. They could well be ambitious, seeking larger roles or an upward move, in which case they will be valuable contacts at a higher level in the future. They may want to promote their own team as high performing, or make their company look attractive to work for. Finding ways to celebrate them as individuals or leaders will help them achieve their goals and build even greater loyalty to your company. In one of my previous roles, we did a major deal with a global technology provider. As part of our ABM approach, we built an entire programme around our main sponsor at the client to showcase him as a forward-thinking leader. We entered his company for innovation awards. We used our relationship with industry analysts to get him on platforms with his peers to talk about what he'd achieved. We provided introductions to journalists that were writing about innovation and put him on event platforms we were sponsoring. These actions not only helped him (and his company) build a positive profile, they also allowed us to shape his narrative about the relationship between our two companies, for example how we were making challenging technology contracts work and why strong partnerships are the key to solving ambiguous and ambitious problems.

Channels

Of course, you have a very direct channel into your existing clients: your account team. Work closely with them to determine what will work for the individuals you are targeting. Ideas include:

- Opportunities for teams to come together, either through hospitality (if companies allow employees to accept it), or professional events such as workshops focused on solutions with authorities in your business. Finding ways for them to access external subject matter experts that are hard to reach can also be effective. Former politicians, academic professors or outspoken journalists can all add to the exclusivity of an occasion.

- Initiate joint corporate social responsibility (CSR) initiatives. Look at societal issues that affect their industry and showcase instances where your company has made a difference. In one of my roles we were engaging with a group of buyers in the financial services sector who were passionate about financial literacy in young people. We entered a partnership with a not-for-profit organization that educated children about financial issues and invited senior executives of our business and from our clients to jointly judge awards and host events. This created a win/win/ win for us: our clients felt appreciated, our chosen charity benefitted from their support, and we aligned our brand with an issue that mattered to the whole sector.

- Help them in their jobs. One year, a client team and I built an exclusive Chief Procurement Officer circle, which met to discuss market trends and exchange best practice. What added particular value was pulling together meeting reports after the event, which included a profile of each of the different leaders, the group's collective advice on what was worth reading and a point of view on trends. This was not only helpful to the senior representatives, it also built our reputation as experts with a valuable network and drove engagement with our business deeper inside their organizations. Separately, our female senior executives led mentoring programmes to help women at the client organization think about succession planning, which helped drive loyalty to our brand at all levels of their business. You can also co-create content with your clients which will help build relationships and advocacy.

- Celebrate key milestones. If you're rolling out a product, jointly celebrate launch day. If there's a technical delivery milestone, create thank you cards for people in the client team who made it happen. I've seen companies take out advertisements on hoardings outside client HQ to celebrate important moments, for example when the number of employees trained has hit a certain target. I also saw one give out hampers to IT people who had to work all night to flick the switch on a key piece of tech.

- Understand what the client's stakeholders are expecting – and at what level of detail – so you can provide success stories to show they made the right choice. Work with your sales and delivery teams to understand the significance of milestones delivered on time and on budget, then package them for the client to share internally. Use infographics and create videos of your team and their team talking about what they've learned through working together.

- Let important clients and their teams have input into, or sight of, the decisions your business is making. Client advisory boards on strategy, product roadmaps or people investments can deepen relationships, improve perceptions of your marketing capabilities at a higher level in the client organization, and generate invaluable advice.

- Support the adoption and usage of your product or service by putting together tailored product demo experiences and bringing experts to the client's office location. This allows customers to engage with you directly in a way that is convenient to them, brings relevant insights to targeted individuals, and will likely generate useful feedback from users.

As mentioned, creating this advocacy also has return benefits for marketing. If a client feels good about working with you, they can help drive advocacy within their broader peer set and lead to case studies and references promoting your business, which we've seen are crucial at earlier stages of the buyer journey. As you engage them through marketing, make sure you ask for reciprocal benefit, or design external events that allow your happy customers to meet the buyers in Explorer and Hunter phases. Capture feedback and seek permission to use it: sales training guru Dale Carnegie suggested that 91 per cent of customers say they'd give referrals but only 11 per cent of salespeople ask for them (Carnegie, 2021). Take the initiative to collect and directly ask clients yourself. As a function, marketing could have more to gain across the buyer framework from these accolades than individual salespeople.

A NOTE ON DISPLACING COMPETITORS

A key objective of ABM is to prevent competitors from breaking the bond of loyalty that you have established with big and important customers. But how do you do just this to your rivals?

If you're in a very established, commoditized, or mature solution environment, breaking loyalty to displace competitors will need to be part of your strategy – but it's hard. It's highly unlikely that you'll be offering an entirely unique service that no one else does, and it's well known that buyers often buy relatively uncritically from companies that they have worked with before. They know that they can trust them, they know how to work with them, and they know what to expect... good or bad.

Sales teams typically use price or other commercial terms to prise prospects out of established relationships. But what can you do from a marketing perspective? Behavioural science suggests that when you give someone something of value, they feel compelled to give you something in return. Consider what you could do to create an opportunity for a conversation. Some ideas include:

- Offer experts from within your business to provide free advice or inviting buyers to an exclusive event. If a potential buyer engages with any of these carrots, it's hard for them to say no to a subsequent meeting and this provides a chance for you to start to build a relationship. Work closely with sales teams to craft the right approach – just showing up and hoping you'll dazzle on price and a nice PowerPoint presentation isn't enough.

- Keep tabs on people. Professionals move jobs frequently – often during an annual *season* (this will vary according to industry and when bonuses are paid). Agree with sales which individuals are likely to matter over a three-to-five-year period and keep an eye on them through platforms like LinkedIn. Job moves provide an opportunity to reset, build or strengthen a relationship. If the mover gets promoted, send anything from a simple 'well done' message to a gift, an introduction to a useful connection, or a thoughtful piece of content that will help them in their new role. Anyone starting a new job is looking for good ideas, insights and help – they want to hit the ground running. What could your company do to add value in this period? Once, when I moved jobs, an agency I'd previously worked with that was not on the rota at the new company did a social media audit and sent it to me in my first week. One of the incumbent agencies sent me a showreel of the best work they'd done with my team, and how they'd collaborated effectively to achieve results. Both were impressive and memorable moves!

- Find triggers. Look for market specific opportunities that could be trigger events. These include restructuring, fines, downsizing, mergers and acquisitions, or the appointment of new board members. When new things happen, opportunities open up. Work with sales and business leaders (even clients) to predict what might come up and prepare marketing to be ready to deploy *in the moment* so you look to be responding fast. At one company when targeting banks, we knew that at least one could be in breach of a new regulation at the end of the first year, but not knowing when or which one didn't stop us preparing prospect and customer communications outlining our solution, to deploy as soon as news hit the market.

If you are speculatively attempting to create moments of opportunity, it goes without saying that your sales or account teams need to be ready to act as soon as a prospect takes up one of these. Work closely with them on your post event or activity strategy, so they are bought in and ready, otherwise this will be a waste of money.

Section 2: Generating new pipeline: using buyer framework within existing clients

It makes sense to try to grow your business at your biggest clients. You know their strategy, budget owners, who has power within the company, and know how to work successfully within their unique culture. This type of marketing will form part of an account-based marketing programme where the objectives are very similar to the buyer framework for non-clients but highly personalized with some shortcuts given what you already know.

It isn't just that you have the advantage as you are already an incumbent supplier. As companies become clients, they increasingly expect the organizations they spend money with to find additional ways to add value to them beyond the contracted service. There are 75 per cent of B2B buyers who say they expect companies to anticipate their needs and make relevant suggestions (B2B Institute, 2021a). This is challenging for sales teams in large, complex businesses as they may not know the full suite of offerings in sufficient detail to bring the relevant service to clients when they need it. This is exacerbated if your business is growing organically but does not integrate acquired solutions into the core or educate sales representatives about the benefits of new services.

How to work out whether to do ABM

A highly tailored approach isn't right for every business though. It can be very resource intensive, so if your business strategy relies on growing prospects in new markets, or budgets are very tightly linked to lead generation, it may incur an opportunity cost you don't want to take. If you're not sure whether to embark on account-based marketing and want to assess whether there is an opportunity for marketing to drive leads within existing client accounts, a good start is to review expenditure at your biggest customers to ascertain how well the money they spend with you is distributed across everything you offer. I've often found that important customers are buying lots of the same things – in part due to how sales or account teams are incentivized – yet the business growth strategy relies on *cross* selling, in other words persuading these important clients to buy other products or solutions. In one business I worked in, we uncovered that only four per cent of large customers were buying multiple services from the company. This insight meant that redirecting some funds to ABM was an easy conversation with the board.

How to use the buyer framework with existing clients

Your targets are buyers in the client who don't know you yet but would be good candidates for other services that you sell. These will be the driver of new revenue streams. It may be that the tax department knows you very well, but the CEO isn't aware that you could support on a strategic enterprise-wide transformation. Buyers may not know that you work with them already (many companies struggle to have a single view of all their supplier arrangements) or that you offer services that could help them achieve their functional objectives. But it is beneficial for them to know this, as now that you have a relationship with their business it is less risky for them to buy something from you. You've proven you have a compatible culture, understand their organization well and can deliver in their unique internal environment.

As Gemma Davies explains in her Insider Insight, smart marketers tend towards one-to-one programmes that focus on deepening relationships with a small number of accounts, with dedicated resources and a customized marketing plan; or one-to-few programmes that cluster groups of accounts, typically by industry. Either way, you can use the buyer journey framework to get greater efficiencies (as you don't need to produce lots of speculative content) and effectiveness (as tight alignment of content to the very specific buyer needs makes it more relevant and likely to be engaged with). You also have more precise information about what channels work than when you're attracting entirely new business.

To unlock more revenue from existing clients, you need to find and deeply understand new buyer targets then design a marketing programme that follows the framework but is tailored to them specifically. Speak to advocates within the client and account teams for unique sources of insight into your new buyer.

Identify precisely who the target individuals and teams are. Look at the client account to understand their strategy, pain points, budget and the industry trends they are concerned about. Use this to identify which of your solutions will be of most benefit to them – you may need to make some tough choices here as Gemma explains in her interview. Once chosen, map out the Horizon Scanners, Explorers and Hunters for your services, what their relationships to your existing buyers are and what you know about their supplier preferences: are they advocates, detractors or neutral? Who influences them internally and how strong are your relationships? Having an audit of who the client's team know in your company – directly or indirectly – will inform your strategy. Research these groups thoroughly – get to know what drives them, what topics they are passionate about, what groups they are part of and who they know in your business or wider networks.

Then create a highly tailored version of the buyer journey framework. You know who the Horizon Scanners and Explorers are and may have marketed to them before. The principles behind the content and channels outlined in previous chapters still hold true, but your insights mean that uncertainties about who is in the target addressable market, what roles they are playing and what types of messages will resonate should have disappeared. You can be extremely differentiated by being very bespoke across the journey. Put budgets to work on aligning your value propositions to specific client challenges. Use what you know about the client's priorities, pain points, internal constraints and budgets to bring your messaging to life in a highly relevant way. Where it is possible, personalize everything you create and keep track of how new people from your target ABM accounts are engaging with the content, making sure to keep account teams alerted of any event attendance, engagement with content or requests for information.

FIGURE 8.1 How to flex the buyer journey framework to drive new revenue in existing clients

WHAT IS DIFFERENT
WHEN DRIVING PIPELINE
WITH EXISTING CLIENTS

ADDITIONAL CONTENT AND CHANNEL IDEAS
TO SUPPLEMENT THE BUYER FRAMEWORK:
ONLY POSSIBLE WHEN YOU KNOW THE CLIENT
VERY WELL

HORIZON SCANNER

You are already trusted to have a point of view on strategy, and can tailor the high-level thought leadership to your client's specific needs.

As you develop thought leadership, consider how you might tailor the outputs to provide industry cuts (one to few) or individual implications documents (one to one). At PwC, the annual CEO survey is tailored for some respondents to show how their company-specific answers compare to trends globally and in their sector. PwC's internal analysts provide bespoke advice and insights that enrich the content and make it more distinctive, which allow teams to have highly valuable conversations with new executives they've not been able to engage with before. Other examples I have seen include creating account specific content linked to surveys (e.g. bespoke infographics benchmarking clients against a wider data set).

You can also use technology platforms to create digital content which can be easily customized by your sales teams with a few clicks of a button. This means relationship managers can choose which chapters or sections to include for their clients, then add in their own personal message to create content that seems designed for this particular client.

Use what you know about these individuals to review your overall messaging. For example, in one of my teams, we looked at a new Chief Technology Officer who had been appointed to a leadership role at a government client from the corporate sector. We wanted to understand whether this person was more motivated by technology or by purpose before deciding how to position our written materials and how to present ourselves at client meetings. Understanding this and adapting our approach meant we were able to get their attention more effectively, and had greater take up on events and content which built the relationship more quickly.

EXPLORER

You can get insight into what matters to them as individuals and know who internally influences them.

Work with the account team to understand who the key existing customers and potential buyers are.

- What is driving the client's reasons to act, its decision-making and possible changes in direction? What market drivers or trends are affecting your buyers? Knowing this will make campaigns more relevant and timelier.

- What are their specific issues and challenges as well as their triggers to act? This will help you articulate solutions in a way that is easy for them to connect what they need to what you have.

- Who are the key people within the account to target? What are their specific professional interests and how will you use this to curate the content that you give to them?

Answers to these questions will allow you to develop bespoke value propositions ahead of making and executing a joint marketing and sales plan. Use the insights to curate or create content directly relevant to individual business needs.

FIGURE 8.1 (Continued)

WHAT IS DIFFERENT WHEN DRIVING PIPELINE WITH EXISTING CLIENTS	ADDITIONAL CONTENT AND CHANNEL IDEAS TO SUPPLEMENT THE BUYER FRAMEWORK: ONLY POSSIBLE WHEN YOU KNOW THE CLIENT VERY WELL
	Commission your SMEs to do some bespoke thought leadership on these topics, or if you have a relevant broader content piece, consider adding a personalized layer that interprets it for your client. If they engage with this content, react quickly: notify the account teams and offer access to internal experts for follow-up meetings. Also make account teams aware of the plan and timings ahead of execution.

Establish with the sales team who they want to unlock new relationships with and use targeted or programmatic advertising to get messages directly to them.

Match named client Explorers to your company's executives then feed thought leadership to your team for dissemination via social media or email. One of my teams used to pull together a regular 'conversation starter' document that went to sales, outlining topical issues that they may hear about in the corridors of the client and our latest, best thinking on the subject. This was minimal extra effort for our team – we'd already produced and packaged the thought leadership – but working with account teams to understand their client needs meant we distributed it much more effectively than sending out a weekly roundup of all the thought leadership with no context.

Create bespoke research. Think about how to deliver the content effectively, such as asking senior executives to send it to the targets in a personalized way.

Give early access to insights to a small group of your customers who are grouped together in your ABM programme – and be sure to let them know that they have something special ahead of their competitors. You can execute this via the sales teams or organize a workshop for individual clients or these groups, focused on discussing their biggest issues.

Provide exclusive insights by doing sector-specific cuts of your overall research and commissioning expert opinion pieces that will make it more engaging for this group. |
| **HUNTER**

You have insight into client strategy and budgets. You know what motivates them at an organizational, functional and individual level.

You may have already sold to some of the influencers before (finance, IT, procurement). | Recreate all the content so it is directly relevant to them (you should already know their strategy and investments, or what specific industry issues will be creating pain points).

If you are driving them to your web estate, create an area where you can put proposition messages that are highly correlated to their business needs. You can also use this area to showcase the work you are doing with their colleagues in other parts of the business and post exclusive thought leadership.

Create exclusive events tailored to their specific needs: introduce them to like-minded people who know you well. |

FIGURE 8.1 (Continued)

WHAT IS DIFFERENT WHEN DRIVING PIPELINE WITH EXISTING CLIENTS	ADDITIONAL CONTENT AND CHANNEL IDEAS TO SUPPLEMENT THE BUYER FRAMEWORK: ONLY POSSIBLE WHEN YOU KNOW THE CLIENT VERY WELL
ACTIVE BUYER You are taking risk out of the decision. You may have sold to them before.	You have proven you can work within their organization and respond already to their needs as a company representative. Articulate precisely how you are currently working with their organization focusing on aligned values, understanding of their cultures and an open dialogue about what you've learned about them to date. Focus with precision on what you know about their functional and individual needs based on your insights. Bring new ideas based on other clients that have similar challenges so that you are seen as innovative.

Across all of these phases, look to get insight from your account teams and existing client relationships to inform tone, style and content. Extreme relevance is key to successful ABM – personalize, tailor and amend what you have so that it feels designed for the specific client or sector (if you are doing one-to-few).

INSIDER INSIGHT

Gemma Davies, Global Account Based Marketing and CXO Engagement Practice Lead, ServiceNow

Since joining ServiceNow in 2018, Gemma Davies has set up and developed an ABM programme worth $12 million in revenue and $132 million of qualified pipeline for the fast-growing Santa Clara-based cloud enterprise software business. ServiceNow has 6,900 customers who rely on its Now Platform® to manage their digital workflows and according to Gemma, who won B2B Marketing's 2019/2020 Marketer of the Year award, the company's multi-layered ABM approach lies at the heart of its corporate strategy. In this Insider Insight, Gemma talks about how to get started in ABM, and the importance of collaboration, client focus, storytelling and metric selection.

STARTING OUT

In late 2017, I connected with the leadership to discuss one of their most ambitious and strategic marketing strategies – driven by a need to shift market perceptions of the company as an IT ticketing tool to a value-based digital transformation platform and build reputation and relevance to the C-suite. This was a board-level initiative and highlighted a shift in the overall strategy to focus on a small number of accounts responsible for significant growth; at that time, there was no marketing plan to support the ambition.

Support from the top, and clear accountability, were critical – our Chief Marketing Officer and our Chief Revenue Officer were our executive sponsors and continue to support and advocate for the strategy across our marquee account programmes. They helped define the scope and the objectives, signed off the first round of target accounts, and helped us sell the vision across the business.

Over the last four years, we have been growing a highly successful ABM practice by embedding an ABM strategy and framework across the business and creating a continual cycle of improvement, innovation, and scale. First established as a pilot in 2018, the ABM Center of Excellence (CoE) has grown from four US-only 'one to one' ABM accounts to the programme it is today, with emphasis on a multi-tiered organization-wide ABM strategy, made up of a series of services all delivered across all three geographies. Moreover, the team has created an additional scale by templatizing the most impactful content and providing expert ABM consultancy to the field, enabling them to repurpose account-specific content and programmes effectively. The success of the ABM CoE has generated attraction and participation from the Executive Suite, Field Marketing, and, most notably, the sales teams.

When starting out, always start with your customer and company goals. Make sure you can tie your programme objectives to what your customers and leadership team care about most. ABM isn't just a marketing imperative: it is a business imperative. Our strategy and philosophy for ensuring a successful business is, in many ways, quite simple. We ensure our customers' success is our success. Our approach is guided by the drive to help customers work smarter, faster, and better – to solve their greatest business challenges. This philosophy is the perfect foundation for our ABM programme, which is centred around understanding our customers and treating them as a 'market of one'.

By aligning directly to our corporate goals and maturity, we were able to demonstrate impact at different stages of programme maturity, all while clearly showing how we were directly aligned to the even bigger long-term company goals. ABM is a significant investment, and it will take time to demonstrate its impact and an acceptable return. Get buy-in early.

'ONE TO ONE' OR 'ONE TO FEW'?
Our ABM as-a-service programme blends two approaches to ensure our resources deliver the most value to our target accounts. A blended approach means we can look at how we prioritize and deliver value to our target accounts more effectively and in a much more informed way. This ultimately has led to higher returns.

In a one-to-one programme, accounts are treated as 'markets of one'. They all benefit from dedicated resources, a customized plan, and content that takes their individual business imperatives and challenges into consideration.

A one-to-few programme carefully segments a greater number of accounts by industry or another common factor, while still considering their business priorities and strategic goals. This method provides greater scalability, which is a perk for teams that have more limited resources or are trying ABM for the first time.

If you choose to adopt a blended approach, don't operate these two approaches in a vacuum. There's a significant opportunity for ABM practitioners to combine them and leverage learnings, resources, and outcomes to help you scale and deliver on programme goals. This advantageous approach will help you better balance short- and long-term KPIs associated with dedicated resources and budget.

CHOOSING SECTORS

There is no substitute for speaking an industry's language and scaling programmes common to cross-industry imperatives across similar accounts. Our global ABM cluster team, running one-to-few ABM programmes, looks for common challenges in a small set of accounts grouped by similar size, strategy, and maturity. And then develops and delivers lightly personalized customer journeys aligned to shared imperatives. We've successfully executed ABM clusters in many industries such as banking and federal. And even identified cross-industry imperatives like supply chain, which are then lightly adapted for industries like retail, manufacturing, logistics, and more.

UNDERSTANDING THE CUSTOMER

Our core objective is to build relevance in our accounts. Customers are at the centre of everything we do. Our first company value is to 'wow our customers'. This requires being forward-thinking about our brand, our products, and the experiences we provide and not settling for the status quo.

Always strive to understand your customers' business imperatives and create value-based messaging and experiences that resonate, or as I like to put it, moving from 'random acts of kindness' to a comprehensive engagement strategy. This is how you establish long-term relationships and trust. Be clear about whom you're talking to – a completely new prospect or a new business line within an existing client company – and what their motivations are. What are their business imperatives, funding commitments, and leadership goals? Then see if your business has a capability to which you can link a value proposition that they will care about. Don't just say how awesome your service is; make sure you know what they're trying to do in advance.

In this context, we've tried to improve our storytelling to bring out the benefits across our business lines and demonstrate the value for buyers and their peers across their organization. You need to be careful, though, how far you align your brand with theirs in your messaging – I was once admonished for using a target account logo on ABM marketing materials. Still, it turned into a good story because it caught their attention! They went on to issue us with an NDA before inviting us to meet with the leadership team. The lesson is: be a challenger, work out where and how you add value, and if you can't, don't even bother to knock at that door.

BUILDING TRUST WITH THE ACCOUNT TEAM

Building trust and a close partnership between the ABM team and the account team is critical – they will become your greatest allies and advocates. To be successful, you need to create a vision and purpose – a picture of success for the business and team, and a framework to educate those around you on what and why you are doing what you do.

Once you have the account team's interest aligned with them on industry insights and account planning, bring them strategic industry intelligence; I promise this will instantly elevate your partnership. Consider how you will position working with them on go-to-market plans to support new business plays and share the success ABM has had with other accounts.

Sales are also the key to decision-maker relationship development. We partner with them to prioritize and identify buyer intent, strengthen value positioning, and extend networking through flagship executive events and engagement programmes across targeted accounts. In many cases, sales will introduce key stakeholders and influencers and enable us to co-create with them directly – this is the definition of customer-centric marketing.

MEASUREMENT AND ATTRIBUTION

Measuring ABM impact is essential to demonstrate the concrete success and influence of the programme. Be mindful that traditional marketing metrics and dashboards will not capture the programme's true value or accurately reflect your reach or impact within accounts. I recommend thinking about reporting across six categories: ABM Reach, ABM Services, Customer Collaboration, Deeper Decision Maker Relationships, Pipeline & Closed Won (Influenced), and Pipeline & Closed Won (Sourced). These allow anyone to see the reach and impact of the ABM programme immediately. You will need to tie any measures directly back to the overall business strategy you defined at the programme's start.

When thinking about your measurement framework, consider how you align and encourage account teams also to take responsibility for their success – if they don't tag their activity in our CRM system, it doesn't get reported in the dashboard and could risk losing investment. However, even with our quantitative data tagged and recorded, we also make sure to include qualitative stories and anecdotes in our reports to demonstrate the power of effective marketing.

PROMOTING ABM INTERNALLY

We don't just use ABM externally; adopting an ABM approach internally has helped us showcase the programme's success to internal stakeholders. Our Center of Excellence is at the heart of this and was designed to drive adoption, encourage collaboration, and create excitement about ABM's potential to drive stronger revenue, relationships, reputation, and retention.

We have also invested in specific training and personal development opportunities to strengthen our individual and team abilities. Over 100 people have now been trained on the two-day ITSMA ABM course. Throughout our ABM optimization efforts, we have ensured that all content is easy to use and has a consistent brand identity. With our bullseye logo, the internal ABM branding easily identifies content and tools as originating from the ABM CoE, which has helped increase our profile and further foster the customer-centric ABM mindset we set out to create.

ADVICE TO BUDDING ABMERS

There is a growing importance of being open to new insights, especially in an age when none of us have a 'lifetime' to master, or even fully understand, every specialism in our business. This is why cultivating a 'growth mindset' is especially important when embarking on an ABM journey.

Research has proven that a growth mindset makes employees better team players; they can learn more or become smarter if they work hard, persevere, and view challenges and failures as opportunities to improve their learning and skills. All of which are key when running an ABM programme.

When successful, this mindset can encourage closer cross-functional collaboration and alignment between teams and individuals in your business, not just between the sales and marketing teams. In my experience, this has resulted in a more thorough and accountable ABM programme for our business and, ultimately, our customers.

ABM wins the toughest customers, changes the most challenging relationships, and represents a level of business integration that most marketing can only aspire to.

ABM is a real team sport, and I'm so proud and humbled to be a part of it.

Attribution

Despite the benefits, many marketing teams have tried and failed to implement ABM. This is often because they've tried to do it as a *side of desk* activity, or it has been misunderstood as a sales support tool and money has been cannibalized into hospitality or other sales support activity which has yielded no return. Attribution of results can be very challenging for either of the objectives outlined in this chapter. In terms of building loyalty, this is a long-term game with results that may only be felt tangentially or considered *owned* by the account management or sales organization. The benefits might also be indirect: building up strong references, case studies and a bank of clients that will speak at your events or advocate on your behalf may not be appreciated as key revenue drivers. When it comes to driving new sales within existing accounts, this is typically forecast. As Gemma mentions, traditional marketing metrics won't accurately capture the impact of the programme. Even where deals are not forecast and are uncovered via marketing, given these clients are known, it is harder to draw direct attribution to lead generation.

Attribution is essential as you will need to work through how to balance your resourcing into these two buyer groups. Building loyalty helps get goodwill from sales or account teams, which could help you create trust as you build your ABM function, and it helps your marketing efforts more broadly. Creating new revenue at existing clients more obviously positions marketing as a lever for business growth. Given it takes time and money to do ABM well, it's important to agree up-front how marketing will demonstrate ROI. Start with asking what the right combination of marketing activities is to justify attribution. Then agree what percentage of the pipeline should be attributed to marketing, and who decides. A joint marketing and sales leadership steering group is an effective way to do this. Sometimes marketing doesn't get enough credit as there's a perception that the relationship was already there. Or it can be that very little marketing is needed for teams to allocate a huge attribution, which doesn't work either. It is clearly suboptimal to ascertain that one email should get millions of dollars in associated revenue, even if it is done with positive intent to show that ABM is working. In either case, define how the deepening of the relationship can be captured and quantified and how marketing will be recognized for its contribution.

It is helpful to align on language and definitions. Figure 8.2 shows a framework I have used in the past.

FIGURE 8.2 Framework to support marketing ABM activity

MARKETING **SUPPORTED** LEADS/ ACTIVITY	MARKETING **ENHANCED** LEADS/ ACTIVITY	MARKETING **ACCELERATED** LEADS/ ACTIVITY
Where there is already forecast pipeline, or where the sales team feel well embedded into the account, but need marketing support to deepen the relationship.	Where you've improved the quality of the leads or relationship e.g. by running workshops with clients or building customization into a product experience, or bringing senior executives together from your business and the client.	Where marketing has accelerated pipeline by identifying and profiling new buyers, opening doors to new teams within the account or run events that have helped unblock conversations.

The types of marketing activities that you do will be driven by what your objectives are but having a clear label for each can help better communicate how marketing and sales have worked together to achieve results. Once you have aligned on what types of activity will be attributed in which way, you can then agree what percentage of pipeline or revenue each campaign should attract, and how you will jointly manage this with sales.

Metrics for both sections

Although there is a clear case for ABM, particularly in more mature B2B environments, be mindful that any money put towards this will be at the expense of attracting new business in new markets. If you have a lead target, you will need to negotiate a downtick in that number to allocate marketing funding to this type of activity – and get the recognition from leaders that this form of marketing makes strategic sense.

At a high level, in this chapter I've outlined two benefits of ABM. First, to finish the buyer framework, keeping those you've been marketing to for months, even years, loyal and driving advocacy. Second, to deliver a bespoke, potentially truncated version of the buyer journey framework into existing client accounts to grow your share of wallet. Across each though, you are looking to deliver more value to your clients.

Precision is essential when defining what success looks like for client marketing. It is a collaborative effort with the account team. Being successful takes trust and entails:

- Joint agreement of a programme's objectives, approach and success criteria.
- Expectations and KPIs that are well understood and well aligned across sales and marketing.
- Time to build the programme, develop relationships, obtain new insights and execute the plan.
- Agreement on frequency of reporting (ABM doesn't move fast) and expectation management as you're trying something new.
- Budget! Doing ABM isn't cheap if you add in agency support and the cost of personalization (even if just adapting existing materials).

As Gemma in this chapter and Peter Thomas in the last both remark: getting strategic alignment at a sales and marketing leadership level is critical to the success of such client-oriented marketing campaigns. With it, you can achieve some of the returns that the ITSMA research, cited earlier in this chapter, outlined. Without it, you run the risk of unrealized marketing efforts.

FIGURE 8.3   ABM metrics

INPUT METRICS	INDICATOR METRICS	OUTCOME METRICS
Measure of how productive the marketing team is	How likely marketing are to hit the agreed targets	How marketing performed related to the marketing and business strategy

Objective: Drive loyalty and advocacy

• Number of product videos or webinars • New client on boarding • Number of customer communications • Number of client advisory boards	• Number of case studies • Client attendance at events • Number of touch points with target stakeholders • Feedback into your marketing: campaigns, messages, creative Marketing enhanced activity: • Meetings with senior leaders and co-hosted events • Joint award wins • Joint PR • Shared platforms at events	Stronger, more robust relationships: • Brand perception with key accounts • Net promoter score or client satisfaction score increase • Number of reference-able clients • Number of case studies • Renewal success rate Clients fully realise the benefits of their investment: • Subscription renewal • Product usage Relationship strength: • NPS/overall satisfaction score • %age clients ranking your business as "trusted advisor" • Sole sourced in renewals or new work

Objective: Drive new revenue streams at existing clients

• Number of accounts in an ABM program. Within ABM, number of custom messaging and thought leadership, events, briefings, number of individuals in target accounts targeted through marketing channels	• New buyer within client attendance at events • Overall number of touch points with target stakeholders • Percentage of priority clients engaged via tailored thought leadership • Number of read/share views of tailored thought leadership • Number of downloads/watch/read of thought leadership by named individuals within client accounts	Discover and drive new revenue streams: • Number of new buyer or influencers within an account identified and engaged with • Number of touch points with named client executives or specific teams that were facilitated by marketing (across all channels) • Time in pipeline (accelerated activity/ leads) • Increased pipeline growth in targeted accounts • Overall average win rate and/or value of ABM influenced pipeline • Percentage of sole sourced opportunities vs competitive bids

IN SUMMARY

- ABM has significant benefits for all parties. For clients it minimizes risks given you're a known entity and have demonstrated you can deliver, for account teams it helps to drive loyalty and position the business as a trusted partner, and for marketing it creates a unified approach around the client and the opportunity to create client advocacy in other parts of the framework.

- You need to be very clear about the objectives, metrics and how you will attribute the success of this type of investment. Sales or account teams can have a loud voice in getting an unfair share of marketing funds to smooth the relationship and increase their satisfaction scores so you must be robust.

- Getting the most out of ABM requires new ways of working, an open mindedness to a different strategy and a high level of buy-in as well as trust.

- The account team will bring knowledge of the client, what the client has committed to in terms of budget or strategy, a view of where you want to build a pipeline, and a team of people invested in the client's success.

- The marketing team will bring additional market or account insights, access to channels to help map relationships or to build profiles of individuals, as well as messaging, creativity, new ideas and skills to execute across channels.

- Finding new buyers in existing accounts means you can increase your share of wallet very effectively. Think back on the three roles that a buyer is playing that I outlined in the previous chapter – you do not need to spend much time at all on the organizational alignment as it is already proven, so you can shift more effort and emphasis to the functional and emotional needs your buyer has. This should give you a huge competitive advantage or dramatically reduce time spent in the Hunter and Active Buyer phases so you can close pipeline faster.

- Keeping your clients happy makes good business sense too. They provide an invaluable source of insight that informs your marketing strategy, references or endorsements to their peers or case studies. You may also be able to use your marketing to drive up their satisfaction with your company – which is a key metric for many businesses.

- Be aware that this is expensive and resource intensive. If you are trying to juggle work across the buyer journey, be clear about the outcomes you are driving and ensure it is of value – and has a value attached to it.

09
Summary of Part One

A B2B marketing strategy with the buyer journey at its heart is a multi-channel plan with content, channels and metrics relevant to each of the five stages described in the previous chapters. Looking across the whole journey means you can assess the amount of work needed to meet buyer needs, allocate the time and money you should devote to each stage and define a seamless experience which satisfies your buyers, allowing you to build up insights into them as they engage with your marketing activities.

Doing a well-integrated, thoughtfully planned marketing strategy and campaign with the buyer journey at the centre is a sustained effort involving huge amounts of content and constant revision. This is the way to drive commercial return over time. This is an iterative process, so at all points seek opportunities to test and learn new approaches and use this insight to refine, course correct or inform your plans. It is my belief that campaigns done partially is what damages B2B marketing because it is impossible to get strong results without sustained activity across the whole journey.

FIGURE 9.1 Summary of buyer objectives, B2B marketers' objectives, content, channel and metrics across the buyer journey

	HORIZON SCANNER	EXPLORER	HUNTER	ACTIVE BUYER	CLIENT
Their objective	Assess how market trends or innovation affects my business.	Formulating problems that need solving, defining a relevant point of view, prioritizing against other things I need to do.	Actively researching options, building business case, surveying competitive landscape.	Shortlisting suppliers, seriously considering services, doing due diligence.	Achieve outcomes I contracted for, get maximum value for money.
Your objective	Position yourself as experts to create or address unstated buyer needs.	Create market for propositions or services – imperative to act.	Differentiate against competitors, be easy to buy from.	Accelerate decision-making and reduce time in pipeline.	Drive loyalty to protect revenue and/or increase share of wallet within accounts.
Types of activity	Thought leadership via blogs, articles, keynote speaker slots, proprietary research pieces, events on topics, webinars, social. Brand promotion: advertising, social promotion, industry body relationships, partnerships.	Opinion pieces: blogs, articles, keynote speaker slots, proprietary research pieces, events, webinars, industry insights, market trends.	Proof points: case studies, benchmarking tools. Decision-making aids: calculators, competitor tables, product collateral with features and benefits, webinars.	Sales support: talk tracks, standard sales decks, RFI/RFP/tender submission. flexes in this). Bid support.	Tools for clients to maximize investment: e.g. product webinars. Account-based marketing, custom messaging and thought leadership, events, briefings. Senior client events, client advisory boards.
Input metrics	Number of journalist conversations. Number of articles, blogs, points of view developed, number of proprietary research pieces, number of social posts, £ spend on promoting thought leadership e.g. through media. Number of third party or industry events or webinars you speak at, number of keynote speeches.	Number of opinion pieces, blogs and articles in third-party publications. Number of keynote speaker or panel slots. Proprietary research pieces and number of events or webinars that you run to promote them. Number of industry bodies or social groups part of.	Number of proof points: case studies, benchmarking tools, decision-making aids: (e.g. calculators, competitor table), product collateral with features and benefits. Number of events – roadshows, webinars, third party.	Number of bids supported. Number of pieces of collateral produced. Number of product videos and demos. Virtual office tours or pitches.	Number of product videos or webinars. New client onboarding materials. Number of customer communications. Number of accounts in an ABM programme. Within ABM, number of custom messaging and thought leadership, events, briefings, number of individuals in target accounts contacted through marketing channels. Number of client advisory boards.

FIGURE 9.1 (Continued)

HORIZON SCANNER	EXPLORER	HUNTER	ACTIVE BUYER	CLIENT

Indicator metrics

HORIZON SCANNER	EXPLORER	HUNTER	ACTIVE BUYER	CLIENT
Journalist/analyst requests for data or comments. Number of social mentions/shares/likes. Number of social followers from clients/prospects you want to engage with. Number of people willing to take part in surveys or follow up interviews. Number of interactions with named influencers. Reads, downloads, views, shares, likes of thought leadership. Number of sign-ups for third-party sessions you are speaking at.	Number of positive media and social media mentions (ideally from targeted client group). Content performance: number of read/share/view of materials or time spent on assets, website visits (from target clients), organic search, visits to opinion pages on your website. Email open rates. Number of interactions with named influencers. Industry body advocates, how active you are in these.	Number of enquiries. Engagement with diagnostic tools. Engagement with product information/case studies Organic search. Email open rates. Visits to product/service – or campaign landing page. Event attendance.	Engagement with collateral – amount of sales-focused content viewed and time spent on collateral. Feedback from sales or clients through purchase process. Number of demos watched, software downloads.	Number of case studies. Client attendance at events. Number of positive media and social mentions from named accounts. Number of touch points with target stakeholders. Number of read/share views of tailored thought leadership. Number of downloads/watch/read of thought leadership by named individuals within client accounts. Shared platforms at events.

Outcome metrics

HORIZON SCANNER	EXPLORER	HUNTER	ACTIVE BUYER	CLIENT
Raised brand profile: • Number of articles featuring your thought leadership or experts • Mentions in target publications • Media share of voice Associated your company with topics buyers care about: • Number of people in your target audience engaging with content	Raised brand profile: • Number of articles featuring your thought leadership or experts • Articles featuring your thought leadership or SMEs in target publications • Industry analyst mentions Associated your company with topics buyers care about: • Number of people in your target audience engaging with content	Improved consideration, acquisition of market share, pipeline generation: • New contacts • Leads • Unweighted pipeline • Conversion rates • Win rate • Length of time in pipeline	Improved market share, competitive advantage and revenue impact: • Closed/won business • Win rate improvement • Reduced length of time in pipeline (revenue hits earlier)	Stronger, more robust relationships: • Brand perception with key accounts • Net promoter score or client satisfaction score increase • Number of referenceable clients • Meetings with senior leaders and co-hosted events Clients fully realize the benefits of their investment: • Subscription renewal

FIGURE 9.1 (Continued)

HORIZON SCANNER	EXPLORER	HUNTER	ACTIVE BUYER	CLIENT

Outcome metrics (continued)

HORIZON SCANNER
- Amount of time spent engaging with your content
- Directly engaged buyers with your proprietary content
- Attendee numbers
- Face-to-face engagement metrics e.g. number of touch points with key buyers
- Anecdotal and qualitative feedback

EXPLORER
- Amount of time spent engaging with your content

Established your company as a trusted advisor:
- Attendee numbers at your proprietary events

Associated your company with topics buyers care about:
- Number of people in your target audience engaging with content
- Amount of time spent engaging with your content
- Face-to-face engagement metrics e.g. number of touch points with key buyers

Expanded reach:
- New buyer contacts made for nurture campaigns
- Number of follow-up discussions initiated

CLIENT
- Product usage

Discover and drive new revenue streams:
- Number of touch points with named client executives or specific teams that were facilitated by marketing (across all channels)

Increased pipeline growth in targeted accounts

PART TWO

10
Bringing the buyer journey together

In Part One, I covered in detail the parts of the buyer journey and a framework for defining the right content, channels and metrics for each part – but clearly, it's just as important to look at it as a whole. In this section we bring everything together.

- First, I dig deeper into the shifting nature of the audience at each stage. As buyers move through the process, the target addressable audience changes – sometimes quite dramatically – in composition and size. Understanding this is critical to ascertaining whether your marketing is working and helps prevent relying on volume or vanity metrics.
- I then cover how to use the framework to decide how much and where to invest your budgets.
- It is easy to fall into the trap of homogenous, undifferentiated and uncreative messaging and execution in B2B. I talk about how you can prevent or correct this using a buyer framework mindset.
- Getting client insights is critical, but often direct communication with clients is owned by sales or account teams and hard to access. I offer some thoughts about how you can use existing marketing activities to inform and improve your strategy.
- When clients are on the move you need to look for clues so you can better service them as they transition from one phase to another – I give some ideas about what to look for and how to design content to give you the maximum insight you can have.
- Finally, I illustrate the cost of a broken journey and give some ideas about how to fix some common mistakes.

This section features an Insider Insight from Jo Pettifer, Chief Marketing Officer, Manufacturing, Automotive, Energy and Utilities and VP of UK and Ireland marketing at Salesforce, who talks about how to use the buyer journey framework to shift the conversation with sales from transactional to value-driven, and gives advice on how to allocate resourcing across the framework and the changing role of digital.

Defining your target addressable market (TAM) at each phase

Different people come into the buying journey at different points. The seniority of the buyers, the roles they are playing, as well as the number of people involved, changes at each stage. This means you need to flex your content so it is appropriate for that audience. You can't assume it is the same person or people going from one part of the journey to the next. Anyone coming into the process later won't have had the same experience as those that have gone through from Horizon Scanner. You need to cater both for those who are part of the journey from end-to-end, and those that come in and out of it. Not everyone in the buyer process will become a lead. Remember too, some of the people in the journey are influencers and some are direct buyers – both these groups need to be considered too. Typically, senior people – often the Horizon Scanners – delegate buying decisions. The decision makers and those who influence them are in turn influenced by their end users.

When mapping out your target market at each stage, remember that it will likely expand as the company gets closer to buying something. You need to ensure that you have sufficient information to appeal to all buyers within each stage, and not see it as a homogenous group. Someone who has come to your site to look at a piece of thought leadership may not be the same person that is going to go on and look at more technical content.

For outbound marketing tactics like email, ensure you have sufficient data to target different groups. If you are embarking on a campaign and only have the data to engage with the *heads* of functional departments, you may only be communicating with a small proportion of your buying set. Defining your audience groups more precisely means you have enough contact information – and the right buyer insights – to communicate effectively enough to support your buyers and having a market sizing against each phase of the framework will allow you to calculate whether you have enough data, for example contact information. It will also allow you to measure the effectiveness of each part of your campaign because you can look at the percentage of the market that you've engaged rather than volume metrics with no context.

FIGURE 10.1 The internal dynamics of your buyers

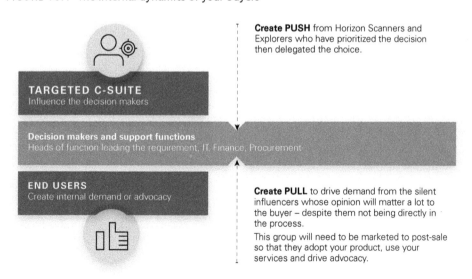

Create **PUSH** from Horizon Scanners and Explorers who have prioritized the decision then delegated the choice.

TARGETED C-SUITE
Influence the decision makers

Decision makers and support functions
Heads of function leading the requirement, IT, Finance, Procurement

END USERS
Create internal demand or advocacy

Create **PULL** to drive demand from the silent influencers whose opinion will matter a lot to the buyer – despite them not being directly in the process.

This group will need to be marketed to post-sale so that they adopt your product, use your services and drive advocacy.

FIGURE 10.2 Fluctuating buyer target addressable markets when purchasing marketing transformation services

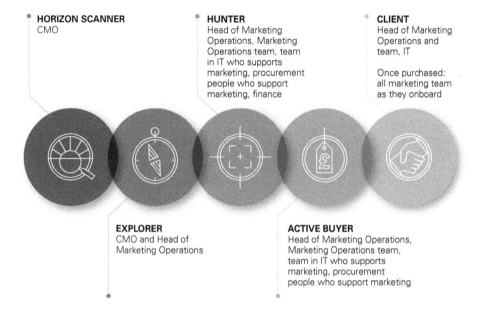

Let's build a scenario to explain. If you want to sell marketing transformation services, you may have the CMO as a Horizon Scanner, the CMO and Head of Marketing Operations as Explorers etc. This is illustrated in Figure 10.2.

Whatever you are selling, define who is in each phase of the journey as illustrated (Figure 10.2). Then against each group, put in a market sizing. If you decide to do a series of outbound communications to the group of Hunters, the number of people you are communicating to is greater than the amount for the Horizon Scanner phase. To assess effectiveness and measure the impact of your marketing efforts, you need to look at the percentage of people within that target group who engaged with your content – not just look at the total volume number which is otherwise misleading. So, if you run a series of outbound communications targeted at people in the Hunter stage and achieved 20,000 people coming to your website and exploring content, that could feel like a strong result, but if you do market research and realize that your potential market could be as big as two million then it shows you still have work to do. Similarly, if you get 70,000 people coming to your Explorer content, but your addressable market is 2,000 senior people, it is not effectively targeted, which means money is being wasted.

Your marketing strategy should define your target market at each phase: what they want, how you can help them and what you know about the type of people in these roles. Just looking at your target market as a single entity will mean that you are not able to be effective and may be missing or mistaking buying signals.

To follow the example above:

TABLE 10.1 Scenario: buying marketing transformation services

Stage	Horizon Scanner	Explorer	Hunter	Active Buyer	Client
Job titles	CMO	CMO and Head of Marketing Operations	Head of Marketing Operations team, team in IT who supports marketing, procurement people who support marketing, finance	Head of Marketing Operations, Marketing Operations team, team in IT who supports marketing, procurement people who support marketing	Head of Marketing Operations and team, IT, all marketing team as they onboard
Typical audience size	Small C-suite audience	Broadening client audience	Broader client audience: functional leads plus support functions e.g. procurement, finance	Specific client audience: functional leads plus support functions e.g. procurement, finance	Precise and typically small very well-known client audience
Types of marketing activity	Articles about the future of marketing, data and insights Position your experts into the market to comment on latest trends, data and changes in the market Advertising promoting your company's brand	Advertising promoting that you have services to support companies Marketing targeted at CMOs like 'How successful companies use marketing data differently' High level benchmarking on how to prioritize outcomes from martech vs. other investments Promote experts at events talking about martech, data and how to effect successful change Joint pieces with alliance or distribution partners Analyst outreach to inform them about your services and get onto rankings	Advertising promoting key benefits of your service Clear articulation of your services and benefits to each buyer type across your marketing literature e.g. • Marketing leads, articles like '10 things to consider when choosing a partner for marketing tech' • Marketing ops: free templates on 'how to benchmark companies' or 'how to work with IT on successful implementations' • Videos targeting IT with technical specifications Videos to upskill finance or procurement on the ROI of marketing tech High-level case studies on clients who have benefitted	Detailed case studies on your process Detailed technical information geared towards the IT team Client reference calls	How to get the best out of your systems – a users' guide The A–Z of marketing tech: what teams need to know User persona documents with benchmarking of skills needed in the new world of automation Training and adoption support

Defining the fluctuations in audience type and volume means more effective resource allocation, better understanding of the buyer's process and more chance of converting interest to consideration and revenue.

Using the buyer journey to decide where to invest

One of my most useful conversations about this was with a private equity firm who told me what they look at as they talk to the CMOs of businesses they invest in. They focused on two metrics: cost of acquisition of the customer and lifetime value. I've subsequently used these as key indicators of performance and a way to communicate with boards about marketing investment to great effect. Look at these two metrics together in the context of your business when determining strategy from both your buyer's and your company's point of view.

If your services are expensive, each deal will yield higher lifetime value, which means you should invest more across the full buying cycle. Given the buyer problem is complex and ambiguous, you will likely need to put more resource into the Horizon Scanner and Explorer stages to support the buyer through a lengthy education and decision process. If you sell a broad range of services and have a well-established brand, you may already work with most of the target companies in your addressable market, in which case spending money unlocking new buyers within your existing clients via ABM might make sense.

While the cost of acquisition when selling higher value transformation solutions, or professional services, is likely to be much higher, so is the lifetime value. Still, high return requires effective targeting. I've seen instances of marketers going after major multi-million-pound deals with a mass market, social heavy campaign, which is unlikely to work as it doesn't cater for the full framework. In these cases, there are only a handful of people who could ever buy your product or service, so devote all your spending to the objective of getting a meeting with them. That's likely to mean engagement with senior buyers at the Horizon Scanner and Explorer stages, when they are open to new thinking, and more engagement from an ABM team in the Active Buyer phase.

If you are selling lower-cost solutions that fulfil a specific buyer problem which is well understood, the overall cost of acquisition needs to be lower; this necessitates a bias towards digital channels and a focus on the Hunter and Active Buyer part of the process.

This may also be true if their problem is well defined or they are looking for a new supplier to replace an incumbent. In this case, the buyer likely knows what they want, so you should be spending more time and money across the Hunter and Active Buyer phases, making sure they get the information they need quickly so you can reduce the length of time it is in the pipeline. You may also want to automate any client engagement post-purchase, triggered by usage, rather than deploying expensive ABM. Similarly, with a lower value proposition, review your marketing plan to make sure the cost of acquisition doesn't outweigh the maximum amount of money a customer could ever spend with you. This can be helpful if your business enjoys large events that don't yield much return. For example, one of my previous teams ran high-end events which were free to participants but cost us around £500 per head. We worked out that the maximum any attendee that converted to a customer was likely to spend over their whole lifecycle was only about three times that. When reviewing the typical conversion rates we had between a 1:3 and 1:4 conversion rate, so at best we were breaking even – mostly we were losing money.

Taking a buyer journey view can help ascertain how much investment to put into any set of activities. Once you have defined your buyer's journey, you can start to plan out your content and channel strategy and consider how much effort and money you need to put behind each part of the journey. Jo gives an example of how she thinks about this at a high level in her Insider Insight interview.

I've mentioned that marketing investments will have a longer return cycle than the fiscal year. When phasing your investments, you may also want to flex when you do a big push into the market according to what you know about the buyer's cycle rather than your internal quarterly sales motion. For example, when I was CMO of a business that sold software products to the education sector, these were primarily bought during just two months of the year and when buyers were ready with budgets, they moved very quickly. Often the sector you are marketing to will have points in the year when budgets need to get set or spent – knowing this will help you balance when you are actively in market because the buyer is ready to spend. Fixing quarterly lead targets without this insight will mean that you could fall behind – and lose internal confidence – early in your own fiscal year.

Using the framework allows you to look at how much money you are spending at each stage, and whether the relative effort seems appropriate given your business strategy. For example:

- If you are trying to move up the strategic curve and upweight your senior relationships with customer groups, you may want to put more effort into the Horizon Scanner and Explorer parts of the journey, particularly if you are already a *go to* supplier for mid-level managers.

- If you are trying to enter a new market which already exists, put money into the Explorer and Hunter phases. You are trying to show the market that your services exist and can answer an already known problem. Being easy to find and top of mind with memorable benefits of working with you will help more than doing macro trend points of view or spending a long time driving loyalty in what is likely a small existing client group.

- If you are an established service provider for parts of your offering, but are trying to get better known for newer, more profitable parts of your portfolio, you could choose to activate your ABM to drive up demand in existing customers as they are more likely to take new services from an existing supplier.

- If your pipeline is sluggish, consider targeted marketing for clients or prospects in the pipeline to try to revive the conversations.

While you need to be marketing across the framework, you can flex your investments into each phase to achieve business outcomes. Whichever way you choose to weight your investments, it is essential that objectives and accountability are shared across marketing and sales functions, which I talk about in the next chapter.

Taking a buyer journey approach to your messaging and creative

Messages accompanying your content at all stages of the buyer journey should give benefits and calls to action relevant to the stage the buyer is in. Your objective is to move them to an associated piece of information, or to nudge them to the next stage of the journey. Ideally offer both to cater for the speed that the buyer wants to go at.

If a cohort of people will carry over across buying stages, review the tone and language carefully across them to ensure it feels like it is an ongoing conversation with similar tone or look and feel – think chapters of a book rather than a series of one-off activities. Make sure that calls to action to nudge people to the next phase are clear. If you suspect that the next phase is likely to be delegated to a buying group with lots of different functional representatives, make sure that you offer different follow-on articles – one for IT, one for procurement, one for the main economic buyer etc. When designing content for the Hunter and Active Buyer stages, remember they may not have seen your earlier phases, so you may need to restate at a high level some of the pertinent findings from the content designed for the Explorer.

I have seen instances of where the next action from provocative thought leadership pieces is to direct readers to go straight to technical sales documents. This is unlikely to work because you've skipped a stage, providing a confusing view of your company. Of course, buyers expect to encounter different levels of technical detail along the journey, but you can't hurry them – a better strategy is to offer similar types of content for the stage they are in, and an option to go to the next stages so they can move at their own pace. Given the TAM may change from stage to stage, you can't rely on those people coming into the process later to have had the Horizon Scanner or Explorer experience with you, and you may need to adapt your materials for these groups accordingly.

The importance of consistency and creativity

Your company's expertise and experience are less likely to stick in their mind if the content's look and feel is variable. Remember that buyers will be dipping in and out of articles, opinion pieces and case studies written by competitors. People need to see information a number of times before they retain it. Your brand logo, look and feel needs to be consistent so that you maintain memorability.

Variance in tone and lack of consistency through the overall buyer journey happens particularly when subject matter experts are writing the thought leadership and more junior marketers are creating sales enablement assets. Read through end-to-end across the buyer journey watching for sharp changes in look, tone or level of expertise. If this happens and is appropriate because your target audience group is different for that particular phase then it is fine; however, if you are nudging people from one piece of content to another and it feels like a dramatic shift, level out your content's tone or put an intervening piece of content in to smooth the flow.

Some buyers may engage with thought leadership months or years before they decide to start buying something, so creativity coupled with consistency is needed to drive salience. Have consistent visual links in the form of your logo and other elements of your brand identity – photography style, colours, tone of voice. This means when they see other things from you, they can connect it with what they remember from the past so any kudos you earned earlier is built upon, not lost. It is important to remember to be creative at all times also. Recent research from the LinkedIn B2B Institute shows 71 per cent of B2B advertisements score 1 on a 1–5 scale of creative effectiveness – not the most reassuring statistic when you consider the amount of money marketers spend on advertising (B2B Institute, 2021b) – and this is the most heavily invested in part of the journey from a creative perspective. Being differentiated at each point is key.

When reviewing look and feel, the good news is that any improvements you make can have an immediate impact. Much B2B marketing is boring and undistinctive, filled with the same stock images of work settings. Where foraying outside the standard business shots, they can stray into trite: silhouettes of climbers scaling mountains in the setting sun to signify overcoming challenges or showing triumph over adversity. Messaging is often just as conventional, as Joanna Brown noted in her interview. Clichés like 'In a fast-changing world, executives need to balance risk and reward' or 'In the war for talent, leaders need to be bold and fearless' abound. Many of us have fallen into the trap at some stage. Avoiding these isn't difficult; it just requires a bit of thought and a commitment to providing clients with genuine insights and a human approach that is rooted in understanding and empathetic to their needs. Choose images that surprise or capture the mood of the market – like the example I shared earlier of the Solvency II project using water images.

Think about how you balance out your tone too. Choose clarity, but don't over-simplify in an effort to be more human. Appropriate industry or functionally specific wording is good: it shows you know what you are talking about and understand the buyer's context. Make sure it makes sense and is easy to understand, but don't fall into the trap of putting technical information into such generic terms that it isn't useful to the buyer any more. This is particularly true in the Hunter and Active Buyer phases – they are looking for expertise, which may necessitate industry jargon.

Of course, if the buying group is very varied or broad, they may need a transla-tor – you can't personalize every piece of content. Sales and account teams play a critical role. They should add context for the clients, help to point out areas that align to their business strategy or create the link between Explorer and Hunter types of content. Making sure that the teams know what content is coming, making it easy for them to navigate it and pull out key messages and creating a central, searchable repository will be fundamental to engaging them.

Getting client insights into your campaigns

At all stages of the journey be ready to adapt your approach. If in doubt, ask your clients. One campaign I was involved with set out to target financial traders about 'the magic of the deal' – but we received strong feedback that dealing implied trick-ery. Even though we loved it, we dropped it.

If you don't feel like you can get direct access to your clients or are loath to test campaign ideas on them (though in my experience they are more up for doing this than you might suppose!) you could use existing marketing channels to get feedback. At the start of a webinar, ask people to do a poll on what images or messages they prefer while they're waiting for it to begin. Or when potential buyers come to an event or visit your stand at an exhibition, ask them to drop their card into a box beside the creative they like best. Try to get feedback internally from your business leaders who know clients well – and find out what the competition is doing. Digital channels make it easy to build in A/B testing from the outset, meaning you don't need to launch a campaign with just one message or image, which might not reso-nate. It is too expensive and important to rely on gut or history. This might be the point where the buyer is actively in market on a ten-year cycle – if you miss your moment, you don't get it back for another decade.

As I've mentioned earlier in the book, buyers want to engage as individuals in their own right as well as being representatives of their function. Try to understand their personality type and content preferences, as this will affect how likely they are to respond to your message. Test whether they prefer headline calls to action, back-ground context, or hard data on features and benefits. You can do this efficiently either by offering options – so buyers can choose whether to view podcasts, video,

FIGURE 10.3 How to refine your messages and position your thought leadership at different stages of the journey

HORIZON SCANNER

C-suite readers will quickly skip to something else if a piece of content starts with too much context and a weak headline. Articles need to deliver a strong point of view. Look at newspapers for inspiration on how to grab attention while at the same time curtain raising what's coming later in the piece. Use a data point high up with a genuinely interesting insight. Keep the first line short – think tweet length. Avoid making it too generic or using marketing speak. A survey targeted at risk managers should say something surprising like '85 per cent of CEOs don't think their risk team are on the case' rather than the more generic and less intriguing 'Risk remains a high priority for the C-suite.'

EXPLORER

Emphasize themes from conversations in the marketplace. Use social listening to gauge sentiment about topics of interest to your target group and use to refine your messaging – or align the tone to feeling. Use data points about what others are doing – or how quickly the market is shifting.

People tend to act when they think that others already are (driven by a fear of missing out), particularly when they don't know what is expected of them in new or ambiguous situations.

HUNTER

Show the product or the solution in action. People want to see what they're going to get and have the opportunity to see inside – whether it is your company's way of working, case study or a product demo. Use videos or interactive diagnostics and monitor how people are navigating to take them deeper into the experience or rethink the journey altogether.

ACTIVE BUYER

Use what you know about them to personalize the message and make it highly relevant to their priorities, strategy or agreed investments. Look at their core values – or annual report – and align tone and style to theirs. Use the way that they talk to or about their customers to inform how you communicate to them.

Would you classify them as formal or informal, authoritative or casual? This insight could inform your messaging. Use images that are pertinent to them. If they are proudly headquartered in a particular city, you could use photographs of it in your literature targeted to them via ABM.

written content or infographic versions of the same content – or split them so half your audience gets one message, the other half another, then optimize for the one that got the best traction.

In one prospecting campaign I worked on, we wanted to get cut through. This group didn't know us well or buy our services and were much targeted by competitors. We wanted to find out what kind of information and tone of voice they preferred. We took 10 per cent of an audience group of several thousand potential clients and ran through a piece of software that used social media posts and publicly available information to categorize them into personality types. This sample group predominantly fell into two: those that liked snappy calls to action for example 'Get this product at this price before it runs out', and those that liked features and benefits. We put two message sets into the market aimed at the group and A/B tested to refine our messaging. The response rate for the campaign was unprecedented – and we were able to dramatically increase the number of leads in the pipeline.

If you have a narrow audience group, look for common interests among its members that you can build into the messaging or images that accompany them. At one company I worked with we wanted to improve our relationship with a very targeted set of senior buyers, all on a one-to-one ABM programme. We did some in-depth research into their interests and found that many of them liked sailing. We started cautiously with A/B tests which showed that the sailing images in our literature had a much higher open rate than more business-style ones. We took sales and client feedback and as a result, entered into a partnership with a sailing team that gave us opportunities to advertise and run events with the crew which improved our attendance rates with this select group of critical senior buyers and influencers.

If you have a broader audience and only know their role or job title, perhaps you can make informed assumptions about their reading habits and what sort of tone and style they prefer. Look at websites or publications targeted at your buyer for insights into how they like to be communicated with, ask people with similar job titles at your company or in your network and engage with sales. Are they likely to enjoy long-form content with plenty of context, or something snappy and creative with a quirky edge? Overall, whatever their preferences are as they get deeper into the buying process, at an early stage when you're trying to attract attention, snackable content helps encourage them into your content ecosystem.

Moving buyers through the framework: looking for clues

After you've worked with internal stakeholders to define the stages of the buyer journey, as well as the objectives of each stage, agree the signals you will look for to indicate that buyers are moving from one phase to the next. For example, if a potential buyer reads a piece of sponsored content on the *Financial Times* website, then clicks to your site for deeper insights on the topic, they could be moving from Horizon Scanner to Explorer. Someone taking part in a proprietary webinar about cloud transformation could be graduating from Explorer to Hunter. If they have started to study highly specific technical implementation information, or are reading a detailed case study, the chances are they're progressing to the Active Buyer phase. If you are capturing information about the job roles of those engaging with your content and notice engagement from a target account – or the seniority level shifting from C-suite to head of department or function – that company may be assembling a buying group or assigning to a more junior person responsibility for researching the competition ahead of a procurement process.

Agreeing these points on the journey will help inform your plan, ensure enough options are given and help sales to know when and how to get involved. Knowing this before starting any conversation will mean your business reps appear better informed. Buyers move at different rates through the journey. Some will need more information than others depending on company size, the scale of the investment, the buyer's familiarity with your business, their risk appetite and their personal standing within their own organization. It's hard to anticipate how quickly they will move and you can only engage sales fully when they are ready. You should obviously try to nudge them towards the next stage, but at the same time there's a danger of making a wrong assumption about the pace they are working at, hence the importance of offering a variety of information options. Buyers can get stuck too as they get slowed by internal process or shifting priorities. You need to be ready for them as they are ready to move to their next phase.

Start by envisaging the full buyer journey from Horizon Scanner to Client. Here are a few golden rules:

- Breaks in the journey, often caused by a lack of content, mean lost leads and wasted money. Typically, companies have Horizon Scanner level articles and strong Active Buyer-oriented sales collateral, but provide little in the way of content for buyers in the Explorer and Hunter phases so it is hard for the buyer to bridge between the two.

- The quality of the subsequent stage of a buyer's journey needs to be as good or better than the one that they are leaving. If you send an email to a delegate at a successful event directing them to a website, that site must be at least as good as the event. Providing a generic email address at the end of a C-suite-targeted piece of thought leadership won't be a satisfying next stage for the buyer.

- If you don't know how a buyer would ultimately be handed off to someone who can make a sale, the journey has no end. There should be line of sight between your Horizon Scanner content and your solution roadmap so you are building future market for something your company can or will offer. Without this, you run the risk of giving the client a problem to deal with, without a way for them to engage with your company to help them solve it. There are many things on a C-suite agenda, so developing points of view on things that aren't in your business strategy to solve means you are helping another company build their revenue at the cost of yours. Refer back to Michael Stewart and Jo Brown's Insider Insights on the importance of being clear about what you will put your brand behind.

Finally, as buyers move through their process, keep an eye out for clues about what and how they are thinking. This will give your sales teams an advantage and help inform your marketing strategy. By designing your content in a way that invites users to provide insights and information about themselves, you'll not only be maximizing

FIGURE 10.4 What buyers want and how marketers can get insights or more value from the content

	WHAT BUYERS **WANT**	HOW MARKETERS CAN GET **INSIGHTS** OR MORE **VALUE** FROM THE CONTENT
HORIZON SCANNER	Inspiring thought leadership that will give them ideas to help shape strategy.	Provide options about where to go next so you can start to narrow down their interests. If they are reading something on the future of work, do they opt next for a technology or people related topic? The answer tells you whether your content appeals more to IT or HR professionals, allowing you to rebalance the mix if necessary.
	Research into issues affecting their market and their competitors.	Conduct a poll to ascertain how far they agree with a bit of content before they move on to the next insight. You can use these stats to re-promote the research e.g. 90 per cent of executives agree with a particular issue being a priority.
EXPLORER	Points of view on what others in their industry are doing.	Where possible direct to the website and create related content to test and learn about what the buyer wants to read next.
	Networking events (with like-minded peers).	Develop anonymized content for prospects summarizing insights from the events, positioning your company as an industry convenor.
	Get information in the way in which they like to consume it.	Provide different variations of the same materials – video, infographic, written or audio – so you can give the buyer choice, and learn which types of format work best.
HUNTER	Case studies.	Ask buyers to outline their problem statement to direct them through to the right case study: this monitoring, regularly looked at, will give insight into common problems.
	Decision-making aids e.g. a diagnostic tool that personalizes insights into how others are dealing with the same issues.	Ask buyers to identify their industry, job role, organization size or country before they access the content. Give sales insights into what their prospects and clients are doing.
	Product or service information and key benefits.	Offer the content in a number of format options to test and learn e.g. whether demo video, talking head or flat content works best. Monitor time on page to see whether you need to rearrange content, give different formats or change your tone to be more direct.

FIGURE 10.4 (Continued)

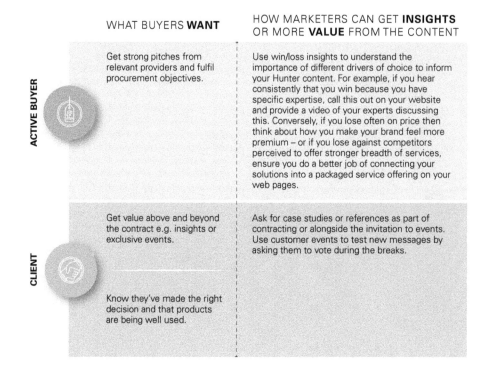

	WHAT BUYERS **WANT**	HOW MARKETERS CAN GET **INSIGHTS** OR MORE **VALUE** FROM THE CONTENT
ACTIVE BUYER	Get strong pitches from relevant providers and fulfil procurement objectives.	Use win/loss insights to understand the importance of different drivers of choice to inform your Hunter content. For example, if you hear consistently that you win because you have specific expertise, call this out on your website and provide a video of your experts discussing this. Conversely, if you lose often on price then think about how you make your brand feel more premium – or if you lose against competitors perceived to offer stronger breadth of services, ensure you do a better job of connecting your solutions into a packaged service offering on your web pages.
CLIENT	Get value above and beyond the contract e.g. insights or exclusive events.	Ask for case studies or references as part of contracting or alongside the invitation to events. Use customer events to test new messages by asking them to vote during the breaks.
	Know they've made the right decision and that products are being well used.	

the efficacy of your content, but you'll also ultimately drive greater value for the buyer by better understanding them. See Figure 10.4 for some examples about how you can do this – and get more from your investment.

INSIDER INSIGHT

Jo Pettifer, Chief Marketing Officer, Manufacturing, Automotive, Energy and Utilities & VP UKI Marketing

Jo Pettifer leads the UK and Ireland marketing organization at Salesforce and is Chief Marketing Officer for manufacturing, automotive, energy and utilities. In this Insider Insight, Jo looks at connecting customers and companies together through marketing strategy, demand generation, brand awareness and product marketing, as well as customer marketing.

STARTING THE BUYER JOURNEY PROCESS

I'm a big fan of a buyer journey approach to B2B marketing. There are lots of different schools of thought about whether there should be a funnel in today's environment, but for me, the act of thinking about what makes buyers engage at the outset then working through where you might take them next is helpful to both the team and the buyer.

First and foremost, before you can even think further downstream about content or channels, ask why on earth would a buyer engage at all? You need to really connect with them at the beginning to spark their interest and even earn the right to begin a conversation. Start with who the audience is – at a persona level – then work through why and how to address them. For example, take the CIO journey. Your first question should be what's top of mind for them? Once you've done this, you can start working through what you have that helps them solve those problems, and what you will do from a marketing perspective once you have them engaged. Think about their influence in the process too – are they the decision makers, or people whose views will affect the decision makers?

We used to segment by company size – enterprise level, mid-market, or small business. But that didn't give our audience enough to connect with. We've really shifted to be buyer-centric, revolving our marketing around their specific challenges. We then layer on how that relates to the industry that they're in because the challenges of a buyer in a retail account will be very different to the challenges to a buyer in utilities, for example. Audience segmentation is key. I'm also a big proponent of telling our story through a customer story. For example, for a CIO in utilities we give insights into how other similar companies have solved the same challenges. This gives you the right to have a deeper, broader, more value-based conversation from both a marketing and a sales perspective.

MOVING FROM TRANSACTIONAL TO VALUE-DRIVEN MARKETING

We have a broad range of existing customers and want to make sure they know how we can add value across the full 360-degree breadth of what we offer – which can be challenging given how fast we're developing new products and services. We have shifted from transactional relationships to value-driven relationships over the last few years. It's not enough to sell something then walk away – or just re-engage when we have something else to sell them.

I always say to my team, 'Put yourself in the shoes of the CIO if you're selling to them.' It isn't good enough to say on one day that you want to talk about cloud, then the next try to push commerce. Instead, think about what the overall story you want to tell is depending on where they are in their journey. That CIO in utilities might be trying to work out how to provide field service excellence or acquire customers from other energy providers that have gone out of business. Starting from how you help them solve that – rather than how you tee up a sales conversation on cloud technology – presents much more value. The product discussion will come further down the line once you've earned the right to have their attention from a more business value-driven approach. I also think it leads to building more loyalty from the outset of the conversation.

ASCERTAINING HOW MUCH RESOURCE TO SPEND AT EACH PART OF THE JOURNEY

Our business strategy means that fundamentally we are measured on pipeline generation. The lifeblood of our growth comes from new business and prospecting. Because of this, brand and the top part of the funnel gets a smaller percentage of our resourcing. Strategically, we think about where we already have good market penetration, and which are emerging. These top line numbers mean brand activity differs depending on market maturity or how well known we are in that industry. For example, we're relatively unknown in that utilities space but in retail we're much better known. This helps us work through what needs to be done at a brand level and allocate investments accordingly.

But we really focus most of our resources on the middle part of the funnel to drive consideration. We work with sales to understand where buyers are coming from, what we know about them and make sure we deeply understand the big bets. We can then focus effort on those priorities in an informed way.

If I had to put numbers against it, I'd say 60 per cent consideration, 20 per cent brand and then 20 per cent supporting sales. The key is to connect them all together so any brand or top of funnel work you do supports consideration – and that your consideration activities are geared towards getting people further down into purchase.

PROVIDING STRATEGIC CHALLENGE TO SALES

Doing this involves a mindset shift for marketing teams. I advise mine to get off the back foot of sales coming to them with a list of tactical asks and orient the conversation instead about what it is that they're trying to achieve. Forget the tactic. Marketing are the experts at pulling together what a tactic is.

Building a new partnership with sales means you can really understand what they need and ask different kinds of questions. If your business is committed to driving a value-based relationship with a buyer, it can lead to interesting conversations with sales: which would they rather have – high value or volume? Having had a sales background, I come to those conversations with that trade-off in mind. The choice is a bigger deal later or a smaller deal now with harder opportunity conversion potential. They can see too that marketing can sometimes get Salesforce into buyers that sales have struggled with.

At an execution level, we agree KPIs for each major marketing investment. For example, with the Salesforce World Tour, every sales leader has a target to deliver. Then they look to marketing to help them drive pipeline. They know that if marketing can deliver 40 per cent of their pipeline number, that means that salespeople are freed up to close or convert deals. It gives them better productivity and they trust us to deliver. In return, we rely on them to make sure that the sales or business development representatives are very well trained for qualified conversations. We give sales constant feedback too – we'll do reviews with sales leaders and give feedback on how their teams are performing against those sales and marketing agreed KPIs. This joint accountability means both teams rarely miss a target.

All of these have really changed the perception of the value of marketing within our business.

THE CHANGING ROLE OF DIGITAL

Web properties are more crucial now than they've ever, ever been. How you respond to the digital engagement a buyer has with your company is a big reflection of your brand. The most frustrating thing is to go onto a company website, see something that piques your interest, fill in the form and then not hear back for three days. If they then call you back your response is probably 'Well, what was I even looking at?' If you offer digital engagement you have to respond rapidly.

It is also important to think about the product offering throughout the journey and customer lifecycle. Most companies have a broad set of solution offerings, but few customers will buy everything from the outset. Marketers need to consider the right sequencing of what they could buy from you according to their needs as a buyer, then lead them on a journey that helps them visualize what the art of the possible could be if they bought both the next thing and the whole thing – with you.

We offer click to buy because some businesses are at a more transactional starting point. We appreciate that for a small business or start-up, our products could be a really big investment, so we want to give opportunities for them to try the product before they decide. This is as much about being empathetic to the customer needs, and realistic about what they can leverage, digest and implement, as it is about keeping the customer lifetime value in mind.

In fact, in a recent survey we conducted called *The State of Marketing* (Salesforce, 2021), I was disappointed to see that Customer Lifetime Value only ranked ninth out of the top 10 metrics/KPIs for marketers. We are clearly thinking too short term about KPIs. While revenue, funnel metrics and web/mobile analytics are important of course, if we are measured on short-term focus, then that's what our teams will focus on. We need to take bolder steps and think much more long term in our relationships and value of the customer.

Once the buying company gets bigger, we think about the whole journey and how we engage across it digitally. The website can help us just better understand what the customer is looking for and learn about where they are in their buying process. We put a lot of effort into understanding what a buyer did on the site, what they engaged with and the number of touchpoints they had with us. We look at how they move through different types of material so we can ascertain when to move them to the next stage. We also analyse what factors might account for journeys differing – is it job role or sector? Lots of time is spent thinking about how long it took them to get from one stage to another – if they moved from industry points of view to technical pages quickly there's definitely a buying signal there.

That means we give sales a buyer that is laden with insight and ready to buy. The first few minutes of their initial touch point with a human being from our company are vitally important to the customer experience. Technology enables us to have a much more educated conversation and buyers expect us to know who they are, what they've looked at, and what they're looking for.

WHAT SKILLS MARKETERS NEED

There isn't a role in marketing these days that doesn't involve data. Going back to the days when I first started, it was probably much more of an art. Now everyone in marketing needs to understand performance, insights and analytics. That can be a scary evolution for marketeers, but it is critical for success. There is a wealth of information and training out there; you need to carve out that path for developing relevant skills. And it is fun too! Taking what you know about the buyer journey and the lifetime value of the customer gives you unprecedented ability to experiment with new things.

It is critical as a leader to evolve the skill set of your team. I make it a priority – in fact it is part of how I measure my leadership team. First and foremost, of course, the pipeline, but second to that, how are they developing their talent?

The cost of a broken journey

B2B marketers usually have much smaller budgets than their B2C counterparts and marketing can be expensive, so making sure you have the right channels and content types mapped to your buyer journey objectives means you will be more certain of getting a good return on the investment. A broken journey means you risk losing leads, insight, credibility with sales and affecting the perception of your brand. Each channel or tactic you use should ultimately lead the buyer to the next step you want them to take. This seems obvious but isn't always the case. A common mistake is to have marketing plans with a lot of brand building such as raising awareness through social posts, search engine optimization (SEO), and paid media, then skipping the Explorer and Hunter phases and pushing the buyer straight to product or services – or passed quickly to sales. This ultimately means sales teams need to work harder, with leads that feel unqualified, which erodes the relationship between marketing and sales. Jo Pettifer talks about how to address this in her Insider Insight when she says '… it can lead to interesting conversations with sales: which would they rather have, high value or volume?... The choice is a bigger deal later or a smaller deal now with harder opportunity conversion potential.' Buyers will perceive you as being very sales-oriented as you are pushing them quickly to detailed product information – and if they don't happen to be in the market for your services at that particular moment, they'll just switch off and you lose the chance to nurture them. Often too, I see dead ends in the journey, for example, teams creating incredible thought leadership for senior buyers with no personalized follow-up. Or there is variable quality across the experience. It is vital that each touch point is as good as the last they had with you.

Critically, by connecting your channels and content across the buying journey, you can learn about what is happening in the buyer's process and how they are making decisions. As digital channels proliferate, you should track how people are engaging with your assets and use this to work out where they are in the cycle based on the information they're looking at. You can offer them choices about which content they go to next, which will indicate whether they are moving on in their decision. Better still, have a set of hypotheses defined at the outset then integrate A/B testing as standard into all of your campaigns so you can continuously learn and adapt as your buyers choose what they want to do next.

How to stop things going wrong

When the buying journey hasn't been sufficiently well thought through, your plan starts to go wrong. Typical reasons why this happens are:

- It is unrealistic. Perhaps you have guaranteed leads with C-suite contacts within a tight time frame, assuming that you will hit 100 per cent of your audience; or your view on conversion rates is too optimistic. Be pragmatic about how much time a buyer will spend in each phase, how much information they will need and what internal constraints they might face that prevent them from moving through the process.

- You've not understood the changing TAM at each phase so don't have the right data to target the right people – or can't understand what the insights into how people are responding to your marketing are telling you.

- You haven't understood the buyer's time frames sufficiently well and may have put your marketing efforts in during a point in the year that you're unlikely to get their attention. Or it could be you are trying to do a major Hunter/Active Buyer push when the buyer's budgets are tight.

- The assumptions you've made about what buyers need aren't right, or you don't know who makes the decision (i.e. you're targeting the wrong people).

- You haven't catered for the buyers' needs across the journey, so you don't have enough assets to fuel the campaign.

- You are only tracking part of the journey rather than looking at all of it and how one phase moves to the other. For instance, you could be just focusing on lead volume rather than quality of leads through to sales and revenue conversion.

- There isn't an agreed definition about what a lead, opportunity or prospect is.
- The hand-offs between marketing and sales are not well structured or communicated.

At the outset, gather your insights on the target market – sector, geography, job function – then make sure you have good quality contact data or a strategy for reaching them. You could have the best solution, the strongest messaging, the best content and an outstanding channel strategy – but if you can't get your messages to the right people then you will not get results. Be specific about who you are targeting as I outlined in the beginning of this section, and as I've incorporated into the marketing strategy template in Appendix Guide 1.

Make sure you are in lockstep with sales and account management teams. I cover this more in the next chapter, but all those across the buying cycle have to share the same objectives as they will rely on each other for insight, will interact with the buyer and will depend on the performance of others to achieve their goals. Sales reps will have great insights into the audience and contacts, will know what messages will resonate at each stage of the buying process, and will verify your objectives and metrics. You need to jointly agree the definition of a lead, who will follow up on each interaction you have with the buyer, KPIs and how to exchange information across the journey. Nurturing leads will likely be a shared endeavour requiring a consistent approach. B2B marketers can provide the insights that come through marketing channels, the background to new leads, and support materials and other responses to any calls to action.

How to fix things when they aren't right

As you look at the whole, here are some common errors I see in B2B marketing campaigns which indicate the full buyer process wasn't considered.

- A piece of thought leadership that is insightful and relevant, hosted on a website and well promoted with advertising and social. Once the reader gets to the end, however, there are no calls to action, so there isn't any way for a buyer to move to the next stage and they are lost. Measuring strong engagement with the thought leadership means it is chalked up as a success; however, it never makes any connection between the thought leadership and what the company sells – so no revenue return and the risk of a deeper disconnect between marketing and sales. *What you should do instead: prompt the reader to go to another, related piece of thought leadership, provide a way to get in touch with the author (not an impersonal form), and put out a poll on some of the issues raised – then promote those findings, for example 35 per cent of people who read this thought leadership agreed – do you? Produce a diagnostic on breaking down some of the issues raised in the piece so that the buyer can start to apply the thoughts to their own business. You are moving people from Horizon Scanners to Explorers.*

- A successful round-table event is held, well attended by senior people who give it positive feedback. An obligatory 'thanks for coming' email is issued, potentially incorporating some of the materials to download... then no further follow-up – there is no data to tell you whether the event was worth replicating apart from a subjective view from sales. *What you should do instead: insist on follow-up from sales or account teams with materials pre-prepared and targets set (this often doesn't happen, usually because roles weren't agreed at the outset), and provide follow-up pieces of relevant content one month, three months and six months later. If you are doing a global series, provide insights from the events done in other countries linked back to what happened in the original geography. You are trying to re-engage Horizon Scanners or Explorers and/or move them to being Hunters.*

- Brand advertising in targeted industry publications, posts and tweets about the company – all showing lots of activities as measured by click-throughs. The spend has been high and the click-through good, but there is no evidence of revenue return so stakeholders are sceptical and funding for advertising is cut. *What you should do instead: think about what your brand advertising is trying to say, then design thought leadership, blogs or even product pages that relate specifically to what is in the ad. Reuse the ad visuals on the pages so that people are reminded where they came from and can see the link between your ads and the services you provide. You are trying to move people from Explorers to Hunters.*

The buying journey also gives you a mechanism to identify when buyers are not behaving in a way that you expect or want them to do, so that you can dig deeper to work out what is going on. This can help you save money or refocus the channel strategy.

For example, in one role I had, we enjoyed strong attendance at webinars targeted at Horizon Scanners and Explorers, designed to share thought leadership and opinion content; however, none of them went on to engage with Hunter-targeted content. After a few of these webinars, we decided to dig in. We realized that the content was so rich that companies were sending their teams as an informal add-on to their own in-house training programmes – some were even giving course credits for it. These attendees would never have bought anything from us, and we would never have achieved return against the objectives we'd set for the channel. At that point we had two choices – either gate the content and only enable certain job titles to attend or offer it as an added-value service for our existing clients through a logged-in area of the website. We did both and were able to maximize the value of the channel because we were able to acquire good data and set those on the journey to becoming customers. We were also able to track attendees from our clients and see whether those that attended more gave us higher satisfaction scores as well as taking the opportunity to cross-promote services and benefits to a defined set of job roles.

IN SUMMARY

- Defining your audience groups more precisely means you will communicate broadly enough to support your buyers – and having a market sizing against each phase of the framework will allow you to calculate whether you have enough data and insights to run a successful campaign.

- At the outset, gather your insights on the target market – sector, geography, job function – then make sure you have good quality contact data or a strategy for reaching them.

- You need to cater both for those who are part of the journey from end-to-end, and those that come in and out of it.

- Cost of acquisition of the customer and lifetime value are key indicators to look at when making a decision on how much to invest. Look at these two metrics together in the context of your business when determining strategy from both your buyer and your company's point of view.

- Marketing investments will have a longer return cycle than the fiscal year. When phasing your investments though, you may want to flex according to what you know about the buyer's cycle rather than your sales motion.

- While you need to be marketing across the framework, you can flex your investments into each phase to achieve business outcomes. Whichever way you choose to weight your investments, it is essential that objectives and accountability are shared across marketing and sales functions.

- Have consistent visual links in the form of your logo and other elements of your brand identity – photography style, colours, tone of voice. This means when the buyer sees other things from you, they can connect it with what they remember from the past and any kudos you earned earlier is built upon and not lost.

- A broken journey means you risk losing leads, insight, credibility with sales and affecting the perception of your brand. Each channel or tactic you use should ultimately lead the buyer to the next step you want them to take. It may be tempting to skip a step in your haste to convert a lead, but it will have the opposite effect.

- Make sure you are in complete alignment with sales and account management teams. All those across the buying cycle have to share the same objectives as they will rely on each other for insight, will interact with the buyer and will depend on the performance of others to achieve their goals.

- This is an iterative process, so at all points seek opportunities to test and learn new approaches and use this insight to refine, course correct or inform your plans – you won't get it perfectly right first time so adopt a test-and-learn mindset and fix things if they're not working.

PART THREE

11
Taking a buyer journey view of brand

Products are made in the factory, but brands are created in the mind
(LANDOR & FITCH)

Brand can be a tricky subject in B2B marketing – it is vitally important and yet less easy to measure compared to other activities. Typically, companies look for trade-offs between brand investment and demand generation – when in fact they are totally intertwined across the buying journey. According to research, B2B audiences exposed to lead generation and creative brand ads are six times more likely to convert (B2B Institute, 2021a). Brand-related investments are doing different things for buyers depending on where they are in their process. In this chapter I will talk about how to use the framework to help you make choices about where to invest in brand and how to talk about the benefits to your business stakeholders.

Promoting your brand

Research shows that companies in B2B that invest in brand outperform their competitors over time. In a study for LinkedIn, the researchers Les Binet and Peter Field analysed decades of effectiveness data for B2B campaigns. They found that campaigns which deliver on brand metrics have four times the impact on the business bottom line than those that don't. They are also more than 50 per cent more likely to move the needle on shorter-term activation metrics like marketing qualified leads. But investment in brand is easily challenged – easy to cut if companies need to release funds and if it's poorly defended by marketers held to yearly lead generation targets (B2B Institute, LinkedIn, 2021b).

Buyers for your services will not be in market all the time – so your brand needs to be *always on* to build low-level salience for when they are ready to buy. Another set of insights from the LinkedIn B2B Institute show that the number of the people who may buy your services actually being in the Hunter and Active Buyer phases at any one time is low. They use the example of buying payroll software or IT services, but this would also be true of any professional services offerings, and encourage marketers to think about how often buyers would want to buy the services you offer.

They may already be buying something you have from another provider, which means they will switch only when their contract comes to an end, or if their incumbent supplier is failing to deliver.

'It might surprise you to learn that up to 95% of business clients are not in the market for many goods and services at any one time. This is a deceptively simple fact, but it has a profound implication for advertising. It means that advertising mostly hits B2B buyers who aren't going to buy anytime soon. And in turn, that tells us about how advertising works: mainly, by building and refreshing memory links to the brand. These memory links activate when buyers do come into the market. So, if your advertising is better at building brand-relevant memories, your brand becomes more competitive.' (B2B Institute, 2021b)

Brand advertising in B2B marketing should focus on building a memory in the buyer's minds, as there may well be months or even years between them seeing an ad and buying something. And because many purchases take years to incubate, the return is seen well after the investment is made.

When thinking about brand architecture and naming strategy, ultimately brand should make you easy to buy from. Clarity over your customer promise, how you use naming to navigate your portfolio of offerings and consistent repetition of key brand assets like your logo help you improve the chances of being thought about once someone is ready to buy. Brand adds value in different ways according to where the buyer is in their journey, so being clear about the objective of each stage helps you to define where to put your energy and investment.

But the value of having a strong brand isn't restricted to buyers at the early part of their process: I detailed in Chapter 4 how important a company's reputation is to Active Buyers. It is the number one reason why buyers chose one company over another: brand drives decision-making as well as attracting new prospects. Similarly, there is evidence that shows strong brands can command premium pricing – and are better able to protect prices in economic downturns.

The benefits of investing in brand go beyond the customer group too. I think of brand as the sum of the perceptions of the market, clients and employees – and if you can shift perception, you can change behaviours. These behaviours will include whether buyers consider your company's services where previously they might not, or to engage with you in more strategic conversations. Raising the reputation or profile of your brand with influencers outside the buying process will help you as buyers seek opinions from their ecosystems, as Michael Stewart illustrated in his Insider Insight.

More broadly, brand investment can support internal transformation efforts or improve employee attraction and retention. It can help you show confidence in a new strategy. Planning your advertising spend around your annual results shows you are putting your money where your mouth is and gives the appearance of boldness. It can help internally to invest during times of transformation, building confidence in your internal strategy. Finally, articulating what the brand stands for, and why employees should want to work there, helps people feel inspired to be part of the journey which supports recruitment and retention.

Being clear with stakeholders how you ascertain the value of investment in brand activities against the buyer journey will help you show how it supports revenue growth and will enable you to better defend why you would fund brand-related marketing.

The difference between purpose and propositions

To present your brand to the market, you need to have a brand idea and messaging which will be informed by your company's purpose. Typically, companies that stand for something bigger than what they sell have more commercial success because they mean more to customers and build inspirational alignment with the buyers who are acting as company representatives and individuals, as well as merely looking for something that fulfils functional needs. Your purpose is your North Star – it doesn't change over time, in fact it is a lens by which you can look at all your actions, messages and how you show up so that you create a consistent organizational message to the market. Proposition messages are linked to external opportunity and buyer insight. These do shift over time – because what you offer to the market will change, taking advantage of market shifts or showcasing new innovation. Mixing the two leads to a decrease in your company's reputation – greenwashing being one example of where companies have got this wrong.

Promoting broad messages aligned to your purpose helps establish or build your reputation as it gives market observers, buyers, employees or potential recruits a *promise* about what you will be like and what they can expect as they engage with your content and services. For your buyers, building inspirational value – the knowledge that your company has an aligned set of values to theirs – is important as they are representing their company when making decisions. Your purpose will build inspirational and emotional value with your buyers across the whole cycle – what you deliver and how you deliver it will provide functional value that is important as they are in the Hunter and Buyer phases. At the highest level, being clear about what you stand for as a business, the values that drive your decision-making and the attributes that underpin the value you add to clients will help you build awareness.

Your company's purpose will also inform your brand strategy – and any ideas, messages and positioning that stem from it. When developing your brand idea think about how it is differentiated from the competition and relevant to your target audience. This gives the target audience not just a reason to choose your brand over the others – but also allows you to build mindshare. In a content-rich world, if you don't stand out or help buyers see why what you have to say will be additive to them, your messaging simply won't get read. In other words, if your differentiation and relevance isn't clear, there is little chance your buyers will engage with you and any investment in brand will not affect the business' bottom line.

Overcoming legacy brand perception

I've often found that in larger organizations, buyers have built a view over time that they know you well, but this can pigeonhole you and make it harder for you to engage them in a broader conversation about what you have to offer. They wouldn't even consider your services – or think to come to you for thought leadership – not because they wouldn't trust you to do it, but because they simply aren't aware of your wider offer. There are several reasons why this might happen. You might have a strong track record and excellent reputation for some things, so it is harder for you to explain that you have a broader skill set. It could be because you have changed business strategy and chosen new areas to grow into – or have found an opportunity to grow into an area that your competitors are slow to respond to. Some companies find that as they grow inorganically through acquisition without taking care to drive new market positioning, they struggle to get the level of cross-sell from their core to the newly acquired services at the rate they'd hoped. Many B2B companies I've worked with suffer from this challenge, which is frustrating as you could be adding more value to clients if only they knew you had what they need. You will be able to get a good sense of whether this is a problem for your company by reviewing financial data to understand what percentage of clients buy more than one service from you. You can also research to understand levels of market awareness for the full breadth of what you do. Lastly, talk to sales about how easy or hard it is for them to have a broader conversation with clients. I come on to talk about how a leading indicator of the success of investing in brand is the quality of sales discussions in Chapter 13.

It can be interesting to observe what others have done to overcome this challenge. Capgemini used brand architecture to shine a spotlight on a specific new thing. When they made the acquisition of Altran, they merged it into their business and launched a new service branded Capgemini Engineering. Clearly you can't do this for every product or service, you need to choose your one, major, strategic investment and really understand whether creating a new brand within your portfolio will help you make the splash you need. IBM's sponsorship of Wimbledon gives them an opportunity to align themselves with another organization known for its pursuit of excellence. But importantly, it also allowed them to make their brand synonymous with innovation and data-led decision-making, which helped shift brand perception of them at a time when they were better known as a hardware business. As the company itself says,

> Since 1990, IBM has been supporting the All England Lawn Tennis Club and The Championships in its mission to be the premier tennis tournament in the world. We do that by continuously innovating, by not being afraid to demonstrate how technology can add to the fan experience while never detracting from it. Speed of serve, real time match statistics provided to commentators and mobile and digital solutions; IBM helps bring The Championships to the world. (Wimbledon, 2022)

Clearly these are very well invested companies with a long-term commitment to building brand awareness and equity. Look at what sponsorships or partnerships might enable your brand to reach new target prospects: they may be smaller or more local, but should genuinely help you get in front of people you can't today.

Specific ways brand helps you at each stage of the buyer journey

Horizon Scanners and Explorers

Horizon Scanners might be in market for a very long time before they decide to prioritize their response to an issue. This means you need to build recall that lasts months, maybe even years. This is important for two reasons. Firstly, advertising your brand works most effectively if it is consistent and *always on* so it builds those memories. Coming in and out of market with brand advertising is forgettable unless your adverts are remarkable – rare in cash-strapped B2B. You are better off having more precisely targeted advertising constantly in market than large splashes in the market that are broadly targeted but over a shorter period. Secondly, for this type of investment to work hard, even if you have high frequency over a long period, it needs to stand out and be memorable, so it must be distinctive. You should do this by having highly differentiated messages, so look to your competitors and make sure you stand out. Understanding precisely what the factors are that will appeal to your buyers and having great advertising that surprises, challenges or reinforces expectations will help you be more salient.

In these phases, you are positioning yourself as experts to create or address unstated buyer needs. As remarked on by the *Cashing in on Creativity* study from the LinkedIn B2B Institute: 'Don't ask customers who don't need your product to "buy now". Instead, you'd be better off targeting future customers with an entertaining ad to get your brand noticed, so it readily comes to mind when those customers buy in the future' (B2B Institute, 2021a).

To grow a brand, you need to advertise to people who aren't in the market now, so when they do enter the market your brand is familiar. This means they are more likely to search for you when starting to move to the Hunter phase.

BRAND AND THOUGHT LEADERSHIP
There are three ways to think about how to use brand in this part of the buying framework:

1 If you are in a newer market, your brand is less well known, or you are trying to establish something entirely new, you will need to use thought leadership to establish your brand. People won't respond to your advertising because they don't know you.

You need to use your ads, media coverage or third-party relationships to promote thought leadership, which in turn needs to cut through the noise so that as buyers read it, they will notice that your company produced it. A steady stream of this type of content will help you build memorability over time and raise your brand awareness in the mind of the buyer. When you are trying to attract the attention of a Horizon Scanner or Explorer, it is likely to be the interesting data, point of view or new insight into a problem that will draw them into your content. This is an ideal opportunity to position your brand as they will be coming for the content but it gives you an opportunity to lodge your company into their mind and start to build memorability. If your thought leadership is very effective, they may start to respond to the advertising that draws them to your content as they have an expectation that you'll have something to say that will inform or change their opinion.

2   If your brand has good standing and is known for expertise in a certain area, then advertising or promotional activity with your brand on it will pull people in to read your thought leadership. For example, when PwC issues new thought leadership such as the annual CEO survey, they get a huge amount of people engaging with it as the brand has market credibility, an engaged employee base who promote it and credibility among senior executives who trust and appreciate PwC's convening power and its ability to help them think about priorities or problems. This can also work if you have a strong partnership with a brand that is well established with buyers, and you have jointly produced and promoted thought leadership.

3   Alternatively, if a brand is well known in one area but is trying to enter a new market or attract a different type of buyer, they can partner with companies better known with that set of buyers to create thought leadership in that new market. At previous companies, we would regularly work with publications such as *Critical Eye* and *Management Today* to write editorial pieces and host events such as CEO roundtables. Deloitte partnered with online news and analysis platform Quartz – a company that appeals to the next generation of business leaders – to start to build their brand profile with younger senior executives. Their thought leadership report is designed to appeal to millennials and Gen Z and uses Quartz's brand with its younger audience and fresh look and feel to reach this target group (Quartz, 2022).

In this part of the journey your thought leadership and brand promotion are synonymous and mutually reinforcing. It is critical that your brand and content teams are working together seamlessly to create a joint plan and that their incentives are aligned.

Brand and the Hunter

Once buyers are specifically hunting for a group of suppliers, they need to know what you do. Your messaging will shift to promoting your services and differentiating you from competitors to help you build pipeline. A clear brand architecture will make you easier to buy from – this can be a challenge for many B2B companies for reasons I come onto later.

DIFFERENTIATION

For the Hunter, you need to be differentiated. When doing work with a leading branding agency, their view was that differentiation and investing marketing effort into standing out versus your competitors was the most effective way of using your brand to generate demand and drive pipeline. This is because the point at which buyers are looking at you and your competitors against each other is when they're getting serious about buying. To check that you are differentiated, take time to look at your competitor's brand. Is what you say about your value propositions sufficiently distinct and relevant to what the buyer is interested in? Certain tropes or ways of referring to things become industry standard, and while it is fine to accept a certain degree of convention if it is what your clients expect, there is a big difference between this and *Velcro-logo*, where companies are all effectively saying the same thing in slightly different language.

Getting insights will help you avoid this. Talk to existing customers about why they chose you as opposed to someone else. Look at your competitor's marketing materials. Print them out and stick them all over a room, together with yours. As you look at them next to each other, does yours stand out or are you in a sea of sameness? Speak to people in your business that have come from a competitor (they will have had compelling reasons for joining you) and will have good insight into how buyers compare you to each other. When in a commoditized market, or one where you have one or two competitors with extremely similar services or products, you must still challenge yourself to do this but may need to get more creative. Look for white space in terms of how you work with clients – are you more collaborative, do you have a longer track record of delivery, do you work with complex sectors? Or think about your people – are they diverse? Interesting? Market leaders?

Brand perception can either help or hinder you across any phase but perhaps most particularly in the Hunter phase. If your services are well known and your company is held in high regard – thanks to advertising that has built memorability or senior influencers you targeted in the Horizon Scanner and Explorer phases enjoying an enriching experience – you will be endorsed and your company shortlisted. Where brand perception hinders you is less about your company being rejected – recent research found that brand rejection in B2B was rare – and more about low brand awareness hampering growth (B2B Institute, 2021a).

BRAND STRUCTURE AND ARCHITECTURE

For the Hunter, brand structure and product or solution naming helps them navigate services in a way that is intuitive and easy for them to understand. B2B brands haven't always been as good at having a clear strategy around brand structure as B2C brands. You need to be easy to buy from, which should inform your brand architecture and product naming. Strong internal voices, choosing the wrong structure to begin with, inorganic growth and poor governance all contribute to a confusing brand landscape and cost your business more money to maintain. This is expensive because you need to maintain them as well as educate the market on their meaning.

Typically there are five ways that companies choose to structure their brand strategy:

1 House of brands: a portfolio of unique, unrelated brands that each have their own distinct offer to a different segment in the market. An example would be Alphabet, which has independent brands like Google and intelligence hardware company Nest because they offer very distinct services to different industries.

2 Endorsement: a portfolio of unique brands that are endorsed by a parent brand. An example would be American multinational conglomerate 3M, who endorse brands like Scotch and Post-it.

3 Sub brand: a portfolio of closely related brands with identities that are visually highly linked to the parent brand. An example is Apple, where iTunes, MacBook, iPhone and iPad have their own names, but are tightly connected to the parent brand by use of colour or logo. Another example is Amazon, where each brand has distinguishing characteristics but they draw on the parent brand's identity through the font or the smile.

4 Masterbrand: a portfolio of products and services offered by a single brand. Examples of this include General Electric, where they support a wide variety of audiences but use the parent brand's gravitas to sell all of them, or FedEx, which uses descriptive terminology to identify functional offerings.

5 Deliberate hybrid: examples include Microsoft, which uses its parent brand when useful in B2B and productivity related offerings like Dynamics, but allows brands like Skype or XBOX to build their own brand equity for consumers.

The reality is that many B2B companies have a non-strategic hybrid. This is based on inorganic growth where acquisitions haven't been thoughtfully integrated into a brand strategy, or it can be because strong product teams push forward with names that might make sense for their specific market but don't look at how naming can enhance the client experience of the whole brand.

Once you have decided your brand structure, you may need to think through how you will navigate some of the challenges or opportunities that your business will face. M&A is a typical one as B2B companies often choose to grow inorganically. If you are acquiring another business and using a Masterbrand strategy, how fast do you want to move to rename it? What are the implications on clients or employee retention? How do you get an unbiased view? If inorganic growth has led to a number of legacy brands, it might help your business to have a cleaner, simpler portfolio which is easier for Hunters to navigate.

In one company I worked at we had 187 brands. This was due to a lack of central control or rigour over naming as well as a period of inorganic growth where the value of the acquired brand names was part of the business case for making the purchase. What this had led to over time was a dramatic reduction of investment in the main brand, so it had fallen into being a house of brands when we didn't have the money to support maintaining these brands in the market. Over 12 months, I led a radical brand strategy refresh, using client insights as well as employee opinion to shape our approach. We decided we'd actively employ a Masterbrand strategy – as it was more affordable, and we were only cross- or up-selling to a very small percentage of our client base, who were buying services we offered from competitors, despite being major customers of ours and our offerings being solid. To do this, we refreshed the look and feel of the overall brand and launched it in conjunction with an interesting partnership at a marquee event with clients, prospects and analysts. We then used a decision tree to help the businesses ascertain whether they should move into the Masterbrand or not – and how. This enabled us to move from 187 brands to 20 in under 24 months.

THE IMPORTANCE OF GOOD GOVERNANCE

Your brand structure decided, you need to keep control. Clear guidelines which flex only if there is a major business strategy change are instrumental to this. They provide brand guardianship as internal teams start to get creative outside the guidelines and stamp out anything that doesn't adhere to the guidelines. Investments into brand will depreciate if you lose control, and precedents are set that are almost impossible to get back into alignment. There can be a high level of creativity that comes out of non-marketing employees when it comes to creating logos, names or identities. The downside to not managing this is that your clients get confused, and your costs will go up. Internally generated brand or logos inevitably end up on external facing presentations and bid documents, or even have their own websites or merchandise created. As well as causing new costs for your business, it dilutes the investment you are making into the core. There is a reason that brands have a financial value and you need to make sure you keep control of yours. If you are challenged by a vociferous organization that has historically made a lot of the decisions, you might want to consider creating a brand council with business, product and sales leaders on it to help you guide or stop things that will erode the value of your brand.

Make sure too that you have clear brand guidelines for your internal teams – marketing and sales – as well as the agencies that you onboard to support you. Offer regular brand training workshops and drop-in sessions for people with questions. Having a network of brand ambassadors can help you institutionalize best practice.

Brand and Active Buyers

Buyers need to have confidence in your brand and will need your brand to instil confidence in others. The slogan 'No one got fired for hiring IBM' endured for a reason – brand reputation can be highly influential as a mitigation for the high degree of risk the buyer feels they are taking. Remember too the Source Global Research data (2021) that showed how brand reputation was the most important thing for Active Buyers. In part, this is because a strong brand reassures the groups they need to influence internally.

One way to achieve this level of trust is to be perceived as a dominant leader in your area. This is where thought leadership, deployed at the early stages of the buyer journey, can shore up positive intent for when the buyer is in this phase of their decision-making. The strength of your brand gives companies the confidence to put you on their shortlist or issue an RFP. The fact that B2B buyers have emotions means that no matter how disciplined a buying process is, they will still use past experience to simplify their decision-making. This may be conscious since the buyer knows they can't learn everything about every potential vendor, or it may be subconscious. In fact, whether or not the buyer realizes it, the decision is often made long before the buying process is completed. As mentioned in the Active Buyer chapter, when this happens – even subconsciously – much of the buying process ends up being an effort to justify the initial emotional decision. Strong brands can lead a buyer to be more willing to try a product or services, take less time to make a decision, be more willing to pay a price premium (or be less sensitive to price increases), and be less inclined to buy from a competitor. Once you have identified that someone is actively buying, think about how you can dial up your brand messaging to them through targeted geographic or programmatic marketing, so that you subliminally surround your customer with your brand.

I've mentioned that B2B buyers are using digital channels to self-inform, rather than engaging early with sales. In tandem, buyers are becoming increasingly sceptical about overtly sales-led messages. Having your sales teams engaged in the earlier parts of the journey means that they are deeply associated with your brand and helps them become guides through the process rather than sweeping in at the end for a sales conversation.

The way in which you *show up* across your marketing, sales, account teams, technical teams and customer services all needs to be consistent with the overall brand promise. You will be looking to build inspirational, functional and emotional value in every interaction that you have. Your brand is the label for how you do things; your unique approaches, expertise and intellectual property. Your people are your brand ambassadors, so how they show up needs to be aligned to your brand promise. Look at your values and what you say about your culture and encourage sales teams to use this as a lens by which they *show up* in the room. Even at a very tactical level, make sure that your brand matches buying drivers – so if consistency is important then make sure all your materials carry your brand in a repeated way. Or if you have bold net zero targets, could you do virtual pitches rather than flying people in?

Brand and Clients (ABM)

For those clients that you are building loyalty with, creating brand affinity between yours and theirs helps build advocacy. While they are buying from you and once they have become a client, your brand will set the expectation whether you will deliver the service they need and whether they can be confident that you will do what you say or deliver the outcomes you committed to. This reputation will help them justify the decision or drive-up adoption of the product or service. Make sure that every interaction you have with them is in line with the promise of the brand they bought from. Creating brand alignment – for example around shared values or CSR – helps create emotional value. Case studies, awards and joint marketing activities (e.g. speaking platforms or analyst briefings) help both of you build brand awareness, which can be helpful both for the company at an overall level and your individual buyer at a personal level as they are building their personal brand internally or more broadly in the buying community. Investing in brand should also help you change the conversations you can have with clients, helping move you up the strategic curve as well as build loyalty.

Creating brand consistency across the buyer journey

When making investments in brand-related activity, consider which area you are looking to affect and what you need your brand to help you do against the objectives you have in your buyer journey. Keeping your messaging, logo and brand names consistent helps you be more memorable, which is key as the length of buying cycles and number of people involved (often in highly competitive environments) means recall is paramount in B2B marketing. Use design to create a holistic brand experience, where every touchpoint is viewed as an opportunity to engage more deeply with the buyer in a way that is consistent with what the brand wants to be famous for. If you change your logo placement, core colours or tone of voice through your journey, you run the risk of undoing the hard work to date as the buyer will have to work hard to connect the new messaging to the previous, and it's most likely that they won't. As they see more if it and look at it every day, internal creative teams will often want to move on more frequently than the buyer can tolerate. Current thinking says that a buyer must see the same message at least seven times (B2B Marketing, 2019) for it to resonate – which is unlikely to be within a short time frame unless you have enormous advertising budgets and a very precise distribution mechanism; or your buyers are in the market repeatedly over short periods of time.

Metrics

Usually when measuring brand effectiveness, companies rank awareness, familiarity, consideration and first choice against competitors, looking at how they perform within each category and the conversion rate between each to understand where marketing and sales need to prioritize resource. The strength of each of these will give an indication of your brand health and help you work out where you need to dial up your brand investment and other marketing efforts.

You can also measure the importance of certain attributes to buying groups and how you perform against them. So if, for example, you research your buyers and decide that being known to deliver superior results, as well as having global expertise and innovative approach, are important you can do a survey to rank both how important these are relative to each other and how your company performs against these attributes compared to your competitors. Knowing this can help you decide what is relevant and differentiating for buyers, which can help you drive up consideration and loyalty.

Many companies do brand equity studies with clients and prospects to measure these. It is certainly worth doing this regularly and over extended periods of time so that you can monitor shifts in sentiment that might affect your commercial aims. It will also give insight into which area of the buyer journey you need to direct investment into. If your awareness is low, then you will not be able to drive sales; people can't buy what they don't know you have. However, if awareness of your company is high but conversion to consideration is low, then you may find that your Explorer and Hunter content isn't strong enough, so you are losing people through their journey. If your loyalty levels are low, then you may want to consider diverting resource into ABM.

In B2B, much of the brand experience buyers get is through your employees. They are ambassadors of your brand. It is sensible to have some questions in any HR-led employee engagement surveys that cover what they think of your brand, what they think clients think of it and how far they believe in some of the core attributes that underpin your positioning. If you see large gaps in how they perceive your company

FIGURE 11.1 How to assess brand health

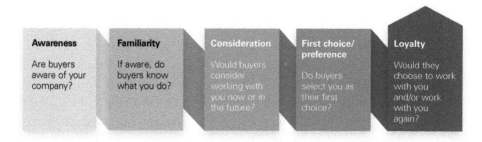

and how you want clients to perceive it, you may need to work with leadership to drive a new employee value proposition. Or if the strategy of the company is poorly understood, you may need to embark on an employee engagement programme. For many customers, your people may be the real embodiment of your brand, so ignoring these signals will jeopardize your brand's reputation in the longer term.

IN SUMMARY

- Your brand positioning is your *promise* to the market and affects your reputation – and therefore your trustworthiness as well as likelihood to win work.

- Your brand should be derived from your purpose, which remains constant as you bring more proposition-led messaging into the market.

- There will always be Horizon Scanners and Explorers in the market so getting your brand in front of them via advertising or thought leadership – or a combination – should be an *always on* endeavour to build memorability over time.

- Once you have developed a brand platform and messaging, you need to promote your brand all the time in the market as people reach the Hunter and Active Buyer phases infrequently.

- Brand is important to Hunters and Active Buyers too: reputation ranked number one of the most important things to buyers in this stage.

- In the client phase, you want to build brand alignment and make your brand highly relevant to their specific paradigm, as this helps your account teams build strong relationships and increases the emotional value that you offer your customer. For those new buyers within existing client accounts, you should be able to more precisely target messages that align your brand proposition to their priorities or strategy.

- Across all of this, your brand needs to stand out. Differentiation makes your brand memorable, which is essential in a crowded market. Draw out what makes you unique and special, and make sure you put it front and centre of your communications.

- Across all your marketing, make sure you are consistent in your brand look and feel, visual/verbal identity and logo placement so that you help build recall to support your brand strategy.

- Flex your brand resourcing to align with your business strategy: be clear about what problem you are investing in brand to solve.

12
Using technology and data to drive results across the journey

There isn't any aspect of marketing that hasn't been enhanced or infused by technology. Understanding how to derive insights, looking at what the signals are telling you and course correcting your plans are fundamental to driving success. As Jo Pettifer said in her Insider Insight, all marketing roles these days rely on being skilled in data and analysis. In this chapter I look at how to use technology across parts of the buyer journey framework to support your objectives, and how to use the framework to make decisions about what technology to buy.

As you start to design your campaigns with the end-to-end buyer journey in mind, technology not only helps you be more efficient and precise when you execute, saving money in the process, it is also an invaluable source of information, which you can be evaluating frequently to enrich, or adapt your plans. This chapter includes an Insider Insight from Kirsten Allegri Williams who was the CMO of Optimizely, that offers digital experience platform software as a service. She talks about the importance of using digital channels to support *micro-moments* the critical but hard-to-detect points in the buyer's internal process where they make major go/no go decisions.

At each phase of the buyer journey, think about how you can use technology to find, target and get insight into your buyers. Your aims should be to:

- Improve your data – better targeting is better-invested marketing.
- Solicit information about your buyers, their wants, needs and style – or gain insight into where they are in their process.
- Provide an at scale personalized experience – technology makes it easy to customize your broader content making it more likely you will get noticed and make you appear more relevant.

While the benefits are clear, many B2B organizations have invested a lot, but seen little return. In a 2020 report, only 13 per cent of marketers thought their stack was good enough (B2B Marketing, 2020). As I come on to talk about in the chapter, this happens for three reasons. The way in which it was bought, solving one problem at a time rather than looking at the whole journey; the fact that so much martech is designed for B2C rather than B2B; and that insufficient investment was put to adoption – specifically making changes to process and updating skills across the whole marketing function – not just marketing operations.

Data across the buying journey

Good data is a critical first step in any campaign. Use your TAM sizing to work out how much data you need and assess how much you have as well as its quality. Acquiring data is a cost that is hard to show ROI on directly, but needs to be done, otherwise you will lose money through poorly distributed content. Marketing that is well targeted is, by definition, more efficient as it helps get better return on investment. Work with your sales teams to do regular hygiene on the data in your CRM system. At one company we gave spot bonuses for every 1000th updated record to keep the data clean. Other companies manage this as part of their sales' operational rhythm. Of course you can buy it too, and use your marketing to prompt buyers to give you richer data, as I have outlined through this book.

At each stage of the buyer journey, score the quantity and quality of your data against the market size. Without regular review and analysis this precious commodity will render your marketing expensive and irrelevant. As you're designing your data strategy, don't forget to consult with your legal or compliance department to help you navigate the complex regulatory landscape around data. Get their input early, ask them to help you put a robust framework in place and scenario test it against the things you want to do so that you maintain your company's reputation. Work through who is responsible for owning and maintaining data – particularly prospect data, as typically once something is in the pipeline it is in the preserve of sales or account management, whereas pre-pipeline can be less clearly defined.

Horizon Scanner

Horizon Scanners are elusive and won't be coming directly to you for information. You will be targeting them via third parties. Ask for subscriber lists from a partner organization, for example when negotiating a third-party event sponsorship, and try to get access to the invitees directly or indirectly through pre- and post-event communications. As mentioned in the brand chapter, you will likely be advertising your thought leadership to this group, rather than your services, so make advertising highly targeted by positioning it in third-party publications that you know your buyer relies on. If you are doing this, think about what they get when they land on your site and make sure you are positioning other thought leadership topics, and promoting your subject matter experts. Remember you're trying to build kudos for your expertise in this phase.

Social listening can be a useful tool for better understanding what your Horizon Scanners (and Explorers) think about particular topics. Use research tools to get information about them at a sector, account, or individual level and use this to inform the content that you want to target them with. Track sentiment about the issues you want to talk about and use this to inform language, visuals and messaging – I gave an example of how to do this in Chapter 6.

Explorer

Start personalizing at this stage. If they have engaged with a third party and come onto your site, refer to the directing source. If they came from an article hosted by a third party, you might want to give a different experience than if they came through a search engine. Make sure that the journey from that third party to your site is seamless and well thought through. In one campaign at a previous company, we A/B tested a page that made explicit reference to the referring source versus one that didn't – the first significantly outperformed the second on time spent on page.

Make sure that as you deploy new adverts to the same group of buyers you change the receiving pages that they go to. Look at bounce rates to ensure that what they got when they landed on your site was what was promised in your ad message. Better use of technology will help you be more efficient in your spending, although it is important to be aware that it is more costly and there is no point deploying your messages to a broad audience group if your target market is a small group of senior buyers.

If you don't have it, you may need to work with third parties to get contact details so you can market to them more effectively. Your aim should be to nudge them from third-party sources to your owned channels, particularly your website, so you can start to capture data and insight into what they are doing. Drive traffic too by optimizing search against terms that relate to campaigns. If you are doing a sponsorship with a media channel, direct to deeper content which is hosted on your site. If co-sponsoring webinars with a third party, try to entice buyers towards your pages in any follow-up messages.

Once you've generated traffic, direct the buyers to the most relevant online touch point to deliver targeted content, capture data and start to build a profile of buyers. You can use your website to enable the buyer to create their own experience through easily navigable content as well as serving them insights that show you recognize their needs and motivation.

Getting them to your digital environment means you can offer helpful additional information as they evolve their thinking, and you can learn more about what Explorers need to move their decision-making on. Your objective is to engage with them through digital brand or campaign experiences, constantly looking for opportunities to get insights or contact data. As mentioned in the buyer journey chapters, design your tactics with data capture in mind. Designing webinars into your journey so that people have to register, gating content, creating diagnostics that require company information, and preference centres can all help.

You will want to have three web strategies which are integrated from a buyer journey perspective:

1 *Your home page.* This is the shop window for your brand, where people will land if they've looked for your company name specifically. They may not know your

full offer as they land there, so think about how you can promote a broad message to them that gives them pause for thought on what your company does. Make it easy for Explorers to navigate to something that might help them – you are trying to engage them in a conversation and keep them with you. Typically, navigation across sites includes issues and capabilities or services offered, but navigation that targets job functions can be very effective in drawing people deeper into a site and keeping them there as it helps them see how your company's offer directly helps them in their role.

2 *Campaign experiences.* These are dedicated areas that can be used to support targeted Explorer, Hunter and Active Buyer activations. These should be designed to deliver experiences that give options to the buyer to move around within the phase they are in, or move them on to the next phase. Catering for both means you may be able to keep them on site for longer and you will be able to learn more about their buying process and format preferences. If you have marketing automation integrated, you can start to personalize content based on where the buyer is in their journey. If you're able to extract their email as they register for an event or download a report, you can use it to give better associated content.

3 *Always on landing pages.* These are most often used to receive users from search as Explorers move to Hunters. The buyer journey objective should drive what you do as they come through using various terms. For example, if they search for something generic like *transformation* and come to your site rather than a third-party one, they are likely to be in the Explorer stage, so offer your best thought leadership. If they search your company name and *transformation*, they may be in Hunter stage as they are looking at the services you specifically have, so offer them a strong proposition and feature content. If they search for the specific name of your product or specific solution, then they are likely in the Hunter/Active Buyer phase. Be smart about where you send them, and if possible have content that is relevant to the buying phase you think they are in and the two adjacent ones so they have options in case you predicted inaccurately. Given the nature of digital, you may as well hedge your bets.

This is also a fertile ground to be testing your approaches and messages. A good strategy is to offer next best content choices which entice them to stay on your site. Think of it in a *T* shape. Horizontally have more on the topic they came to your site for, and vertically give choices to go deeper into the topic, providing functional or sector insights for example. Offer format choices so you can optimize your campaign spend towards those that buyers prefer and keep a close eye on bounce rates and time on page.

As you scrutinize your web assets, look at where you are directing buyers to next and make sure it is as good as the page they landed on. Above all, don't let someone get lost in your web estate; provide clear signposts to what you'd want them to go to next and make sure you've got enough content to cater for this part of the journey. If you are moving straight from an article about prioritization of long-term climate response to a page that pushes a product, you run the risk of losing them at an early stage of your content relationship.

Hunter

Your goal is to nurture these leads and make sure they can access the information they need to directly compare you and your competitors. Make sure that your content is optimized for search terms associated with your services (these are likely to be different to the more topic- or theme-driven level for the Explorer as mentioned above). Web content needs to be well laid out and navigation easy so they can find what they need quickly. At this stage, any barrier to entry to fulfilling their research aims could cost you a place on the shortlist. Provide detail about your products or services in action, make sure case studies are easy to find and pull benefits out early on the page. Hunters will come to your site with specific objectives which you need to meet as seamlessly as possible.

Lead nurture campaigns start in earnest at this point in the buyer journey because Hunters are more likely to respond to it given where they are in their journey – they want easy access to your messages. Marketing automation can help you make nurture efficient and allow for different user journeys depending how Hunters are engaging with your content or channels. Start personalizing content according to what you know about the buyer or people like them. Depending on what type of company they are from, you may want to show how products work, have trial demos or give access to parts of them so they can look inside – think back to Jo Pettifer's example at Salesforce. Chatbots can help with site navigation and answering questions that your Hunters have. At this point you will have a number of outbound marketing activities such as emails, event invitations, access to exclusive content or new insights to deliver relevant content and messaging. Support this with display and website retargeting to nudge them in their journey. Test and learn as standard.

Once a lead has been flagged as ready based on a pre-agreed criteria with sales, route the lead and alert sales so they can follow up. Many marketing automation systems have been designed with a B2C buying journey in mind, so one thing to consider when implementing lead scoring is using the buyer journey and thinking through the dynamics of it. You might be weighting job seniority for example, but if you know that once a decision moves from Explorer to Hunter, the research is delegated to someone more junior within the organization, it might be a good idea to upweight a more junior job title score in the Hunter or Active Buyer content, otherwise you will lose the opportunity to convert the lead.

Use digital channels the way that they were intended; having a flat, brochure-ware website is a waste and won't give you new insights. Interaction will drive this. Think about infographics, calculators and benchmarking tools, all of which give a richer experience to your Hunter and provide new information about what they're doing. Think carefully about sub navigation and service pages; make sure that the *elevator pitch* on sites is strong with the call to action both clear and something that your business can respond to quickly. Remember Jo Pettifer's anecdote about lazy follow-up and how responding well to digital signals is a key part of how your brand shows up.

Remember too that some of your Hunters influence the sale and aren't direct decision makers. Create pathways for them through your site so you don't get confused by the signals that buyers are giving you.

Active Buyer

As leads convert into serious buying intent, use technology to reduce or remove friction in the buying cycle.

- If you are part of a competitive tender or pitch process, you can create an entirely bespoke digital experience. Post Covid-19, we're used to running virtual sales discussions. Use technology to enrich the pitch. Supplement with personalized video or create a way for buyers to explore offices or delivery centres virtually. You can create a shared online space where sales can solve problems in real time with customers – or respond to their questions fast.

- Build a tool for sales reps to take into client discussions, or get prepared ahead of time, where they can look at topics that are on their buyers' minds and familiarize themselves with the services your company offers.

- Increasingly buyers will want to have the choice of whether they want human or digital interactions. If you are selling digital services or products, *click to try* or *click to buy* and trial demos mean that buyers can go further through their process without engaging with salespeople if they don't want to. Ensure that you have lots of calls to action across your pages and encourage buyers to actively engage with you.

- Offer multiple ways to get more details – you're trying to get engagement. Exclusive news, data and insights to show what the product contains, the specifications that IT may need, all encourage people to fill in contact fields, which provide an invaluable data source for your teams.

- Renewals might be an interesting digital opportunity for your business. A recent McKinsey study showed that 86 per cent of B2B buyers would renew a service digitally if they were able to (Maechler et al, 2017). If buyers have been through the sales process once, you may be able to secure upgrades, repeat subscription or renewals entirely virtually through a logged-in experience, which may be a better experience for your buyer at a much lower cost to your company.

Clients

As outlined in Part One, you have two objectives within your existing client: driving loyalty or finding new buyers within an existing client account. In both instances technology can help you.

- Driving loyalty: once the contract is signed, support onboarding through digital training, welcome or introduction materials, walk-throughs and demos. If you are in services, consider a dedicated FAQ and open forum for your client to ask questions. Some software companies also allow client procurement teams to monitor usage so that they can reallocate licences online and use the opportunity to promote new thought leadership or training to their internal end users. It should be easy to get real time access to experts or customer support – reduce the effort to get in touch with your team. Create a logged-in area for all your customers to crowdsource the Q&A. You can seek real time client feedback as they progress through adopting your product or reach critical milestones in the contract.

- Creating new pipeline within existing accounts: once you have devised your plan with named targets or buying teams at an existing client, build a social outreach plan mapping your executives to theirs, measure engagement and use technology to build content that account teams can customize on a platform. Do highly targeted social listening to understand how your company is perceived and track specific things that are happening in the client account or sector that you could help them find solutions for. Alerts on company M&A, leadership changes, and regulation can all be served to the sales teams and used to start a campaign that is well targeted to buyers. Use technology too to assess whether your SMEs are achieving the reach that they should, and inform them about topics that are trending, performing well or where they could be being more provocative.

Across each phase of the buyer journey, think about how you can use your owned channels – particularly your website – to create moments of interest, or to counteract any doubts your buyer might have. As Kirsten cites in her insight, with good buyer and firmographic data, you can cater for the pivotal decision moments that are unlikely to happen when your sales team are in the room.

INSIDER INSIGHT

Kirsten Allegri Williams, former CMO Optimizely, SAP SuccessFactors

Kirsten has more than 20 years' experience in B2B marketing. She has worked predominantly in the tech space including in several leadership positions at software company SAP. She was most recently Chief Marketing Officer at digital experience platform software company Optimizely. Kirsten is a digital first marketer who deeply understands the technology ecosystem needed to provide an optimal B2B buying experience. In this interview, she gives her thoughts on harnessing micro-moments to influence major decision points in the buyer journey.

THE ROLE OF DIGITAL ACROSS THE ENTIRE BUYER JOURNEY

Over my 20 years in B2B marketing, we've always relied on a traditional, bottom-up way of building tactics. For too long, we've been tethered in an unhelpful historic funnel-view of the world. But this doesn't fulfil what is needed for the complexity of buyer engagement today. You now need digital engagement strategies across the entire buyer journey, not just at the e-commerce or targeting part of it. As digital channels mature, the increased complexity they bring has become a permanent feature of the landscape. Applying the lessons of the past helps to some extent, but marketers need to get much more creative about what they are doing to accelerate the journey when sales teams are not involved.

The work we do on brand and content is really the only thing that senior internal people at most companies actually *see*. Their view of marketing's contribution is literally what's in front of them – typically big brand advertisements. A stakeholder in a typical leadership team has incredible demands on marketing and assumptions about what good looks like, but if they can't see it realized in the form of an advert, they may think marketing isn't happening. The reality of buyer engagement these days is that they are doing a lot of self-discovery through digital channels. This means marketers need to be clearer how we're targeting the addressable market, showing the whole experience for buyers in a visual way – supported by metrics. Only looking at volume metrics might cause people to underestimate the power of any specific digital experience or touchpoint.

THE POWER OF MICRO-MOMENTS

An inclination towards big brand bursts, because of this historic view of what good marketing looked like, makes me wonder whether all the science around frequency is false when we think about the impact of our work on the buyer. There are so many different micro-moments in the buyer engagement with your business. Every interaction could be a magical one – the one that made the difference between buy/don't buy, or them choosing your business – but it could be so small that people in your organization don't even know it was the deciding factor.

The next frontier for us as B2B marketers is how we understand and capture the impact of that moment. Today, we don't know what the ultimate trigger was for a buyer to say, 'I'm going to buy now, I'm not going to wait.' It's likely an emotional response – something you put in front of them hit a chord. It's almost impossible to measure the impact of what motivated them at that critical point. It isn't likely to be at a brand advertising level, and it isn't in a sales interaction. It is deeply buried in the sphere of exploration, research and decision-making. We really don't yet know or understand when all those *unlock* moments happen along the buyer journey, but we're starting to learn.

Let me give you an example. I was talking to a CMO in the media and entertainment industry who was describing that they had lost a significant amount of money during Covid-19. We were discussing how they needed to dramatically change their business model to come back from that. He was battling tremendous pressure from shareholders and many competing visions from his stakeholders about what was best for the business. After a series of conversations, he decided not to move forward on a piece of digital strategy work. For him in that moment, it was too hard to put that level of investment ahead of revenue. I think a lot about that micro-moment, that decision point, and I ask myself: What was it that persuaded him into a *no go* rather than a *go*?

SURROUNDING THE BUYERS

We know that the buyer process is sprinkled with micro-moments that profoundly impact whether someone gets into a buying frame of mind, likely very early in their process. The next question is: How as a marketer do you surround that buyer and equip them with everything they need to move at least into a further evaluation or deeper exploration? Think about the example above. This was at a really early stage of the thinking. It was far ahead of sales funnel – it was at the tipping point of whether he could move from thinking into buying. And in those micro-moments, we're navigating context, baggage, culture, risk and change appetite – all of which impact how fast the buyer can or will move. And then there is that moment where buyers must take a leap into the unknown, that moment when they are making big bet investments, putting their personal reputation on the line. They are having to go out there into something unknown to advance their business.

Successful B2B marketers need to be there at that critical moment of decision-making. We need to understand all the challenges, roadblocks, objection handling etc. that swirl in a buyer's mind about whether to take the decision. This could be a real do or die moment – a make or break for their job at a particular company or even their careers.

So, to the B2B marketer, I'd say, challenge yourself to think differently: understand the motivations in the buyer that you need to anticipate, using data and industry insight – then ask yourself how to get creative in that moment. There are so many opportunities for surrounding that buyer frequently, to educate them. Typically, we don't do a lot of this in marketing, but it's foundational. It's when we need to step up to help them so we can drive a value-based relationship with our brand long before we create a human connection with them.

ANTICIPATING BUYER NEEDS AND CREATING MOMENTS THAT MATTER

As you're looking at the investment mix across your buyer framework, I'd encourage you to think about how much content, effort and expertise we are really bringing into that mid-framework content strategy. Digital is your friend here. You will be facing multiple buyers across different industries and sectors. There are huge variations within the target addressable market. This provides an amazing opportunity for creativity, but it's not at the strategic brand advertising level or even at the tipping point for converting to sales activity. Instead, we need to cultivate and accelerate those future buyers that are just thinking that they might need to do something in a more speculative way. This is the opposite of the big charismatic brand moment – this is the comparatively quiet long game. Marketing plays a hugely important role in guiding their buyers through that, often lengthy, consideration process.

It's difficult to evaluate the risk profile of the buyer, but we have to do it. We need to understand it so that we motivate people to act or move their thinking onward. In those micro decision moments, what does it take to tip the buyer over into the next phase? You've got to get people over the line – not by using fear tactics but by using aspirational content that recognizes what that buyer's likely to be battling with inside their organization. This changes depending on the size and scale of their company. That's why you have got to have great data and salespeople who understand their sector or business well. Then, you can assess their context and build marketing to really respond to it on a deep level.

THE ROLE OF DIGITAL

I speak to a lot of customers and CMOs in our industry – we all know we have a long way to go to understand the full power of the digital experience.

We think of meta tags in search engine optimization (SEO), we need it in the design system of how we deliver digital experience. Marketers use analogies like Lego blocks, with buyers selecting their own experience based on component parts. All of the parts need to fit the buyer or influencer and their specific journey. This involves an immense creativity. You have to fit all the different permutations of an experience together. You have to give full consideration to every micro-moment you can create or influence. To do this, you have to invest in creative and in a digital framework for that creative to be responsive. There's no substitute for a commitment on this front. Without the investment, it's like trying to play chess without the full complement of pieces on the board. It's just much harder to win.

What's the end goal? A relevant, content-rich opportunity for the buyer to come to a decision on their own terms. The days are long past when you can guide them yourself. There are now too many different ways into the buyer journey to do that. You've got to pour your best minds and resources into the challenge of designing that long, complex middle part of the journey. The end result doesn't always look as glamorous as the highly visual, high expense video and advertising campaigns, but there is just as much magic in it. It would be great to see the industry celebrate it someday.

Test, learn and analyse

Across all your activity you want to be insights-driven and efficient. Technology supports data collection and augmentation. Analyse performance data, automate where possible and use AI/machine learning to improve efficiency. You can also A/B test where you have two or more messages running at the same time with the same purpose to the same audience to assess, which have better impact measured through interactions. A/B testing has been proven to drive dramatic business results; Microsoft company Bing's experiments with colours showed that slightly darker blues and greens in titles and slightly lighter black in captions improved user experience. When rolled out to all their users, the colour changes boosted revenue by more than $10 million annually (Kohave and Thomke, 2017). It doesn't get done systematically in B2B, partly because the numbers of visitors to websites is lower than in B2C (and because of underinvestment in data science) but doing it will increase the performance of your messages and efficiency of the buying cycle. Test different copy so that you can learn which approach works best. Try out different calls to action – for example something factual 'x per cent of people who use our product save money' versus something direct 'You will miss this offer if you don't sign up this month'.

Using tech tools – particularly digital done well – will help you create a more curated, content-rich and relevant experience for your buyers.

Using the buyer framework to help choose technology

Having a technology stack that truly enables the marketing team is now an imperative if you want to respond to signals buyers are giving you, personalize at scale, demonstrate ROI and drive productivity. This has led to a proliferation of marketing technology and providers. Scott Brinker's Martech landscape graphic shows over 8,000 vendors (Brinker, 2020), and Martech Alliance recently put the global market for Martech at $344.8 billion (Charlton, 2021).

TABLE 12.1 How to use technology tools across the buyer journey to gain insights

What you are trying to do	Horizon Scanner	Explorer	Hunter	Active Buyer	Client
Get contacts, information or data	Advertising respondents, thought leadership readers, third-party site referrals, third-party event attendees	Previous site visitors, third-party and proprietary event attendees, LinkedIn contacts, web visitors, webinar sign-ups, retargeting ads	Target account outreach (email, social, events), affiliates, nurtured leads, sales triggered contacts, past event attendees		Nurtured leads, sales triggered contact, past event attendees, target/ pursuit account outreach
Solicit information using tech channels	Lightly gated content, landing pages, paid campaigns, organic search, virtual events	Exclusive gated content, landing pages, paid campaigns, sponsorship referrals, organic search, channel options, webinar or event registrations, interactive white paper	Personalized welcome, lead nurture journey, infographics, quizzes, demos, diagnostic tools, price calculators, competitor comparison based on Hunter input, call back request/get in touch, product or location tour	Demos, diagnostics, price calculators, online FAQ, call back request/get in touch, buying influencer content e.g. a video for an IT person buying marketing technology, technical details, product or location tour	
Personalize	Use referring source to tailor experience	Dynamic landing page, A/B testing, keyword referral alignment, on-page BOT	Dynamic content, identity matching (if you have a logged-in space), returning user insight, lead scoring, depth of content engaged with, next best action recommendation	Next best action, pitch microsite	Logged-in area where information served is tightly aligned to account insights from sales, CRM or client's business strategy

Using technology to transform how you engage with customers or create more productivity in your marketing organization is a given, but it can be challenging to work out how to think about and organize your tech investments, as well as understand the ROI it provides. Having led several marketing transformations re-platforming websites, consolidating multiple CRM systems and introducing marketing automation, I have seen at first hand the time, effort and cost that goes into making this successful. This is because many B2B organizations have bought technology but not looked at it in an end-to-end way. Often teams are looking at the efficacy of pieces of the technology stack in isolation, such as the website, the CRM, or marketing automation, or they are organizing governance by tech vendor rather than taking a systematic view of how each part of the system needs to link to another to make it work to its full potential. This leads to inorganic, sometimes chaotic technology solutions that are not joined up and not realizing the investment that was hoped for.

Solve for this by using the buyer journey as a base for prioritizing your investments. Take your buyer journey then map what technology could help you according to each stage or across the whole. I've given an example (see Figure 12.1). Map in what you have already bought against a diagram like this to assess what you have, where gaps are, or where you have duplication. Weight the parts of the journey

FIGURE 12.1 Using the buyer journey to prioritize technology investments

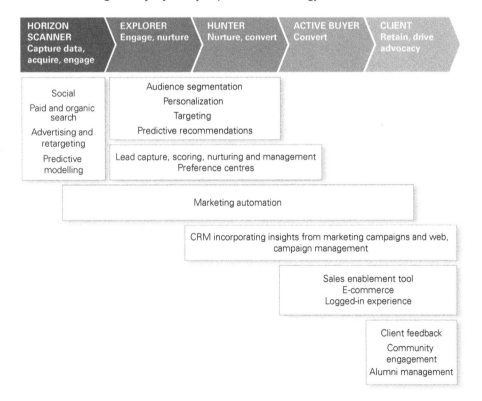

where you need the most help. For example, if you are growing your business, you may want to make sure that data capture, modelling and reach in the Horizon Scanner and Explorer stages take priority over e-commerce.

Looking at the stack this way could also help you discover critical dependencies between technologies otherwise overlooked or underappreciated. It is very difficult to use marketing automation to target existing clients or get insights to do predictive modelling if the data in the CRM isn't sufficiently high quality. In that instance, you'd be better off diverting funding into adoption of your CRM or a mass purchase of data for a period of time, instead of any additional technology investments.

Often too, technology has been put in but processes haven't been updated, or teams insufficiently upskilled. Labels don't always help. *Marketing automation* implies that things will get easier or less labour intensive, but sometimes the work just shifts elsewhere in the team. If you want to build audience journeys across a campaign – rather than just a single tactic like an event – you may be able to streamline the time and effort it takes to contact the buyer at each point of the journey, but that may mean hundreds more pieces of content need to be created. So, it doesn't stop with the IT investment; having a technology-enabled ecosystem involves entirely rethinking how your team thinks about content production, overall processes, skills mix and how they collaborate with each other.

IN SUMMARY

- Your tech strategy has at least three aims: to improve your data, solicit information about your buyer, and provide an at scale personalized experience.

- Use your target market sizing to work out how much data you need and assess how much you have as well as its quality. Acquiring data is a cost that is hard to show ROI on directly, but needs to be done, otherwise you will lose money through poorly distributed content. Score the quantity and quality of your data against the market size.

- Marketing that is well targeted is, by definition, more efficient as it helps get better return on investment. Work with your sales teams to do regular hygiene on the data in your CRM system.

- As mentioned in the buyer journey chapters, design your tactics with data capture in mind and at each stage of the buyer journey.

- You will want to have different web experiences which are integrated from a buyer journey perspective: these should revolve around your home page, campaign experiences and *always on* landing pages.

- Across all your activity you want to be insights-driven and efficient. Analyse performance data, automate where possible and use A/B test as standard.

- Ensure processes are updated and teams sufficiently upskilled as you develop and update your tech.

- Having a technology-enabled ecosystem involves entirely rethinking how your team thinks about content production, overall processes, skills mix and how they collaborate with each other to ensure you can maximize data capture and ensure a smooth customer experience.

13
Return on investment, managing agencies, setting targets and a new partnership with sales

I believe that marketing should make money not cost money. I like the famed management consultant Peter Drucker's quote, 'Business has only two functions – marketing and innovation.' But it can be very challenging for B2B marketers to know what impact they have had on revenue growth. I think that this is because both variables – the investment and the return – are challenging, as I talk about below. Marketing metrics not well aligned to objectives become confusing for the business to understand. In addition, the impact of parts of the marketing spend is not realized within a fiscal year cycle, which means that marketers need to explain it to leadership and finance in a different way compared to other functions, using the buyer journey framework to help.

The return depends on what the objectives are for each part of the buyer journey. Using the framework will help you explain what business outcomes marketing money is achieving. It also helps you challenge thinking from business stakeholders who have strong opinions about what should go into the marketing plan, who push for expensive commitments based on subjective views about what will attract clients or insist on continued commitment to certain things every year. The buyer journey will help you have more precise conversations with stakeholders about the growth market is driving, and give a mechanism to assess the downstream commercial impact of shifting resources from one part of the journey to another.

In this chapter I talk about the challenge of short-term thinking when considering return on investment for B2B marketing. I have alluded to this throughout the book by offering indicator as well as outcome metrics in each stage of the buyer journey. Educating buyers, enticing them to buy and capturing them at the point when they are ready – rather than when you need to hit a target – is a multi-year ambition, so you need to reframe when the ROI will hit. You will get it, but not perhaps within a quarter if you're trying to market something complex or new.

I then focus on agencies and how to get the best out of them, given how critical they are in supplementing capacity and capability – and how much of your costs they take up given tight B2B budgets. As part of this, I feature an Insider Insight from Tom Klein, CEO of Stein IAS, which is a leading B2B marketing agency. He talks about how to be a good client, the changing demands from B2B marketers and its impact on agencies as well as giving advice on how to get the best out of agencies and share commercial goals.

Finally, I discuss how to set targets that are aligned with your business, and how to use this exercise to reframe the relationship between marketing and sales. Much has been written on this topic, but I suggest that the buyer journey framework might be a good galvanizing opportunity to get better alignment on roles, resourcing and ROI. This partnership is so critical to the buyer experience, it is worth spending time and effort getting it right. In this section, I have another Insider Insight, this time from Ismail Amla, Executive Vice President of Professional Services at NCR Corporation. In it he offers a provocative view about the changing dynamic between marketing and sales in a digitally enabled buyer environment.

The challenge of return on investment

I mentioned in the introduction that both sides of the investment and return can be challenging for B2B marketers.

On the investment side, marketing plans comprise activities that have been done year after year with little real understanding of whether or how they yield results. In fact, often they are justified by a sense of anti-return – or spending simply to prove a point. I've heard expensive events defended through sentiments like 'customers will think that we aren't in the market anymore'. Events or sponsorships are even committed to without consulting marketing. The marketing team is then on the hook for achieving return on investment, even though objectives and return weren't agreed up-front. Added to this, it can be hard to know the true cost of an activity. It is straightforward to know how much it was to take part in a major event, but marketing teams rarely load in the cost of their labour to put it on. If you're not inclined to use time sheets, then at a minimum you should use salaries to give you an indicative sense of what it costs to execute the marketing activities and use this to negotiate out of things that are resource intensive but commercially unfocused.

On the return side of the equation, sometimes the business is measuring the wrong things. I have had many conversations with senior sales leaders in the past simultaneously asking 'Where are my leads?' and asserting that 'No one knows our brand in this space.' These two objectives are related in the buyer journey, but at different points and are achieved through a different mix of content and channels; if you try to measure the impact of brand awareness through sales leads alone, without connecting it up through the buyer journey, then investments are likely to fall short on anticipated returns. And when you measure the wrong things, you make false trade-offs. Often in B2B environments, short termism takes primacy, typically due to marketing historically being considered sales support or because marketers haven't been able to make the case for brand investment. This means money isn't allocated according to the buyer's journey; rather it is assigned to hitting quarterly sales numbers, which forces marketing to be more focused on the Hunter or Active Buyer stage, at the expense of Horizon Scanner, Explorer or Client where it might yield more enduring return or build critical future pipeline.

Investment in marketing end-to-end won't yield results that align neatly to your company's financial year. For example, it might take nine months of Horizon Scanner activity, then six months to move from Explorer to Hunter, followed by a four-month procurement process. If buyer timelines look like this, it is more likely that you will get return on your investment in year two. A recent LinkedIn study showed that 46 per cent of digital marketers have budget allocation discussions every month and there are 77 per cent of marketers attempting to prove the ROI of their marketing campaigns within a month of them running (LinkedIn). This is not long enough to change brand perception or make yourself memorable in the minds of your buyers not yet in market to buy something. You will never hit the Horizon Scanners or Explorers and the company will be at the mercy of just waiting for RFIs rather than building relationships way ahead of the Active Buyer process.

Often too, marketers try to measure the effectiveness of a marketing tactic by channel, without taking into account the purpose it serves in the context of the buyer journey. For example, teams compare event with digital spend in an attempt to reduce cost per lead. The risk of diverting funds to cheaper channels is that they won't address the needs of the buyer and they provide a poorer quality experience. It might be plausible to replace face-to-face events with webinars, particularly since Covid-19, but ditching all event types to fuel digital spending could undermine your chances of providing buyers with valuable time with your company representatives. If buyers want to spend time with peers or sales reps to help them work through a problem and competitors offer this experience, buyers will build rapport with them and you will lose out. This tactic-led approach might also lead you to look at an isolated activity against a specific buyer journey objective without considering fully where in the framework it could yield best return. When reviewing overall spend in one of my past teams, we saw events weren't getting good return for lead generation but wondered whether they might have benefit at other points in the journey. We found they were particularly helpful when trying to unblock stalled pipeline, or to accelerate people from Explorer to Hunter, so shifted how we measured what events were helping the business achieve. We revised who we invited, agendas, who should attend from our business and reframed how we articulated the benefits.

A more helpful approach is to look at the combined set of tactics and their effectiveness within each stage rather than trying to evaluate each channel in isolation. It is rare that a buyer will only come across one of your channels; in fact, if you've got a good plan, they shouldn't, so look at what the right module or package of marketing is to achieve a particular outcome. If you want to move someone from Hunter to Explorer, is thought leadership plus event plus a diagnostic tool more effective than thought leadership plus a diagnostic tool only? Or might it be more effective to put the assets in a different order?

Without a buyer journey view and with this pressure to justify short-term return, marketers run the risk of putting all investment into the most short-term lead conversion – which is arguably the place that sales need it least. It jeopardizes your longer-term pipeline and isn't a realistic way to think about the time lag of marketing spend versus revenue return. Work through evidence-based buyer time horizons across each phase of the journey to manage expectations around when the money you spend will lead to a sale. You may need to flex this as you learn more, but at least you've got a starting point. I would advocate you building a rolling three-year view of ROI, which will help you be more accurate and realistic about how you will make money for the company in the longer term.

Working with agencies

Agency spend can be one of the biggest line items in a B2B marketer's budget, because under investment in skills and resourcing necessitates buying in capability and capacity. Given the typical size of B2B budgets, making sure you get good return on this money is critical. Whether spending on production (creation of ideas, assets and channels) or distribution (things that get the work into buyers' hands like paid advertising or social promotion) you need to make sure you really manage the relationship and the budget carefully.

Whatever criteria you have for choosing an agency, to create great work you need to like each other. When agencies pitch, I find it helpful to set aside time for a chemistry session. This will help you see how the relationship could work when you're in execution. Like for the buyers you are trying to reach, if you are doing anything that is complex or new, it is likely that you will have periods where you won't agree or where the work isn't hitting time or budget parameters – so it is important to get on with and respect each other! It is interesting to understand too what makes a good client for them – and be very honest with yourself about whether your company would be. For example, I had one agency tell me that their best types of clients are those that are organized with lots of check-in meetings – which at the phase of the transformation we were in, with people leaving and processes changing, we were not in a position to be. Some agencies like more access to your clients and stakeholders, and how comfortable you are in doing this will likely depend on the reputation that marketing has within the company and what stakeholder perception is of agency spend. You need to get the best out of them, and they know what internal environment they operate most effectively in, so this can be a good way of checking alignment from the outset.

Once you've hired an agency, make sure that they are well briefed (there is a template in the appendix) and you're clear about how you will work together. Most marketing teams I've worked with have had agency relationship management high on their list of training asks, and agency spend can be much higher than it needs to be because of this skills gap. If your team is junior and not used to working with agencies, they can iterate through agencies, not realizing that they are racking up costs, given agencies typically charge by hours used. If marketers are not entirely clear about what the end result needs to be – or haven't engaged well with internal subject matter experts – they may be making a huge number of rounds of revisions. I've seen cases where small changes can go back and forth seven to ten times – each time incurring more cost – and adding time to the deliverable.

To stop this, be clear at the outset what the final deliverable will be, precise about format and how many rounds of review are needed. This will prevent runaway, expensive iterating, and force you to be complete with your feedback rather than giving it piecemeal, which again incurs additional charges. Finally, make sure you're all clear on the timelines and pay attention to the speed at which the agency has assumed you will give feedback. Agencies know how long their processes take, but don't know yours. This can cause delays in the timelines/deliverables – and you will be incurring agency resource costs that are not actively working on the project because their time has been ring-fenced for your work. Tom Stein gives some great advice about this in his Insider Insight.

Keep an eye too on who from the agency is involved in each stage of the work. It is unlikely you will need a senior creative on something you know is a small piece of transactional work or if an agency has bigger B2C clients you will be outspent, so they may put their senior talent onto more lucrative clients. If it is particularly important that a specific person from their team is part of a particular phase of your project – or at a critical meeting – you should be clear about that from the outset. If you have negotiated a flat rate for the work, you should still do this so you don't jeopardize the relationship you have with the agency. They shouldn't feel they're doing more than they expected or are using up additional time. They are trying to run a business too.

Flag immediately when an agency isn't getting it right. There is no point persisting with a poor performer – particularly if they are engaging with senior stakeholders as your choice of agency reflects on you.

When you finish a project, whether you will be working with the agency again or not, you should do a debrief and feedback session. This will enable you to share and learn from each other. What went well? Celebrate hitting milestones, the end outcome of the work and any highlights in how you worked together. What didn't go well? What did you learn about how you operate under the pressure of getting the deliverable done? Could you have briefed better? Given clearer direction? Was your feedback timely enough? Did you get what you expected? Was the quality where you needed it to be? Finally, what did you learn? What advice would you give each other as you go into another project? How could they have been a better agency partner, and how could you have been a better client?

INSIDER INSIGHT

Tom Stein, founding partner of B2B specialist agency Stein IAS

Tom is Chairman and Chief Growth Officer of Stein IAS. He's been a B2B marketing leader, thought leader and innovator for more than 35 years and is part of the leadership team that propelled Stein IAS to global B2B Agency of the Year at the Associate of National Advertisers nine times over the past 12 years. He has worked with leading brands such as pharma company Merck, HSBC, NCR, Western Union Business Solutions, Juniper Networks, ABB, Ingredion, Samsung and many others. In this Insider Insight, Tom discusses what makes a great client/agency relationship, as well as the importance of considered courage.

WHAT MAKES A GOOD B2B CLIENT?

The three most important qualities are clarity, candour and trust. The lack of these typically explains why the average agency/client relationship lasts no more than three years, often less. I see situations constantly, whether in a new business or existing business context, where the agency must make assumptions or informed guesses and ends up working off an ambiguous or incomplete brief. On the flip side, it's up to the agency to challenge the client and make sure every brief is a good brief. If a lack of clarity persists, things will go south quickly. When client stakeholders aren't on the same page, the result is rework, frustration, inefficiency, cost overruns and ineffective work. Every time. A good client also will be candid and direct in all regards – about reactions to work product, about company inner workings and politics, and evolving internal perceptions of the agency. With clarity and candour come trust. With trust comes better and more effective work – and an always improving body of work. There also develops an appetite for placing bigger bets (with the risk of doing so being shared), which of course leads to breakthrough work... and a long, happy and productive relationship.

THE CHANGING DEMANDS FROM B2B MARKETERS AND THE IMPACT ON AGENCIES

In the past, the role of B2B marketers was largely sales enablement: messaging, collateral, websites, events, lead generation. By and large, the care and feeding of the sales organization. That was and remains very valuable work. But over time, the best B2B marketers have evolved to become growth enablers and, in some cases, growth drivers. And the big question for B2B marketers is whether they are taking orders from the business or driving a growth agenda. This massively affects the demands from B2B marketers and the impact on agencies. Strategies to help drive growth. Connecting brand to demand and demonstrably delivering impact. Digital interaction approaches that deploy intelligent experiences up and down the funnel. Creative ideas that become strategic assets to drive businesses forward into the future. The demands on and from B2B marketers are great; the opportunities for marketers and agencies are commensurately great. My belief is that marketers need agencies that can run alongside them as true marketing partners, and not merely communications partners, to instigate growth and provide the expertise and ideas that add the greatest value to marketers' organizations.

SIMILARITIES AND DIFFERENCES BETWEEN B2B AND B2C

The ongoing conversation around B2C and B2B marketing being a lot more similar than they are different has a lot to do with digital. Things like frictionless customer experiences, accessibility and simplicity are now as important in B2B as in B2C. As a result, B2B needs to improve the quality of the immersive experiences it provides and the use of technology to streamline the buying cycle and process. The B2H (business-to-human) conversation also is front and centre – and brings B2B closer to B2C. That's a good thing. But that being said, B2B is still and will always be different than B2C. A global professional services firm buying a seven-figure solution is not an individual decision maker. There are multiple decision makers, decision breakers and influencers involved in a high-stakes, potentially career-defining process. Jobs can hinge on the decision and the level of sophisticated information that needs to be imparted over time (and the relationships that need to be forged and sustained) make B2B a different animal to B2C.

WHY AGENCIES AND MARKETERS FIND IT HARD TO SHARE TARGETS

Measuring success is an art and a science. But here's where things inevitably fall down: when targets set by marketing team and agency aren't truly internalized by all key client stakeholders, reaching them becomes far less meaningful. For example, you can deliver the 5,000 MQLs promised, but there is still scepticism among the client stakeholders about the value delivered. A good agency can meet most KPIs. The question is, does everyone who matters on the client side truly agree that these are the KPIs that will move the business forward? Are the CEO, CRO, CFO and business unit leads going to be jazzed by the result? There will be a lot less friction and drama when marketing and sales, at minimum, agree the targets. And not just at a lip-service level.

Another point about targets: it's long been cited that only 20 per cent of CEOs genuinely trust their CMOs. This mistrust tends to cascade into the agency relationship.

It certainly explains the short tenures of many CMOs (and of many client/agency relationships). While some B2B CEOs are natural-born marketers, many are not – nor are they trained as marketers. They don't have intuition about it. They don't have an abiding belief in the impact of marketing and not surprisingly are sceptical about investing in it. Developing a shared language with the CEO and others in the C-suite about targets is one important way forward.

HOW TO THINK ABOUT COMMERCIAL STRUCTURES

Whether you use a retainer structure, or monthly billing against time expended, everything's manageable and workable if there's a clear plan and process in place. The challenge comes when things pop up, or if the work gets very ad hoc. That's when it becomes hard for the agency to manage time and costs on behalf of the client, and to stay profitable itself. So, if you've established priorities, workstreams and deliverables according to plan, and then three new projects pop up, there's bound to be a knock-on effect. Most agencies don't magically have staff or resources to throw at these projects. It can be a very significant resourcing challenge. Naturally, the agency and client have to adapt as need arises. But ideally, you should have a very clear sense of what you're trying to achieve on a quarter-to-quarter and annual basis.

A VIEW ON DISCOVERY COSTS

As an agency, you don't ever want to be in a situation where the client says, 'You guys are four months into discovery and research, we've just spent a huge amount of our budget on it, and there's no in-market activity to show for it.' This goes back to the earlier point about clarity. The client and agency must have an early conversation about discovery and set crystal-clear expectations about what needs discovering and how the insights are going to be applied. The client needs to be willing, able and actually excited to invest in the discovery agreed to, including the time frame and process.

WHAT IS YOUR ADVICE FOR GETTING THE BEST OUT OF AGENCIES?

Clients can get more out of agencies by trusting them to do what they're good at, and by being a true advocate for the agency within their own organizations. Don't constrain the level of creative ambition – something that typically happens in regulated industries, or due to inherent conservatism, or because of corporate cultures. You'll get more value if you take deliberate risks together, calibrate them and understand the potential outcomes. Great marketing comes from considered courage. Interestingly and unfortunately, B2B agencies rarely get fired for inadequate strategy or creativity. They get fired for operational and account mismanagement issues – for being unreliable. Tight execution is hugely important. Great strategy, creativity and content change the game.

Understand and be better at strategy. Real strategy changes things. It means turning left instead of right. It means making leaps in product and positioning. It means harvesting deep insights and applying them in a way that leave competitors' heads spinning. It's about doing something that can meaningfully, materially, significantly change the course of affairs, and it doesn't exist nearly enough in B2B. If you do something fantastic strategically, whether it emanates from the client or the agency, and ideally from collaboration between the two, it's going to win in the marketplace. It's going to make you famous. And it's going to drive growth, full stop.

Getting more for your money

Budgets in B2B marketing are typically low compared to B2C companies. If you are in a transforming company, or a business that has very tight margins, or one that is impacted by unexpected market fluctuations, marketing is often the first place that is looked to for hand backs or cuts. While this isn't the sensible decision, it happens all the time so you might as well be ready for it. There are a few things you can do to have a great impact on a small budget, or to try to maintain the same impact as your budget gets cut.

- Use cheaper alternatives: consider where you could replace things that achieve similar objectives with another. Webinars are more cost effective than face-to-face events. A proprietary event or client round table could be more effective than a third-party event for the Explorer or Hunter. Check you are effectively harnessing your whole organization to amplify content to help reduce promotional activity.

- Use the right tool for the job. Do you need a gold-plated marketing solution? I think of it as having a Ferrari in the garage to do a weekly trip to the supermarket. When working with agencies, they may push you towards a bigger spend, a splashier activation or a more highly polished video, but it might not be necessary for what you need to accomplish.

- Make incremental investments and commitments. Rather than asking for a lot of money in a company that is sceptical about marketing, outline the full ask then ask for part of it now, which would give a small return in a shorter timeframe, as a way of proving yourself into the bigger case.

- Negotiate hard with vendors and suppliers: knowing how to leverage your negotiating position can help you get lots of things for free. If you are paying to go to an event, get attendee lists to enrich your data. Make sure your materials are in post-event literature to amplify your message. Third-party organizers could supply you with targeted attendees for an exclusive round table. If you're working with an agency and spending a reasonable amount of your budget with them, ask them to give your team some training, or help you brainstorm new ideas you could take to the business. Get insights into what their other clients are doing and ask creatives to share examples of work they think is cool or ground-breaking.

- As well as negotiating to raise the value of your investments, you should also negotiate down on every cost. I'm surprised at how often marketers take the first price they are given from suppliers. You could also do what I've suggested you do with your own clients – offer to provide references, case studies or proof points in return for reduced fees. Or do some workshops for them so they can learn about how to become better at dealing with their clients. For events, there should be room to negotiate on every first price you're given, and if you're operating on a very reduced budget, look at inventive ways to create the same impact at lower price, for example offering cocktails versus champagne, canapés versus sit-down dinner. You can even look at using edgier locations rather than the traditional hotels and package it as part of the experience.

- Ask agencies to partner with your high performers: this helps them build skills and gives agencies invaluable insights into how your organization and team works.

- Be precise and targeted: doing mass market promotion is expensive and in B2B is unlikely to yield the results you need. You would be better off spending less money on a very precise group of buyers than more money on anyone who might be interested in your services. Think about advertising for example. Advertising in transport hubs is great if you have a lot of money, but programmatic digital will probably get your company in front of your target buyer more often at a fraction of the cost.

Aligning targets across the buying journey to form a new partnership with sales

As mentioned in the introduction, the historic roles of marketing and sales in B2B have altered forever. Buyers are increasingly looking to a broader range of channels, choosing to engage with sales teams later in their process. There is no longer a single hand-off from marketing to sales.

Jointly deciding objectives, roles across each part of the framework, and feedback on how you'll continuously help each other optimize the buyer experience is key to building successful near- and longer-term pipeline. Both Jo Pettifer in the previous chapter, and Ismail Amla in this section talk about this dynamic in their insights. Sales need to help marketers understand the buying dynamics and support the early stages of the journey, otherwise marketers will be scattered in their targeting and produce vanilla content. They also need to be ready to continue the experience that has been established through the early stages of the buyer journey in a meaningful way. I've seen several interesting and engaging thought leadership programmes generated by marketers or internal subject matter experts with leads carefully cultivated, only to be handed to a salesperson ill-trained to have the strategic conversation you've set up. I've referred already to the fact that many of the interactions with the buyer are moving to channels traditionally owned by marketing – the insights from these need to be used by both teams to improve the value added to the buyer.

Of course, end revenue is the goal, but as mentioned earlier in the book, buyers engage with marketing activity well ahead of any sales motion – sometimes by years – so looking at in-year return could jeopardize future pipeline. Sales leaders often push marketers to take a percentage of their pipeline as a marketing target. But that's the wrong way to look at setting targets.

Helping each other across the buyer journey framework

In B2B marketing, no part of the journey is ever 100 per cent marketing or 100 per cent sales. Each function has a role to play in supporting the experience. The companies that do best are those that work in true partnership with each other and figure out how to collaborate in the right way across each of the stages in service of fulfilling buyer needs rather than on hitting sales targets alone. Set and agree targets across the framework up-front, then have a mechanism for holding each other to account and getting feedback to decide whether you need to course correct your investments.

As you plan each stage with sales, you must get completely aligned on:

- Who is in the total addressable market in each part of the buyer journey. Be clear on specific job titles – don't settle for generic answers like 'all the C-suite'. The detail of which job titles are in each phase will help you target more effectively, and ensure you have enough clean data to do it. The size of the market will help you work out whether the number of people responding to your marketing is good relative to that sizing.

- What the buying stages look like, how long you think buyers will spend in each stage, and what information they will need. Typically, the longer the pipeline, the more likely it is that you will need to continue to market to that buyer during it. This means you need to have a conversation about whether marketing resources are better directed at this Hunter/Active Buyer phase to keep the pipeline alive, or whether your efforts should focus on putting new Horizon Scanners into the pipeline. Test this with research and ongoing feedback into your campaigns.

FIGURE 13.1   How marketing and sales can complement each other's efforts across the buyer journey

MARKETING   **SALES**

HORIZON SCANNER

- Content and channel strategy
- Thought leadership production and distribution into owned and earned marketing channels
- Brand messaging and advertising
- Event and webinar management
- Sponsorship and partnerships
- Market and buyer insights (e.g. channel preferences)
- Competitive intelligence (e.g. bold marketing moves, messaging, sponsorships)
- TAM sizing and data quality
- PR
- Analyst outreach

- Input into thought leadership topics and channels
- Review messaging and campaign ideas, help articulate business challenges and solutions
- Distribution of thought leadership through social channels and directly with target buyers
- Attendance at events, follow up
- PR and analyst interviews
- Identify key job titles and target buyers
- Help refine TAM sizing
- Competitive intelligence

EXPLORER

- Thought leadership production and distribution into owned and earned marketing channels
- Produce and promote multi-channel content, make it easy to find e.g. via search
- Event and webinar management
- TAM sizing and data quality, look alike profiling, white space analysis
- Persona insights, campaign journeys
- Content streams aligned to core topics
- Analyst outreach, awards

- Subject matter expertise, opinion pieces
- Social sharing of content
- Comments on thought leadership or target client posts
- Authored content
- Attendance at events, follow up, invite prospects

HUNTER

- Thought leadership production and distribution
- Proposition/solution/services advertising and benefits-led content
- Event and webinar management
- Lead nurture, trigger-based marketing
- Design diagnostic tools
- Create collateral, case studies and high-level technical information

- Input into solution-level messaging
- Subject matter expertise
- Attendance at events, follow up
- Response to direct buyer outreach
- Provide proof points
- Create digital content e.g. videos on solution benefits

ACTIVE BUYER

- Detailed case studies
- Product demos
- Click to try or buy
- Easily accessible solution information – oriented to direct buyer and influencer groups
- Sales talk tracks
- Bid support and packaging

- Pitches
- Bid materials
- Buyer outreach
- Pipeline management
- RFI/RFP response
- Follow up on lead generation activities (form fills, marketing qualified leads)
- Commercial discussions and close
- Win/loss reviews

CLIENT

- Exclusive content and events
- Case studies
- Client advisory boards, round tables
- Account-based marketing
- Logged-in experience
- Trigger-based usage campaigns
- NPS score
- Awards submissions

- Pitches
- Bid materials
- Buyer outreach
- Pipeline management
- RFI/RFP response
- Follow up on lead generation activities (form fills, marketing qualified leads)
- Commercial discussions and close
- Win/loss reviews

- How long something takes to sell. This informs what targets marketing should be willing to take within a year, and the time it might take to realize marketing investment. Using the buyer journey, you can agree how long you would expect a buyer to spend at each stage, as well as what the clues and cues are for when buyers might be ready to move to the next stage.

- A realistic conversion rate – from the buyer's perspective, not a work back from what the sales team needs to hit a number. For example, if a concept or problem is quite new, it will take much longer for a buyer to decide that it could be a priority for them – or if a new crisis emerges, they will be reprioritizing their own resources, which will significantly impact your plan.

- What signals there are that the buyer is moving from one stage to another. If they move from reading an opinion piece to looking at a case study on your website, does that indicate that they're moving from Explorer to Hunter, and will marketing or sales respond? For example: a buyer attends a round table aimed at senior buyers.

  o If you jointly predict this could be a move from Horizon Scanner to Explorer or a lateral move within the Explorer phase: add to marketing nurture journey.

  o If you think this is a move from Explorer to Hunter or a lateral move within the Hunter phase: sales to follow up with outreach within pre-agreed timeframes.

- Critically, define what a lead *looks* like – what level of seniority, how much marketing they need to have had and how ready they need to be to buy, i.e. will a sales rep talk to someone who is speculatively thinking about buying something in the next two years, or would it be better to service that buyer with lead nurture marketing material? This may lead to the type of conversation Jo Pettifer talks about – volume versus value.

- When sales will take leads: some teams like to take them very early in the cycle – particularly if they want to make a more consultative sale. Some effectively want a buyer on the end of a phone ready to sign a contract before they'll accept it. I would argue that taking the lead too early or expecting it to be so overly nurtured are both suboptimal, but having the discussion and a clear, documented agreement is an essential starting point.

- When sales will focus attention on cultivating early pipeline versus closing later stage deals. This will be dependent on how your reps are commissioned but it is important as you may need to provide marketing air cover to earlier stage leads – in Explorer and Hunter – as sales are looking to close deals at the end of the financial year.

- KPIs for how quickly leads will be engaged with, and agreement that sales reps will be trained to have the right discussions, will give feedback on campaigns that aren't working and that they will turn up to events. You might need to decide how to share the responsibilities too. For example, if putting on an exclusive round table may necessitate a direct follow-up – is this marketing or sales' responsibility?

- If you are supporting cross or upsell strategies, agree attribution for how you will acknowledge marketing's contribution to known accounts, or forecast pipeline: I referred to this in the account-based marketing section of the Client chapter.

- How you will feedback to each other about team performance to support each other in achieving your targets and how you recognise each other's contribution.

Get sales input into messages up-front – they should be your testing ground for any campaign ideas. During a campaign, ensure that there are good feedback mechanisms – with clear handovers or hand backs – when working jointly on the leads. Using the buyer framework to reframe responsibilities can be a helpful way to rethink incentives too. In one role, we gave forgiveness on commission for sellers to come into the early stages of the process, and in marketing we had targets on closed/won business and pipeline contribution to make sure marketing was focused further down the funnel too.

As you develop your plan, step through it together from the buyer's perspective to ensure that you have an agreed response plan between sales and marketing. If a buyer has got a lot from a webinar and your company doesn't engage with them for months, any warmth will wear off. Or if they simply opened an email, they don't want to be mobbed by an enthusiastic salesperson. By the time your buyer is engaging with sales through marketing channels you have already built the expectation of their first human interactions. Each marketing activation needs to be as good as your best sales or account rep, each sales engagement needs to be as good as your best quality marketing output.

Working together to create insights

As you design shared campaigns, think through what insight each of you can bring to enrich the stages that the buyers are in and clues to inform how you think about when buyers are on the move. It is in both your interests to learn what the buyer is doing – this is no longer the preserve of sales.

Doing this well relies on a seamless information flow from sales to marketing and back again. If you position yourself as an insight-giving, learning organization with the buyer journey at heart, you will build a more successful relationship. Digital gives a rich seam of data and insights, but it can be easy to forget in the grind of execution to harvest these, look for patterns or useful information to pass to sales.

FIGURE 13.2   Marketing insights to sales and sales insights into marketing

MARKETING TO SALES   **SALES** TO MARKETING

**HORIZON
SCANNER**

- How people are navigating thought leadership on your website, so you both know what topics buyers are interested in
- Contract for data from third parties (e.g. partners or event organizers) to build marketing data sets and improve targeting
- Competitive intelligence: how they are engaging with the market more broadly

- Feedback from third party events on which topics or speakers resonated, the questions asked, to help shape thought leadership
- Sector trends, pain points and shared challenges across client groups
- Competitive intelligence: how they are engaging with clients directly

EXPLORER

- Profile of events key buyers are speaking at so sales can attend
- Topics getting traction on social and web properties
- Insights into where people are going next from opinion pieces – either horizontally to other opinions or down into services: this will show where they are in the buying journey and whether they are moving

- Topics getting traction on social, in sector publications and client conversations
- Feedback on quality of events and attendees to inform future year spend

HUNTER

- Event registrations so sales can meet Hunters face to face in a targeted way
- Provide diagnostic results to sales with insights by sector or function about how buyers are thinking about specific topics
- Web page performance to improve product demos

- Review or input into materials to ensure they are at the right level of detail for buyers
- Act on leads at an agreed point then feedback on readiness so that the handover point can be adjusted

ACTIVE BUYER

- Audience profiling to give insights into specific likes, personality, styles
- What worked in other pitches that teams were involved in
- Constructive challenge to pitch practice and documents

- Sales win/loss insights to inform whether messaging or marketing content needs to be altered

CLIENT

- Marketing to provide insights into C-suite changes within clients through intelligence tracking

- Client feedback about what marketing resonates, or input into campaign ideas
- Surface high levels of satisfaction with the deal/product so that case studies can be sought

Similarly, sales are focused on the near term when they could scale their value by inputting into marketing materials or channels, creating future pipeline.

Setting targets

I've suggested throughout this book how you might set targets mapped according to the buyer journey, based on what is realistic from a buyer point of view. Agreeing and aligning these is important otherwise you could end up with unrealistic targets, compounding the narrative that marketing isn't effective. Common areas of misalignment include handing over leads to sales too early, which frustrates the buyers as they get an unwanted sales-led intervention before they're ready. Another area of tension is where marketing hands over leads which sales doesn't respond to in a timely way. Agreeing up-front shared KPIs allows you to hold sales to account for otherwise wasted marketing investment.

If you're struggling to set targets:

- Estimate conversion rate using a floor and ceiling approach. So, if sales assert that 15 per cent of Explorers will become Hunters, opt for a 5 to 20 per cent range. This shows you're willing to work with a target, but that you're advocating a data-led, test and learn approach.

- Many marketing departments lack meaningful insight without a view of what good looks like. Data presented in a standalone way – 17,747 views, 1,091 reactions, 100 shares on LinkedIn – means it is hard to know whether numbers are good or not. Use TAM numbers to extrapolate a percentage or look to industry standards for help with targets the first time, accepting you will have no insights until you execute using your own data, and be in a position to set a benchmark to track improved performance over time.

- Use the TAM and buyer journey framework to put in reasonable assumptions. For example, if you sell HR systems that get replaced infrequently and have a TAM of 10,000 HR buyers, look at what is a reasonable number of them to be looking at your content at each phase of the journey – and how many of them are likely to be in the market looking for services at any one time. If, in this case, you assume three per cent of them will be in the Hunter stage in any one year that means the number of people you are marketing to in the Hunter stage is 300 – which paints a very different picture of how you market and target than if you took the traditional view of 10,000 potential buyers across all the stages of the cycle.

If you and the sales teams aren't really sure where to draw the line in terms of readiness to buy, and/or you're putting in marketing automation so testing and learning about lead scoring, then having inside sales teams or sales development reps can be a good investment. These resources can sit in marketing or sales and they don't need to be senior. Their role is to do the first outbound call or contact to leads as they come in through digital channels (or are scored). This touch point provides insight into who is in the buying group, the buyer's timeline and how they are assessing their needs. This team will also be able to test whether the leads coming through are the right level of seniority, have enough buying power, are even interested or are ready to buy. This insight will help you flex your scoring or make better agreements with sales on readiness of leads without having more senior (and expensive) sales resources spend their time on what might end up being junior or disinterested leads. For this team to really add value, you need to make sure they are sharing insights across marketing and sales, and you should adapt your tactics accordingly. They should be able to give insight into whether your assumptions about people being ready to move to the next stage of the cycle are correct, whether you are targeting your marketing effectively and whether leads could be passed through more quickly or need more nurturing.

Is it time for a full-scale overhaul?

As you look to improve the buyer journey at every point, acknowledging the shift towards marketing owned channels, an interesting question to consider is how far to use the framework to dissolve silos entirely by creating combined teams around what buyers want to achieve. A recent article cites an example of a company who segmented their buyer journey into *learn*, *buy*, *order/install*, *adopt* and *support*, then established an internal team comprised of marketing, sales and customer service to serve each part of the journey (*Harvard Business Review*, 2022). Forrester suggests that within the next five years, progressive companies will not have sales and marketing but will organize themselves around the buyer journey. As buyers choose a multi-channel experience across the full buyer journey, and as marketing, digital channels and sales converge, it might be time to rethink your internal structure to attract, acquire and convert a new breed of buyer. In fact, as Ismail talks about in his Insider Insight, legacy businesses can learn a lot from new market entrants about using marketing to create an experience of your company that is served by sales, rather than directed by them. If your company is transforming its front office operations, rather than making incremental improvements to traditional ways of working, this might be time to take a buyer journey view of all the teams involved.

INSIDER INSIGHT

Ismail Amla, Executive Vice President of Professional Services, NCR Corporation

In this Insider Insight, Ismail, currently Executive Vice President of Professional Services at NCR Corporation, provides a provocative view on the future of sales and marketing. He draws on more than 30 years of sales experience in global companies including IBM, Capco, Accenture and American compliance company CSC to provide insights into how the functions can operate most effectively together, as partners, in service of the client.

A SALES PERSPECTIVE ON WHAT GOOD LOOKS LIKE

The three key metrics that matter to sales leaders are length of time in the pipeline, conversion rate and sales value. Although all are effectively owned by sales, they can be hugely influenced by marketing. If you have an effective relationship, the impact of marketing on the growth line is more transparent – marketers don't have to convince anyone of their value. You can see the correlation between marketing activity and both sales productivity and pipeline velocity. If you have seamless interfaces between the departments including the use of data and aligned objectives, you'll also be able to collaborate better to drive revenue and client value.

QUALITY OF SALES DISCUSSIONS AS A LEADING INDICATOR OF RETURN ON BRAND INVESTMENT

Obviously, some activities – like brand building – take a long time to impact sales, whereas other activities are much more clearly aligned to the sales process. To understand the value of broader brand building, I think about how it gives me permission to have a different conversation with a buyer. Measuring return on things like thought leadership needs to be in the quality and type of discussion my sales teams can have. Having a shared marketing and sales objective here is important: you may be setting up your company as a thought leader extremely effectively, then the salesperson could be really bad at following up. They need to be confident enough to maximize the opportunity that the thought leadership created to have a more strategic conversation. So just as sales ask marketing to provide a quality lead, marketing should demand a quality follow-up from sales. If you think about it like this, the sales conversations are a leading indicator of the longer-term effectiveness of your brand or thought leadership activities.

IF YOU'RE STILL WORRYING ABOUT SALES AND MARKETING, YOU'RE ALREADY BEHIND THE CURVE

We are starting to see much of the decision made well before a buyer contacts the salesperson – some even moving online without any contact with sales at all. This means much of what used to be done in sales is today largely considered to be marketing activity.

Whereas in the past, you wanted your non-sales channels to be as good as your salespeople, now it is the other way around. Marketing builds the expectation of the experience of the brand, which is challenging given most people compare you to the last experience with a company that they had – whether it is B2B or B2C. Every experience that your company gives a buyer needs to be the standard for the next experience they have, and each needs to be deeply rooted in your customer promise. I believe that over time sales, marketing and customer service will all be responding to how the client wants to work – which is mostly online. As this happens, the job of sales becomes very different. In the past, sales was black book-led. Then it was process-led. Now it is increasingly content- or insight-led. This shift is happening and there are still huge swathes of organizations and people in denial. Legacy companies are spending time worrying about an incumbency challenge of making existing sales and marketing departments work better, whereas newer companies are obsessing about making better digital experiences to drive demand that sales can service. If you assume that sales and marketing are a singular motion to the client, then the salesperson who has prided themselves on being an individual needs to change their behaviour to create a consistent experience for the client. Tailoring the experience to make it personal for the client, using insights and data means sales need to change their approach.

USING DATA AND CONTENT TO CREATE RELEVANCE

Added to that, there is a digital footprint your buyer is creating – they're using particular key words, consuming content, visiting your competitors' websites. If you put that data together with what you know from their social media footprint, you get a sense of what they're interested in, who they are following. All this leads to a rich seam of information and insight, identifying buyer intent as well as channel preferences. This behavioural information means you can create really meaningful, targeted activities for your buyer. We've never had so much content – we just need to know how to put it all together to drive insights.

If you think about the B2C experience, you have a cart that you load then click to buy. The B2B equivalent to that is understanding what signals and triggers the buyer is giving digitally – then providing the next best action for them to take. So if they've downloaded a paper on cryptocurrency, be innovative around what you could offer next, don't just leave it at that. Send them a wallet with some currencies to spend on your products perhaps or give them NFTs in return for feedback on company strategy or product. All of this new technology too means that the day-to-day relationship on the ground changes to one of relationship management rather than sales. Similarly, if you look at a brand like Tesla and their narrative that they've not spent a dollar on marketing. They have used existing platforms to get their message across so they can be buyer preference-led. They create great content that is easily accessible in the channels their buyers are in anyway. They'll sell to you in the showroom but by then they are servicing an existing requirement to buy something – you wouldn't have made the effort to get there otherwise.

ADVICE FOR MARKETERS

Think of mass customization and creating an Amazon-like experience for the B2B buyer: easy to navigate with options suggested, then work back from that. Don't think about putting marketing effort into creating sales support – they should be able to service a well-informed lead. Focus instead on getting that lead educated and excited about the idea of buying from you then let sales service that demand.

IN SUMMARY

- Marketers often try to measure the effectiveness of a marketing tactic by channel, without taking into account the purpose it serves in the context of the buyer journey. A more helpful approach is to look at the combined set of tactics and their effectiveness within each stage rather than trying to evaluate each channel in isolation.

- Work through evidence-based buyer time frames across each phase of the journey to manage expectations around when the money you spend will lead to a sale.

- Chemistry sessions are useful when choosing an agency. This will help you see how the relationship could work when you're in execution.

- Always ensure agencies are well briefed, be clear about timelines and timings, and never iterate through the agency – collect all stakeholder feedback beforehand and send through one set of amends. At the end of a project, have a debrief/feedback session to understand learnings.

- There is no longer a single hand-off from marketing to sales. Jointly deciding objectives, roles across each part of the framework, and feedback on how you'll continuously help each other optimize the buyer experience are key to building successful near- and longer-term pipeline.

- Set and agree targets across the framework up-front, then have a mechanism for holding each other to account and getting feedback to decide whether you need to course correct your investments.

- Agree who is in the total addressable market in each part of the buyer journey. Be clear on specific job titles, what the buying stages look like, how long you think buyers will spend in each stage, and what information they will need. Decide what a good lead looks like, how they will be handed over to sales, how quickly they will pursue them and how you will give feedback to each other on the quality.

- As buyers choose a multi-channel experience across the full buyer journey, and marketing, digital channels and sales converge, it might be time to rethink your internal structure to attract, acquire and convert a new breed of buyer.

AFTERWORD

The purpose of this book is to help ambitious junior marketers change the traditional marketing relationship with buyers. That is to say it's no longer about how we sell to them, rather it's about how we respond to their needs as buyers going through multi-year complex decision-making processes.

It's a new way of thinking that accommodates the many nuances in buyer behaviour rather than assuming the simplistic view that it's about a singular set of buyers making a linear series of rational choices (i.e. the traditional funnel model). Instead, the framework allows for your content strategy, channel choices and metrics to flex according to the buyer objectives at each phase, creating a highly tailored experience that builds traction and helps your buyer make the right choice. It lends itself to a new way of assessing brand investments, choosing and using technology and how you gauge return on investment. It also helps bring about a new type of collaboration with sales which in turn will support your company's growth ambitions and create a better buyer experience.

I hope that the buyer journey framework gives you the structure and tools you need to be very successful in B2B marketing.

APPENDIX
Helpful frameworks and templates

In this appendix I have included templates that I've found useful in the past. I have collated my responses to questions I'm often asked by mentees and team members.

Guide 1: A marketing strategy template

Background and business challenge

- What is the business challenge that your solution addresses?
- How does it map to the challenges that buyers are facing at a high level?
- Information on competitors: how are they positioning themselves? How do you stand apart from them?
- What are your genuinely differentiating solutions, services or brand propositions?
- What does the ideal client look like: for example, industry, organization size and complexity, number of employees?

Client value proposition

- What do you offer?
- Why should the target audience care about what you say?
- Why does it help them? Can they save money? Get access to experts? Increase productivity? Enter new markets?
- What are the reasons to believe and proof points?
- Are there regional/country differences to consider?
- Key audience takeaway: what is the main message you want to get across? What makes you distinguishable and why should the buyer care about it? Is it easy to understand the benefits and does it feel relevant to them?

Objectives

For each stage of the buying journey, outline what your objectives are, the goals that you will set and targets, alongside outcome, indicator and input metrics. Once you have it, use the insights in Chapter 10 on 'bringing the buyer journey together' to portion out your budget allocation across each stage.

Map your strategy against the buyer journey

Table A.1

Stage	Horizon Scanner	Explorer	Hunter	Active Buyer	Client
What job roles are you targeting?					
How many of them are there (target addressable market)?					
Buyers, influencers or both?					
What are their primary challenges (industry, function, societal)? What are their problem areas, aspirations and behaviours?					
How does your solution help them?					
Who are the stakeholders outside your client groups, e.g. academics, trade bodies, etc.?					
Market insights including what their drivers of choice are.					
What do you know about people in these of roles – for example are they likely to be analytical or conceptual?					
What channels to they tend to prefer?					
Content: What is your buyer trying to do or learn? What information do they need?					
What do you know about format preferences?					
How do they like to be spoken to? As a peer? An authority? Formal or informal?					
What do you want them to think, feel or do?					
How will you know if they are on the move or ready to move to the next stage?					

BEFORE YOU START, CHECK

- Have you got or can you generate new thought leadership? This is particularly important if you need to engage with Horizon Scanners or Explorers.
- Do you have enough content, case studies, references to support the full journey?

- What SMEs (subject matter experts) do you have, and do you have enough?

- How will you get and store contact details for prospects and clients?

- Once you have buyer job titles, how much data do you need before you start marketing in earnest and how long will it take you to get it?

- Do you have existing customers for other products and services that might be a new market for this campaign? Or do you have existing clients who can give feedback or help you get insights?

- What are the key dates for this campaign? Are there any key external milestones or events to take into account? When do you need to be in the market by? If you work back from when the pipeline needs to be converted to sales, have you started early enough?

- Do you have agreement on how long each phase will take, and have you agreed KPIs including lead hand-off to sales?

- Do you have an internal activation plan, e.g. sales training and enablement?

- What are your key dependencies and/or barriers to entry?

- Are there any risks to the plan and how will you manage them?

- What hypotheses about the buyer journey will you test?

Guide 2: A way to think about events

Views on events can be highly subjective, making them one of the most sensitive areas of B2B marketing. For this reason – and because they can be expensive and consume a large part of your budget – it is important to have a good strategic framework aligned to the buyer journey. There are a few areas to consider before you commit funding: the event type, how to choose what you do, making sure it lines up with your overall buyer journey objectives and managing expectations.

Type of event

Ask yourself, where do your buyers go to, why and when in their process? What do you want to provide for them and what value will they receive? For example:

1 Large scale summits strongly position you as leaders in a market. Buyers come from far and wide to attend, look forward to them and prioritize them in their diaries because they hear from exciting speakers, mingle with peers and learn enough to justify a day out of the office. To host these, you need to have sufficient brand *pull*.

2 Roadshows can deliver a consistent message to customers in several locations. Ensure all have the same agenda, so that as the location varies, you can capture

insights from one to use in post-event communications for attendees of other events. These will likely be very specific to your company and what you want to talk to attendees about, whereas summits should be more market-issue led. Buyers want to know what you're doing to solve their challenges and will appreciate that you come to them to tell them about it.

3 Round tables provide intimate occasions for you to discuss how you can help buyers in the stage they are in. Use your convening power to provide peer-to-peer forums.

4 User or customer forums provide the opportunity to seek specific feedback on products or strategy from existing customers.

5 Webinars typically attract large numbers of people wanting to hear about your thought leadership and solutions in a way that is efficient (low cost, time limited) for them.

Be choosy about what you decide to do

This is particularly important because of cost. Without a clear sense of why you want to host, sponsor or even attend an event and what you want to get out of it, you will really struggle to get any return on your investment. Ensure the event provides a platform for you to speak to people that it is otherwise hard to reach, and ensure what your internal stakeholders want to talk about line up to the solutions or products that you sell. Remember Michael Stewart's advice in the Horizon Scanner chapter. Be targeted. Don't sign up for too many events and make sure others understand clearly what the investment case is.

Make sure the event experience aligns with your objectives

When thinking about how you want to show up, make sure it is aligned with what you're trying to do across your marketing. So if you are positioning the business as a technology-first, digital brand, think carefully about how this translates into an event format. If you are using events to showcase thought leadership to Explorers, do you have something compelling and new to say? If you are using it to showcase products or case studies to Hunters, is there a way you can do this that really stands out?

Manage expectations

It can be useful to document how you make decisions about events. That means everyone can see what you and your team consider before you commit and understand the reasons for your decision. Events can be emotive, so having an impartial framework agreed with internal stakeholders helps explain why, for example, you've

Table A.2

Type of event	What you want to achieve	How you know you've achieved it
Summit	Profile, market awareness	PR, media share of voice, customer attendance and feedback
Roadshow	Market awareness, sales	Leads, accelerated pipeline
Roundtable	Market awareness, sales	Customer feedback, leads, unblock or accelerate pipeline
User groups	Feedback on products and customer loyalty	Customer feedback, usage, retention, product development
Webinar	Market awareness, sales, drive adoption	Leads, increased understanding of product benefits, usage
Hospitality	Targeted relationship building	Brand awareness with targeted group, number of target clients attending hospitality events, pipeline acceleration, increased number of references from existing clients, client feedback
Third-party event	Sales	Leads

decided to spend money on it rather than on something sales might prefer to do. Events are the most time consuming and expensive types of marketing; the rationale for doing them must be rigorous.

AN EXAMPLE OF HIGH-LEVEL GUIDING PRINCIPLES

We will only do third party events when:

1 There is a *must go to* event for a customer segment – we know that it attracts the type of people we can have profitable conversations with.

2 We need to access a new market and get attention from buyers who don't know us well yet.

3 We can accelerate sales of existing services by accessing a large group of potential buyers.

4 It is high-value hospitality where we can generate a shared experience between our senior leaders and our customers that will deepen the relationship and help with retention.

We will only do proprietary events when:

1 We have something new to tell the market.

2 There are KPIs against how many attendees we can attract and what level they are.

3 We need to get customer feedback on a specific part of a strategy.

4 There is an opportunity to bring existing clients in front of new buyers.

We will only do corporate hospitality when:

1 We need to gain access to executives that are otherwise hard to reach. If using hospitality for this purpose agree who, specifically, you are trying to reach. Then research these individuals and see what interests they have, and whether these overlap with the event you may be targeting. In one of my roles, we wanted to reach a number of people who lived around a northern city in the UK so we sponsored a local arts organization to show our commitment to the area as well as providing hospitality near them. Remember that in some industries many executives won't or won't be allowed to accept a gift.

2 There is an ABM programme in place, and we want to provide opportunities to deepen relationships by providing a shared experience between your account teams and existing clients. If this is the objective, be clear which clients you want to be there and set shared targets with sales, for example that 75 per cent of those invited will feature in an attributed case study in your marketing literature within three months of the event, or 25 per cent of them will speak at one of your proprietary events.

There are as many poor events out there as there are good ones, so think hard before you commit funds. However good the event, you would fail to achieve the expected ROI if the opportunity provided no more than a chance to have a casual encounter with existing customers. As Jo Pettifer talked about in her interview, hold sales teams to account for ROI against strict KPIs for attracting leads or building new relationships.

Remember too the advice on deciding follow-up activities. If your leadership has met someone interesting at a round table, who will follow up and do they know they are on point? If a salesperson took a business card, what is their KPI for following up and how will this be monitored, tracked and recorded?

Guide 3: An agency briefing template

As covered in the agency section, how well you brief agencies will profoundly impact not only the quality of work and cost of it, but the calibre of talent you get supplied by the agency. Constructing a brief well doesn't just mean answering the questions as follows, it means ensuring that these topics have been debated and aligned with your business. Don't shortcut the answers or make assumptions – that means that your investment in the work will not yield return. When you're assessing the work, go back to these questions – and answers – to stay true to your strategic intent rather than being carried away by a creative idea that won't achieve your original objectives.

Remember too that usually your target market isn't marketers or agencies, so what appeals to you won't always resonate with your prospects. Using research and insights to inform answers to the questions in the brief, and how you assess the work will help make sure your messages land with them, not marketing creatives!

QUESTIONS TO ANSWER IN AN AGENCY BRIEF

- Who are we talking to? Make sure you add account type, industry, geographic area as well as job type, title and what role(s) they might be playing in the decision-making.
- What do they think about this now? What do they think about your company? What expectations might you need to overturn?
- Will this help us stand out from our competitors and does it align with our brand strategy?
- What are the top three to five challenges they face on a day-to-day basis?
- What are the top three challenges in the industry that impact them?
- What does our product/service/offering do to help with these challenges?
- What are we selling or promoting?
- What is the buyer journey overview? How will this campaign or piece of work support your buyer journey objectives?
- What should they think or do after seeing or engaging with this work?
- What action are we asking them to take?
- What is the main message?
- What points support this message?
- What is the call to action? How will this help move the buyer in their decision-making?
- What else should the agency know or consider?

Guide 4: How to build a personal brand

A personal brand is how your subject matter experts market themselves and their value to buyers. Any representative of your company is the face of it on direct channels like social media. And whether they like it – and are owning it – or not, they already have one. Personal brand is your reputation – how you bring who you are to what you do. You need to take ownership of it as in today's market, buyers expect it. If you are starting to position your company as one that builds trust with its customers, but your social profile has scant information and no photo, it will erode your brand message.

When talking to SMEs and encouraging them to think about their brand – or indeed, if you are doing it for yourself, think about:

- What makes you unique?
- What is your competitive edge?
- What three words come to mind when people think about or talk about you in a professional context?
- What do you want to be known for?
- How do you interact with people and issues in the world around you?

The way in which you show up in person or online needs to reflect your skills, talent and authentic style – but it needs to be appropriate for the situation that you are in. If you are being an ambassador for your company, you should also think about how you are reflecting the company's culture and whether it is authentic to that too.

Start thinking of yourself as a brand. Audit your online presence so it is consistent with that brand – and audit yourself often, and with honesty. Think about what platforms you want to be present on and make sure you are committed to spending time building your profile. If you're on social media, you need to post regularly. If you want to be on the events circuit, you need to present. Don't just be an expert on your owned channels – make sure you are out there engaging with the market and clients regularly.

Guide 5: Some thoughts on managing your own skills

As I mentor marketers, a recurring question is how they should be thinking about professional development. Typical questions I get asked range from how to get promoted, what fundamental skills are needed to develop as a marketer, how to increase external visibility and how to navigate effectively in an organization to get exposure and build networks. Of course, you will need technical skills to become an expert in digital, creative, writing etc., but there are some fundamental skills that I believe will help you no matter what role you are in. These will also help you as you look to advance your career as much of it covers the business fundamentals that are expected from a professional working in the B2B environment.

Commercial acumen

You need to know how your business makes money. How well do you understand your balance sheet and annual report? Do you know how sales sets targets for driving revenue or pipeline? Do you know how teams are expected to report on forecasts, progress and pipeline – do you know how sales convert leads to the next stage? Do you know how your board thinks about quarter or year-end – and what matters to finance at each point in your financial year? Do you know how profitable your products or services are?

All these – and more – increase in importance as you start to work with finance or write business cases. You need to know your context to be able to situate the value that marketing will create. Getting answers to these questions should be reasonably straightforward, but you may need to go to sales or finance to get them – they aren't always included in general onboarding or in standard marketing training that you may get from your company. I've found that being able to use finance terms and being adept at understanding how sales are relaying activity or results has helped when looking to secure or protect marketing funding

Getting the basics right

As a marketer, there are some things you are just expected to do well, and in my experience, this isn't always the case. There are three in particular: being able to write well, being able to write and deliver an excellent presentation through engaging with impact, and data/analytics skills. Wherever you sit in marketing, it is not only helpful to be able to do these very well, but it can also erode the perception of your competency if you can't. Unfortunately, this is true even if you're not a copywriter, creative or data scientist. There are plenty of courses – take time out to master these areas.

Some thoughts on public speaking

This is a common hate. Public speaking is as much about confidence as technique. I used to detest it – and felt physically sick every time I was asked to stand up and present or speak, but with time and practice I've come to enjoy it. You do need to be good at it to get ahead as a marketer – people expect it of you, more than in many other functions – and you only get better by doing it. There are plenty of books and courses that can help you on specifics. Things I find useful are:

- Keep slides very light – use pictures only if you can – and learn your script using images to prompt you so you don't forget any points. This makes for more visual interest and makes you look much more confident as you aren't using words which you could be tempted to read. I think you look better using cards than reading from a script but either is better than looking at your slides and reading from them.

- Always start by introducing yourself – full name, including surname and role – and potentially a very short personal or professional anecdote. It means you break the silence and gives you a chance to ground yourself in the setting. It helps the audience to see you as a real person and somehow exudes confidence. If you go straight into the presentation without doing this, it makes you seem like you are desperate to get it over with.

- Understand from event organizers what the set-up is – are you standing or sitting? Stools or chair? Will you be wearing a microphone? This helps you dress appropriately (as a woman it can be awkward to have a lapel mic put on if you're wearing a dress, and leads to a lump in your line, or having to hold the mic – something with a waistband is better, a skirt, trousers or even a belt) and you'll be able to picture yourself doing the session ahead of time. If you're speaking in an internal meeting room, will you stand or sit? Where do you want to sit? If there's a window facing outside, I like to be with my back to it as I don't get distracted. Try to sit across from someone you know will nod and smile as you speak. Think about how you can arrange yourself for success within the room you are in.

- If you're on video, is your lighting flattering? Does the background look good and are your surroundings tidy? If you're in marketing, you can put your logo up behind you if you want to cover any blemishes you might not want a senior stakeholder group to see.

- Think about the rule of three – it is easy to remember three things against each topic area and will help you keep track of where you are in the presentation.

- Personal anecdotes, client stories and data make your message memorable.

- If you hate the idea of answering questions, a great tactic can be to finish your presentation with a question. Usually, human behaviour takes over and your first couple of hand raisers are likely to attempt to answer your question or comment on it – with luck you can use up all your time having your question answered – but worst case, it gives you some breathing room between the rush of getting to the end of your presentation and the anxiety of facing into the ambiguity of question taking.

- Look at people you think do it well – comedians, professional business speakers, people within your company – and try to diagnose what they are doing that could help you get better. Do they use questions? When do they pause? How do they start and finish?

- Get feedback. It can feel excruciating, but it will help you immeasurably. Start with an internal meeting where you have a friendly peer – ideally someone outside marketing – or your boss and tell them beforehand what you wanted to get across then check that you did. Ask for thoughts on how you could have had greater impact. Did you use too much jargon? Did you hold the room? Did you come across as assured and confident? What are the two or three things they'd suggest for you – and then ask them the next time to check you did something differently.

As I mentioned, this is such a common area that people dislike, but at a certain point in your career it will really matter that you can do it well. Start early and take as many chances as you can – even if it is giving a short update on a team call – to get used to it. I always remember doing a huge conference with a very senior business professional. Everyone kept telling me that he was an incredible public speaker – informal, personable, relaxed. He could just get up and speak with conviction. I was a bit surprised then to be in the event space with him on stage until midnight the day before as he practised, rescripted, got feedback, re-practised – all so he could look off the cuff the next day.

Developing networks and managing senior level relationships

Taking time to network and build relationships across the organization is key to working effectively within it. Something I suggest to my teams as a useful first step is to make a plan – by which I mean, write something down in a spreadsheet. Include who you want to get to know within your organization, why and how you will do it. Do you need someone else to help you make the introduction? Commit to when you want to do it by. Then review it – ideally with your manager – on a regular basis to ensure you are keeping up with your commitment to yourself to network. Once you've started to build or extend your network, then add an area where you keep track of what you have said you'll do in terms of follow-up and an idea of how often you will re-engage with them and keep track of that too.

When working through how to approach more senior people, think about what you can bring that adds value. Get hold of a piece of insight or information they might not be aware of as that will give you something to talk about and pique their interest. As a marketer, you will have things that others don't – client anecdotes from an event or trends on how people are engaging with your content or offer that they won't have had from anyone else. Think about what might interest the senior person you're targeting and be prepared with information – specifically about buyers or clients – rather than progress on projects.

Have your internal pitch in your head and ready to go – a minute's worth of bio: who you are, your experiences, skills and interests. If you are meeting someone for the first time, the first likely question is 'tell me a bit about yourself' so be ready with it – particularly if you're feeling nervous about the meeting as it will give you a chance to orient yourself while giving a strong first impression.

Negotiation and prioritization

B2B marketing teams often feel overwhelmed as the number of asks are high and resourcing tends to be tight. This means balancing demand for marketing with the supply of money or headcount is an ongoing challenge. In addition, if you're transforming from a more tactical, reactive function to something more strategic, it is likely you'll need to say no to things that stakeholders think are a good idea. The other reason why this can be hard, is that marketers tend to be amiable, helpful people who want to support the business asks, so it can be challenging for us to say no to things, even if we know that we'll struggle to get the work done.

In terms of allocating your own time, it is worth having a conversation with your manager about what you think you can uniquely do or bring to the team. This doesn't need to be confined to tasks you've done before, it can be about attitude, ability to build relationships, speed of delivery. This will help you scope out how you can uniquely help make the project successful. This will mean you can have a grown-up conversation with them when you feel like too much of the work you are doing could be done by others more effectively and that you're not spending enough time doing work only you can do well.

When discussing ideas with stakeholders, it is worth remembering that no one likes hearing no. And what they are asking for is incredibly important from their perspective – they don't necessarily get to see the breadth of the asks you are managing. What can you offer in return? Or how can you position the work you are doing as having greater value for a broader number of buyers? Does your plan lead to value over volume for example? Be confident and clear about what the time or money will be spent on instead and how it is better from a buyer/customer perspective. Make sure you anchor your views in into commercial reality – so x will give more revenue than y – or create a better client experience. It might be that you feel like the business has asked you to prioritize something else, so you've diverted scarce resources to that leaving no time for anything else. If they disagree, at least you are part of a three-way conversation with another business owner/sales lead rather than on your own saying no to someone who wants something. You're making a strategic prioritization instead of loading more into the team with no clear plan for achieving it.

Similarly, they don't know what it takes from a resource perspective to get something done. The more seamless an event is, the easier stakeholders think it was to execute – whereas it probably means more rather than less work went into it! And there tends to be an underweighting in perception of what it takes for digital to do well. Finally, I have talked about the importance of thinking about the whole buying journey rather than one-off tactics – which takes more time, care and energy to do well, as it is deeper and richer programmes of work.

Building your external presence

With social media, this has never been easier; however, it does take a level of commitment as it is easy for it to fall down the to-do list and never actually happen. As a starting point, you should look at the guide on how to build personal brand and use as an input into your plan for what you want to do. In particular, what you want to be known for, what topics you want to be seen as an expert in and where you have something credible or interesting to say. Then look for opportunities.

- Create a blog on LinkedIn and post frequently. It helps if you've spent time building a good network first so that you build your profile more quickly, so build your network first before you start. Once you've published, ask some of your team or peers to comment on or like it so that you feel like you are getting traction for the effort you're putting in.

- If there are companies that organize webinars or discussion events on topics you're interested in, attend some, put yourself on the organizers' radar and then send them your bio and offer to help with any they have coming up.

- Suppliers and agencies want to be at events but would like their clients to give case studies or the customer perspective on the work they've done. This may well give you a bigger stage than you would have been able to achieve on your own.

- Approach publications that specialize in marketing to see if their journalists are looking for interviewees on specific topics – or case studies or references.

- Look at B2B marketing awards and enter some so that you can build the profile of the team and the work – and you can often then write testimonials into the awards websites, even if you don't win.

- If you are passionate about specific issues – diversity, reliance, coaching – this provides even more extensive opportunities for you to build your profile. Make sure they are in line with your personal brand – and that you have something relevant and real to say. Again, look to specialist events, publications and start to blog/post on the topic.

Across all these areas for managing yourself, the critical thing is to take the time to do it. It can be so easy to get bogged down into the tasks at hand but putting time aside to do this will bring real rewards. Setting targets and agreeing them with your manager can help – but you also need to hold yourself to account for this investment in your broader skills. You will become a better marketer as a result – and be a more effective business professional.

Guide 6: A marketing competency framework

When assessing your team, it can be difficult to compare performance across different areas of technical expertise. An effective way to do this can be to create a set of competencies that outlines expectations by level. This gives you something for the team to benchmark themselves against, and a fair way to discuss performance and promotion potential across these diverse experts.

In building a competency framework, it makes sense to have a set of job responsibilities that all job levels shares. Expectations against these responsibilities change depending on both their level and the type of work they do. Performance is critical, but culture is too. To build the right culture, having a set of core behaviours and attributes will provide clarity on how you expect people to do the work, as well as what you expect them to do, can be helpful.

The benefits of having a competency framework are:

- Clarity about what it takes to be successful in the team with a consistent, role-agnostic way to talk about performance.

- A means to identify the right skills in the team for success today as well as future marketing capabilities required to deliver on your business objectives and growth strategy at an individual and team level.

- Greater transparency for team members as they plan their career: providing a clearer understanding of where people *sit* within the team and what their opportunity is for advancement and development.
- Better alignment between managers and teams so people get the support they need and can put in place a clear, agreed plan to develop capabilities.

Use your specific business priorities to assess what makes sense for you to have in your capability framework. To get you started, here are some suggestions for how you can frame the competencies and ideas for what could go in them.

An example of how to think through the process:

- First, work through the elements of an effective marketing team for your business at a high level. What are the core things that it would take for you to be effective as a whole team? In this illustration I've chosen client value creation, quality execution and being part of – or building – a high-performing team.
- Then break those top-level elements into some component parts – or capability areas – and define them. In the example below, I've broken the top three into seven sub-capability areas: customer insights, commercial acumen, partnership with the business, innovation, delivery, leadership and talent development.
- Everything should be underpinned by behaviours and attributes: teams can be highly successful performers but do it in a way that isn't right for the culture of the organization. Integrating this into the framework means that you send a signal to the team and set clear expectations on behaviour.

Table A.3

Client value creation			Delivering exceptional work		Being part of a high-performing team	
Buyer insight	Commercial accumen	Partnership	Innovation	Delivery	Leadership	Talent development
Understands customer needs and wants deeply, and champions new opportunities for them	Maximizes impact on business performance and the ROI on all marketing activities	Acts as a strategic adviser and trusted partner to the business	Drives innovation across the business and challenges market conventions	Manages complex and integrated marketing plans and budgets	Shows up as an expert, thinks and acts in best interest of the client, and leads by example	Drives results, raises the performance bar and develops others
Behaviours and attributes expected at each level						

Lastly, for each of the areas, define what you are expecting by level so people know what they need to do to achieve a high-performance rating or get promoted.

Below are some tables that bring this to life to explain how the framework works in practice:

Competency: Client value creation
Capability: Buyer insight

Table A.4

Client value creation				
Buyer insight	**Junior level**	**Next level**	**Managerial level**	**Senior level**
Understands buyer needs and wants deeply, and champions new opportunities for them	Basic understanding and awareness of buyer needs developed by joining buyer events and reading buyer insight reports	Uses understanding and awareness of buyer needs and market trends to inform execution Confidence to share knowledge and ideas with wider marketing	Proactively seeks opportunities to meet buyers, understand their needs and pain points (e.g. attends internal and external events) Uses buyer insights, and a broad knowledge	Spends significant amounts of time with buyers, and uses insight and market trends, at both a global and local level, to champion the buyer internally and instigate new buyer initiatives and opportunities Stays on the cutting edge of buyer needs,
Understands buyer needs and wants deeply, and champions new opportunities for them	Aware of industry trends through reading relevant publications and researching industry information	team and business stakeholders – e.g. sharing buyer insights on team calls Recognized by stakeholders for effectively supporting priorities and proactively keeping business stakeholders informed Demonstrates basic knowledge of how propositions solve buyer challenges	of how our services solve buyer challenges, to drive and tailor impactful campaigns that align to business priorities Understands the bigger picture and how work aligns to and supports this Appreciates long-term and short-term business objectives and prioritizes work based on it	market trends and evaluates the market, our competitors, our brand and business to identify new opportunities and effectively differentiate our market positioning Is highly credible with the business and influences decisions and priorities, and shapes marketing programmes that challenge buyer thinking and perceptions Brings a full marketing discipline perspective to deliver marketing programmes that drive growth and revenue for the business

Competency: Deliver exceptional work
Capability: Innovation

Table A.5

Delivering exceptional work				
Innovation	Junior level	Next level	Managerial level	Senior level
Drives innovation across the business and challenges market conventions	Demonstrates a courageous and innovative mindset Suggests ways to work, smarter working Willingness to learn and share knowledge/ ideas with others	Proactively inputs into the broader marketing plan Basic understanding of market conventions Appetite to try new things and able to identify the link between channels and outcomes	Demonstrates a courageous and innovative mindset, and delivers bold and creative marketing campaigns Frames and contributes to thought leadership Uses insight and brings new ideas and thinking to challenge the way we do things and improve productivity and performance of the team	Creates an environment for innovation, taking risks, and is heavily involved in defining and driving thought leadership Champions the end-to-end customer experience, and is not constrained by remit when looking for opportunities to improve
			Understands competitive landscape and produces marketing that is differentiated Identifies the most appropriate channels and uses new tools and techniques to get the best outcomes	Uses deeper knowledge and expertise to bring new ideas and thinking to challenge the way we do things and improve productivity and performance of the team Challenges conventional thinking and can synthesize information

Competency: Build and be part of a high-performing team
Capability: Talent development

Table A.6

Build and be part of a high-performing team				
Talent development	Junior level	Next level	Managerial level	Senior level
Drives results, raises the performance bar and develops others	Curious and willing and able to learn and take on work Peer-to-peer knowledge sharing Helps shape, input and own development plan by seeking guidance from manager	Acts as an informal mentor for more junior members of the function Proactively manages own and assists others' development plans	Understands the performance distribution curve and knows the talent within the team Manages people and sets stretch targets for themselves and the team Proactive management of own development plans Understands company processes and policies related to people management Exhibits learning and puts it into practice	Coaches and mentors others, removes subjectivity to provide honest and candid feedback Passionate about talent development, and empowers team members to make their highest and best contributions Raises the performance bar across the team, recognizing and rewarding performance, and making tough calls on people issues to remove underperformers and blockers Identifies development opportunities for themselves, the team and the function

What makes this a compelling framework for the whole team is that there are things that are held in common across all levels, and then it is broken down by level. This means that if I'm a manager, I can see what is expected of me, for example I need to proactively manage my development plan, and understand what I need to do in order to get to the next level (coach and mentor others). I can then take the initiative to start to demonstrate these competencies as I make my case for promotion. It also means leaders can use it to talk about the accomplishments of their people in a common way when it comes to performance reviews.

As well as what you do, how you do it is critical too. Providing clarity to teams on what you expect from them culturally and what the attributes of high performance are will help you have constructive conversations with your people and your peers. These need to be relevant for your organization, team and sector, but I have put some ideas here to help you as you get started.

Core behaviours and attributes

Junior level

- Enthusiastic and highly driven
- Curious and hungry to learn
- Proactive and a self-starter
- A team player and willing to go above and beyond
- Effective communicator
- Demonstrates basic business and commercial acumen

Next level up

- Basic level of knowledge and/or strong interest in industry
- Execution oriented and able to deliver results
- Takes accountability for maximizing the impact and ROI of the work they deliver
- Highly collaborative and team-orientated
- Clear communicator
- Confident sharing new ideas
- Interested in learning about other areas of the business
- Demonstrates basic cost and budget management

Next level up/manager

- Good understanding of the industry
- Execution and outcome-orientated, and takes accountability for the results of the team
- Drives collaboration and alignment across marketing and business horizontal teams
- Highly effective and authentic communicator and listener
- Leads through influence and engagement rather than power

- Analytical and insight-driven

- Courageous, innovative and bold in their approach, and challenges current thinking and status quo where possible

- Pushes boundaries, takes sensible risks and learns from mistakes

- Good understanding of the broader business and able to confidently and effectively navigate the organization

- Commercially aware and demonstrates ability to manage complex campaign budgets

- Role model and mentor for junior team members

Senior manager/director

- Deep understanding of the industry

- Focuses their team on execution excellence, and takes accountability for the results of the function

- Enables and drives collaboration across marketing and business horizontal teams

- Experience leading teams in matrixed organizations through influence and engagement

- Able to build rapport and develop strong partnerships with senior business leaders and clients

- Leads the commercial focus of the team and prioritizes in alignment with business objectives

- Passionate about team development, and takes proactive steps to support the development of people across the marketing function

These attributes will become core to your employee value proposition as well as the promise you make to the rest of the organization about how you will show up. Being clear about what is expected – or having that clarity if you're more junior – means you're more likely to be successful and deliver client value.

REFERENCES

Almquist, E (2018) How digital natives are changing B2B purchasing, *Harvard Business Review*, March, hbr.org/2018/03/how-digital-natives-are-changing-b2b-purchasing (archived at https://perma.cc/H33A-JHCF)

B2B Institute, LinkedIn (2021a) Cashing in on creativity: How better ads deliver bigger profits, June, https://business.linkedin.com/marketing-solutions/b2b-institute/b2b-creative (archived at https://perma.cc/YP7X-A4RN)

B2B Institute, LinkedIn (2021b). Advertising and effectiveness and the 95-5 rule: Most B2B buyers are not in the market right now, July, business.linkedin.com/content/dam/me/business/en-us/marketing-solutions/resources/pdfs/advertising-effectiveness-and-the-95-5-rule.pdf (archived at https://perma.cc/B4E3-BMKK)

B2B Marketing (2020) It's time to stop binge shopping your martech, April, www.b2bmarketing.net/en-gb/resources/articles/its-time-stop-binge-shopping-your-martech (archived at https://perma.cc/XPP3-445J)

Barnes, H (2016) In enterprise tech, sell broadly (within an account) is the only answer, Gartner, Sept, blogs.gartner.com/hank-barnes/2016/09/27/in-enteprise-tech-sell-broadly-is-the-only-answer/ (archived at https://perma.cc/K766-UCAQ)

Blum, K (2020) Future of sales 2025: Why B2B sales needs a digital-first approach, Gartner, September 2020

Brinker, S (2020) Marketing technology landscape graphic, chiefmartec.com/2020/04/marketing-technology-landscape-2020-martech-5000/ (archived at https://perma.cc/X4NU-JSUX)

Bryan, J (2019) The power of the challenger sales model, Gartner, August 2019, www.gartner.com/smarterwithgartner/power-challenger-sales-model (archived at https://perma.cc/7WQK-3SFD)

Burgess, B (2022) *Account Based Growth*, Kogan Page, London

Carnegie, D (2021) Asking for referrals and the tale of a (half) a million pound question, October, www.dalecarnegie.co.uk/asking-for-referrals-and-the-tale-of-a-half-a-million-pound-question/ (archived at https://perma.cc/EP79-3AU3)

CEB (2012) The Digital Evolution in B2B Marketing, Marketing Leadership Council

Charlton, G (2021) Global martech industry worth $344.8bn in 2021, Martech Alliance, www.martechalliance.com/stories/global-martech-industry-worth-344.8bn-in-2021 (archived at https://perma.cc/HW7F-HRJ9)

Gartner (2022) The state of marketing budget and strategy, www.gartner.com/en/marketing/research/annual-cmo-spend-survey-research (archived at https://perma.cc/5XS3-XFE6)

Hedger, J (2019) B2B Marketing. The marketing rule of 7, and why it's still relevant in B2B, July, www.b2bmarketing.net/en-gb/resources/blog/marketing-rule-7-and-why-its-still-relevant-b2b (archived at https://perma.cc/CJM3-XKYS)

IT Services Marketing Association (ITSMA) (2022) ABM Benchmarking Study 2022

Kahneman, D (2000). Experienced utility and objective happiness: A moment-based approach, *Choices, Values, and Frames*, edited by D Kahneman and A Tversky, Cambridge University Press

Kohavi, R and Thomke, S (2017) The surprising power of online experiments, *Harvard Business Review*, September, hbr.org/2017/09/the-surprising-power-of-online-experiments (archived at https://perma.cc/8LDP-AGNV)

Landor & Fitch (2010) Products are made in the factory, but brands are created in the mind, landorandfitch.com/en/articles/thinking/landor-and-fitch-talks-branding-in-the-big-book-of-marketing (archived at https://perma.cc/E3UW-2KUB)

LinkedIn (2018) B2B buyers don't want personalisation, they demand it, March

Linkedin Marketing Solutions (2019a) From brand to demand: How to cultivate meaningful marketing impact, business.linkedin.com/content/dam/me/business/en-us/amp/marketing-solutions/images/insights-and-research/advertising-insights/pdfs/From_Brand_To_Demand.pdf (archived at https://perma.cc/D5UU-WEG4)

Linkedin Marketing Solutions (2019b) The long and short of ROI, October, business.linkedin.com/marketing-solutions/success/insights-and-research/marketing-ROI (archived at https://perma.cc/3BXW-U5QS)

Linkedin Marketing Solutions (2022a) The war on brand, business.linkedin.com/marketing-solutions/content-marketing/b2b-trends/the-war-on-brand (archived at https://perma.cc/A78T-5TW7)

Linkedin Marketing Solutions (2022b) Five principles of growth in B2B marketing, business.linkedin.com/marketing-solutions/b2b-institute/marketing-as-growth (archived at https://perma.cc/CX4F-JYBG)

Linkedin Marketing Solutions (2022c) Advertising in trusted environments that deliver results, business.linkedin.com/marketing-solutions/b2b-playbook/building-trust (archived at https://perma.cc/YN56-ZM93)

Maechler, N, Poenaru, A, Rüdt von Collenberg, T and Schulze, P (2017) Finding the right digital balance in B2B customer experience, P. McKinsey & Company, April, www.mckinsey.com/capabilities/growth-marketing-and-sales/our-insights/finding-the-right-digital-balance-in-b2b-customer-experience (archived at https://perma.cc/GTD2-3USB)

Miller Heiman (2018) CSO insights. The growing buyer-seller gap: Results of the 2018 buyer preferences study

PwC (2022) Annual CEO survey, www.pwc.com/gx/en/ceo-agenda/ceosurvey/2022.html (archived at https://perma.cc/NCY9-UYFG)

Quartz (2022) The resilient generation, sponsored.qz.com/deloitte/the-resilient-generation/ (archived at https://perma.cc/6E9A-VESD)

Ramaswami, R (2021) Future of sales 2025: Deliver the digital options B2B buyers demand, Gartner, March, Sales organizations must adapt to b2b buyers' digital-first preferences for future of sales. (gartner.com (archived at https://perma.cc/PA58-MNDA))

Romaniuk, J. Brand rejection in B2B: Incidents, reasons and implications, B2B Institute, LinkedIn, B2B Rejection.indd (linkedin.com (archived at https://perma.cc/YP7X-A4RN))

Romaniuk, J, Sharp, B, Dawes, J and Faghindno, S (2021) How B2B brands grow, B2B Institute, LinkedIn, business.linkedin.com/content/dam/me/business/en-us/marketing-solutions/cx/2021/images/pdfs/final-how-b2b-brands-grow-white-paper.pdf (archived at https://perma.cc/4SFP-45AG)

Rothman, D (2015) How to sell marketing automation to your C-suite, blog.marketo. com/2015/07/ebook-how-to-sell-marketing-automation-to-your-c-suite.html (archived at https://perma.cc/84SU-GCSA)

Salesforce (2018) 5 ways businesses can meet expectations of the connected customer, June, www.salesforce.com/au/blog/2018/06/new-report--5-ways-businesses-can-meet-expectations-of-the-conne.html (archived at https://perma.cc/5ZEM-EK2V)

Salesforce (2021) *The State of Marketing*, 7th edition, August

Simpson, J (2017) Finding brand success in a digital world, Forbes, August, www.forbes. com/sites/forbesagencycouncil/2017/08/25/finding-brand-success-in-the-digital-world/?sh=7488ba09626e (archived at https://perma.cc/9JYR-B8U5)

Source Global Research, February 2021

TrustRadius (2021) The 2021 B2B buying disconnect, November, www.trustradius.com/ vendor-blog/millennial-b2b-buyers-what-you-need-to-know-about-the-new-wave-of-decision-makers (archived at https://perma.cc/9JYR-B8U5)

Wimbledon.com (2022) Official partners, www.wimbledon.com/en_GB/atoz/official_partners.html (archived at https://perma.cc/L2F3-A7BQ)

INDEX